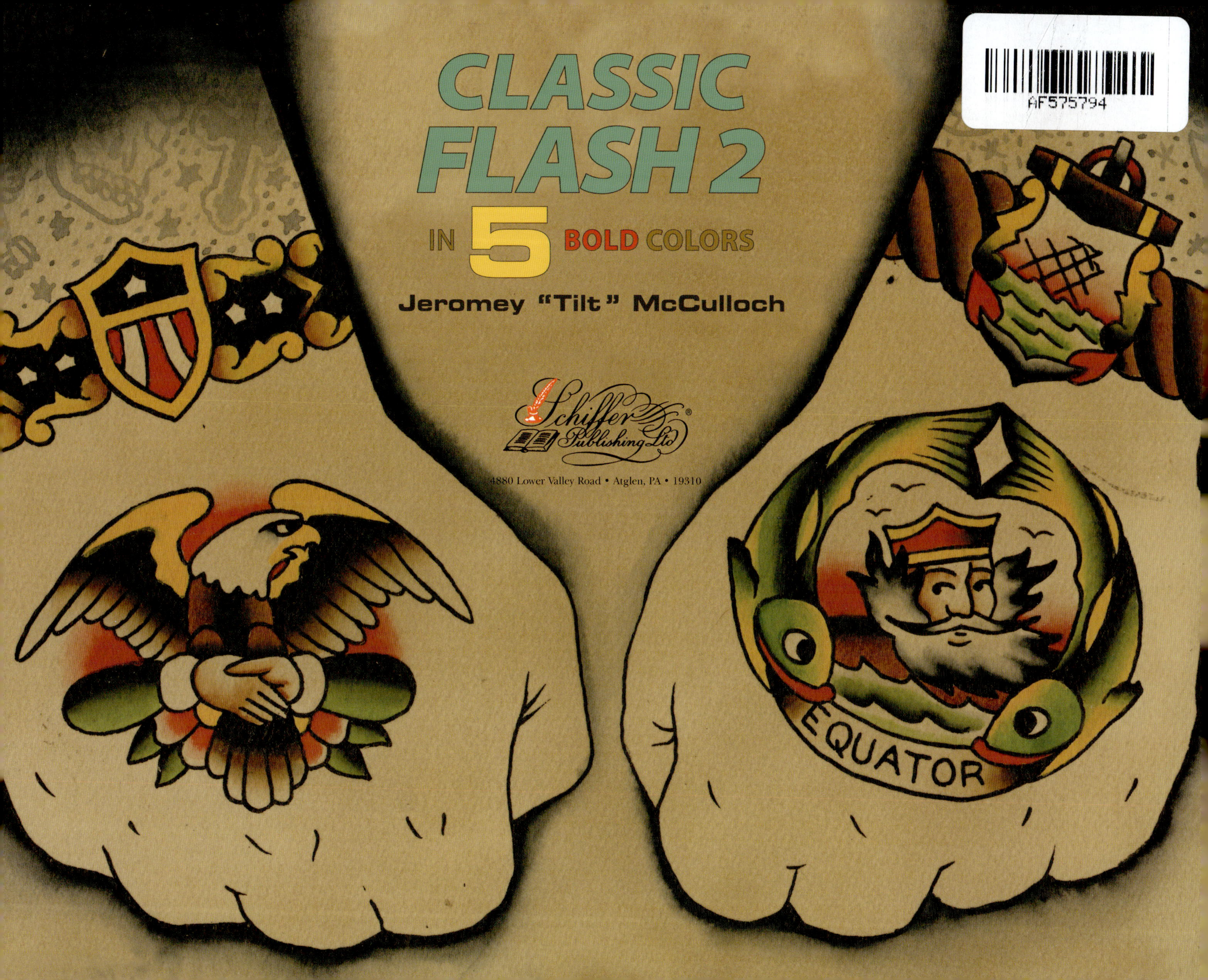
CLASSIC
FLASH 2
IN 5 BOLD COLORS
Jeromey "Tilt" McCulloch
Schiffer Publishing Ltd
4880 Lower Valley Road • Atglen, PA • 19310
EQUATOR
AF575794

Also by Jeromey "Tilt" McCulloch:

***Classic Flash in Five Bold Colors,* 2009.**
ISBN: 978-0-7643-3165-7, $25.99
Available from Schiffer Publishing Ltd.

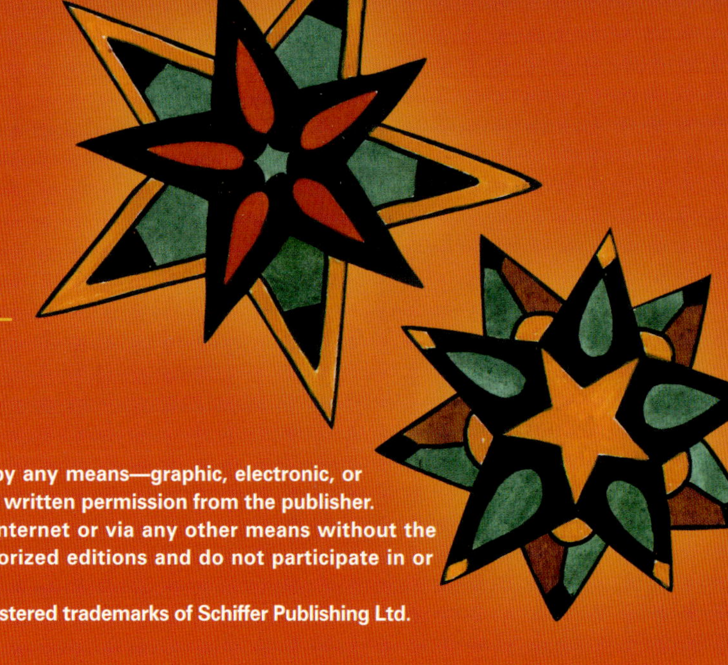

Library of Congress Control Number: 2011928588

Designed by DANIELLE D. FARMER
Cover Design by BRUCE WATERS
Type set in Myriad Pro/Zurich BT/ A Charming Super Expanded

FSC
www.fsc.org
MIX
Paper | Supporting responsible forestry
FSC® C104723

ISBN: 978-0-7643-3867-0
Printed in China
6 5 4 3

Schiffer Books are available at special discounts for bulk purchases for sales promotions or premiums. Special editions, including personalized covers, corporate imprints, and excerpts can be created in large quantities for special needs. For more information contact the publisher:

Published by Schiffer Publishing Ltd.
4880 Lower Valley Road
Atglen, PA 19310
Phone: (610) 593-1777; Fax: (610) 593-2002
E-mail: Info@schifferbooks.com

For the largest selection of fine reference books on this and related subjects, please visit our website at www.schifferbooks.com
We are always looking for people to write books on new and related subjects. If you have an idea for a book please contact us at the above address.

This book may be purchased from the publisher.

Please try your bookstore first. You may write for a free catalog.

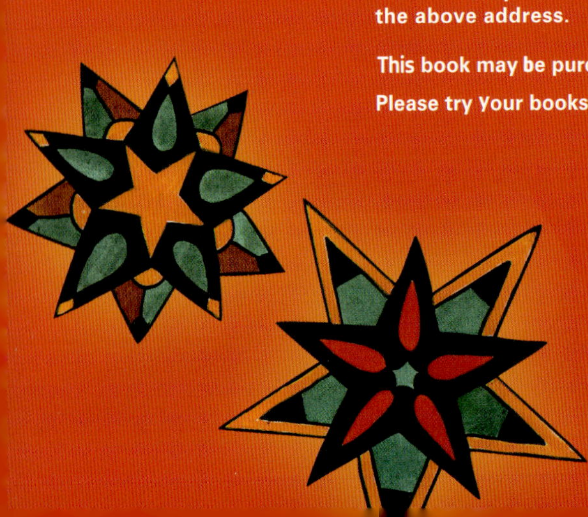

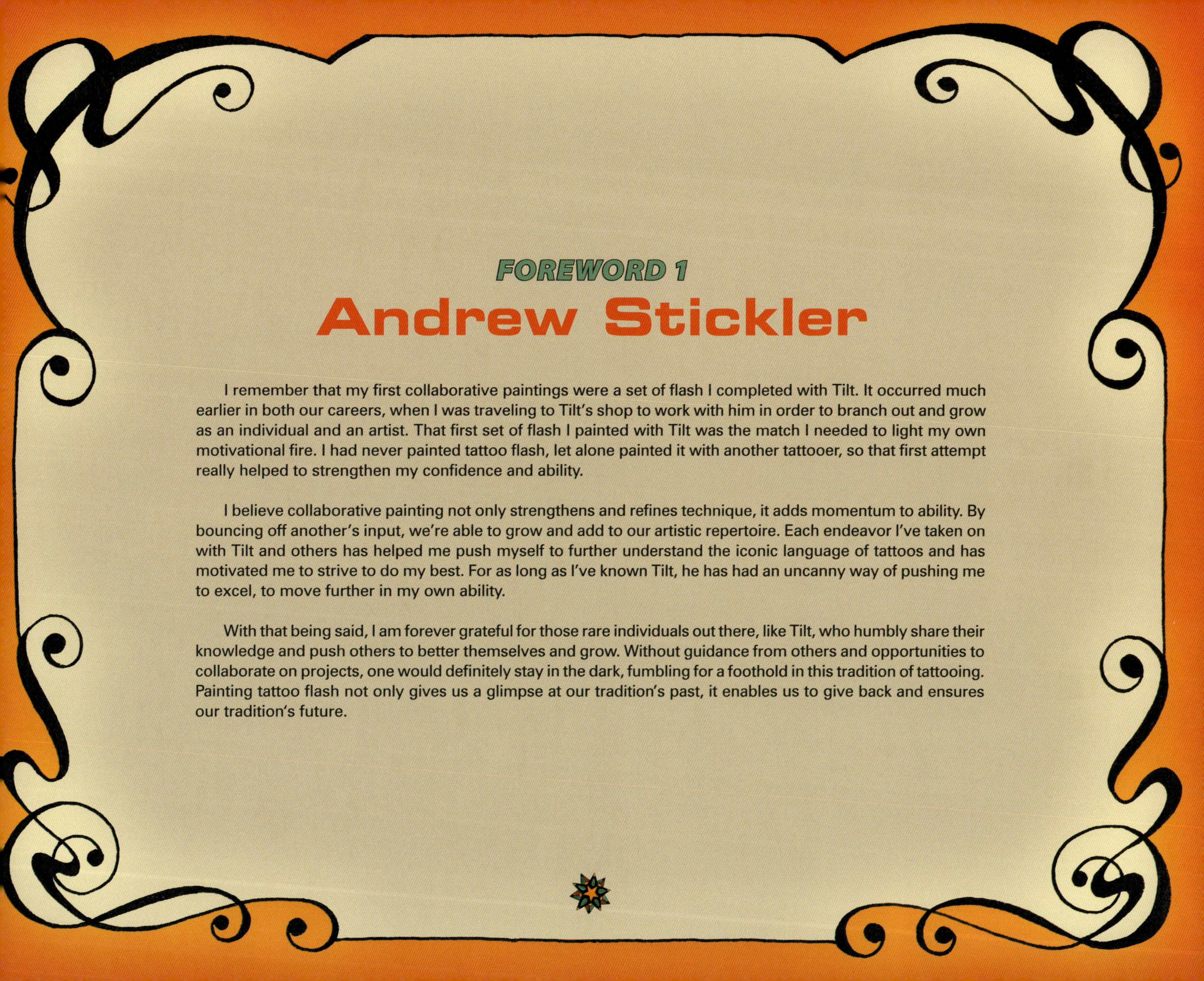

FOREWORD 1

Andrew Stickler

I remember that my first collaborative paintings were a set of flash I completed with Tilt. It occurred much earlier in both our careers, when I was traveling to Tilt's shop to work with him in order to branch out and grow as an individual and an artist. That first set of flash I painted with Tilt was the match I needed to light my own motivational fire. I had never painted tattoo flash, let alone painted it with another tattooer, so that first attempt really helped to strengthen my confidence and ability.

I believe collaborative painting not only strengthens and refines technique, it adds momentum to ability. By bouncing off another's input, we're able to grow and add to our artistic repertoire. Each endeavor I've taken on with Tilt and others has helped me push myself to further understand the iconic language of tattoos and has motivated me to strive to do my best. For as long as I've known Tilt, he has had an uncanny way of pushing me to excel, to move further in my own ability.

With that being said, I am forever grateful for those rare individuals out there, like Tilt, who humbly share their knowledge and push others to better themselves and grow. Without guidance from others and opportunities to collaborate on projects, one would definitely stay in the dark, fumbling for a foothold in this tradition of tattooing. Painting tattoo flash not only gives us a glimpse at our tradition's past, it enables us to give back and ensures our tradition's future.

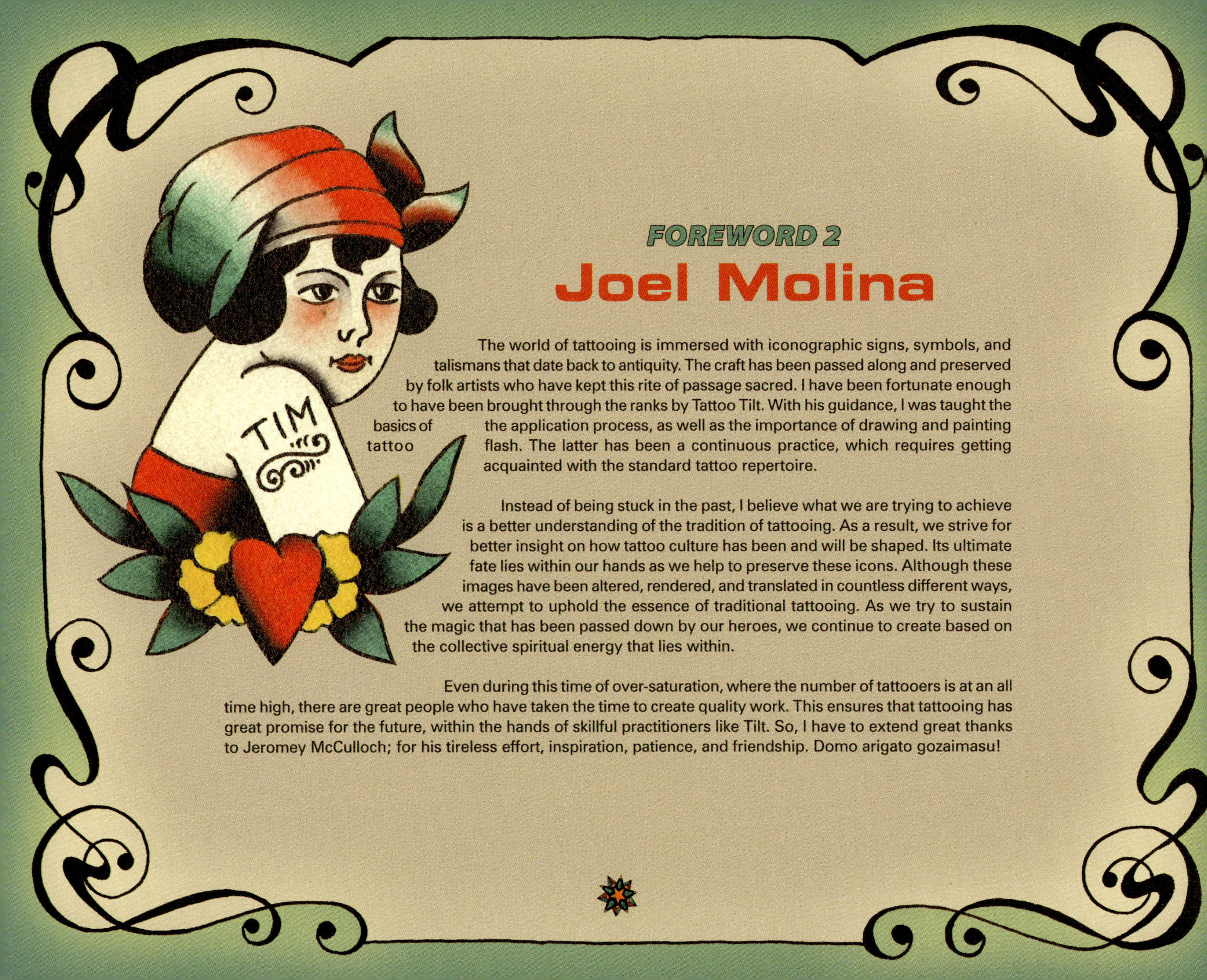

FOREWORD 2

Joel Molina

The world of tattooing is immersed with iconographic signs, symbols, and talismans that date back to antiquity. The craft has been passed along and preserved by folk artists who have kept this rite of passage sacred. I have been fortunate enough to have been brought through the ranks by Tattoo Tilt. With his guidance, I was taught the basics of tattoo the application process, as well as the importance of drawing and painting flash. The latter has been a continuous practice, which requires getting acquainted with the standard tattoo repertoire.

Instead of being stuck in the past, I believe what we are trying to achieve is a better understanding of the tradition of tattooing. As a result, we strive for better insight on how tattoo culture has been and will be shaped. Its ultimate fate lies within our hands as we help to preserve these icons. Although these images have been altered, rendered, and translated in countless different ways, we attempt to uphold the essence of traditional tattooing. As we try to sustain the magic that has been passed down by our heroes, we continue to create based on the collective spiritual energy that lies within.

Even during this time of over-saturation, where the number of tattooers is at an all time high, there are great people who have taken the time to create quality work. This ensures that tattooing has great promise for the future, within the hands of skillful practitioners like Tilt. So, I have to extend great thanks to Jeromey McCulloch; for his tireless effort, inspiration, patience, and friendship. Domo arigato gozaimasu!

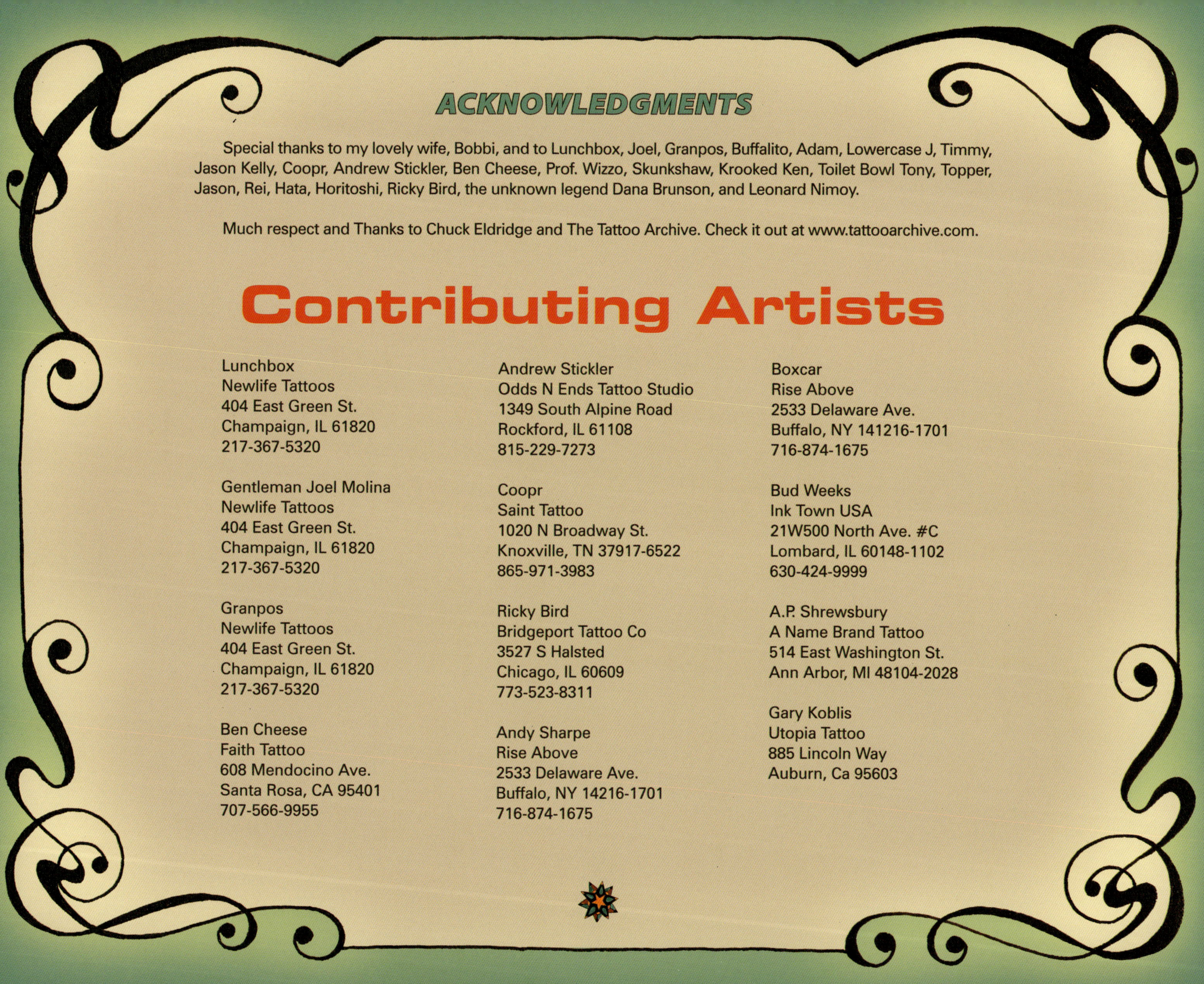

ACKNOWLEDGMENTS

Special thanks to my lovely wife, Bobbi, and to Lunchbox, Joel, Granpos, Buffalito, Adam, Lowercase J, Timmy, Jason Kelly, Coopr, Andrew Stickler, Ben Cheese, Prof. Wizzo, Skunkshaw, Krooked Ken, Toilet Bowl Tony, Topper, Jason, Rei, Hata, Horitoshi, Ricky Bird, the unknown legend Dana Brunson, and Leonard Nimoy.

Much respect and Thanks to Chuck Eldridge and The Tattoo Archive. Check it out at www.tattooarchive.com.

Contributing Artists

Lunchbox
Newlife Tattoos
404 East Green St.
Champaign, IL 61820
217-367-5320

Gentleman Joel Molina
Newlife Tattoos
404 East Green St.
Champaign, IL 61820
217-367-5320

Granpos
Newlife Tattoos
404 East Green St.
Champaign, IL 61820
217-367-5320

Ben Cheese
Faith Tattoo
608 Mendocino Ave.
Santa Rosa, CA 95401
707-566-9955

Andrew Stickler
Odds N Ends Tattoo Studio
1349 South Alpine Road
Rockford, IL 61108
815-229-7273

Coopr
Saint Tattoo
1020 N Broadway St.
Knoxville, TN 37917-6522
865-971-3983

Ricky Bird
Bridgeport Tattoo Co
3527 S Halsted
Chicago, IL 60609
773-523-8311

Andy Sharpe
Rise Above
2533 Delaware Ave.
Buffalo, NY 14216-1701
716-874-1675

Boxcar
Rise Above
2533 Delaware Ave.
Buffalo, NY 141216-1701
716-874-1675

Bud Weeks
Ink Town USA
21W500 North Ave. #C
Lombard, IL 60148-1102
630-424-9999

A.P. Shrewsbury
A Name Brand Tattoo
514 East Washington St.
Ann Arbor, MI 48104-2028

Gary Koblis
Utopia Tattoo
885 Lincoln Way
Auburn, Ca 95603

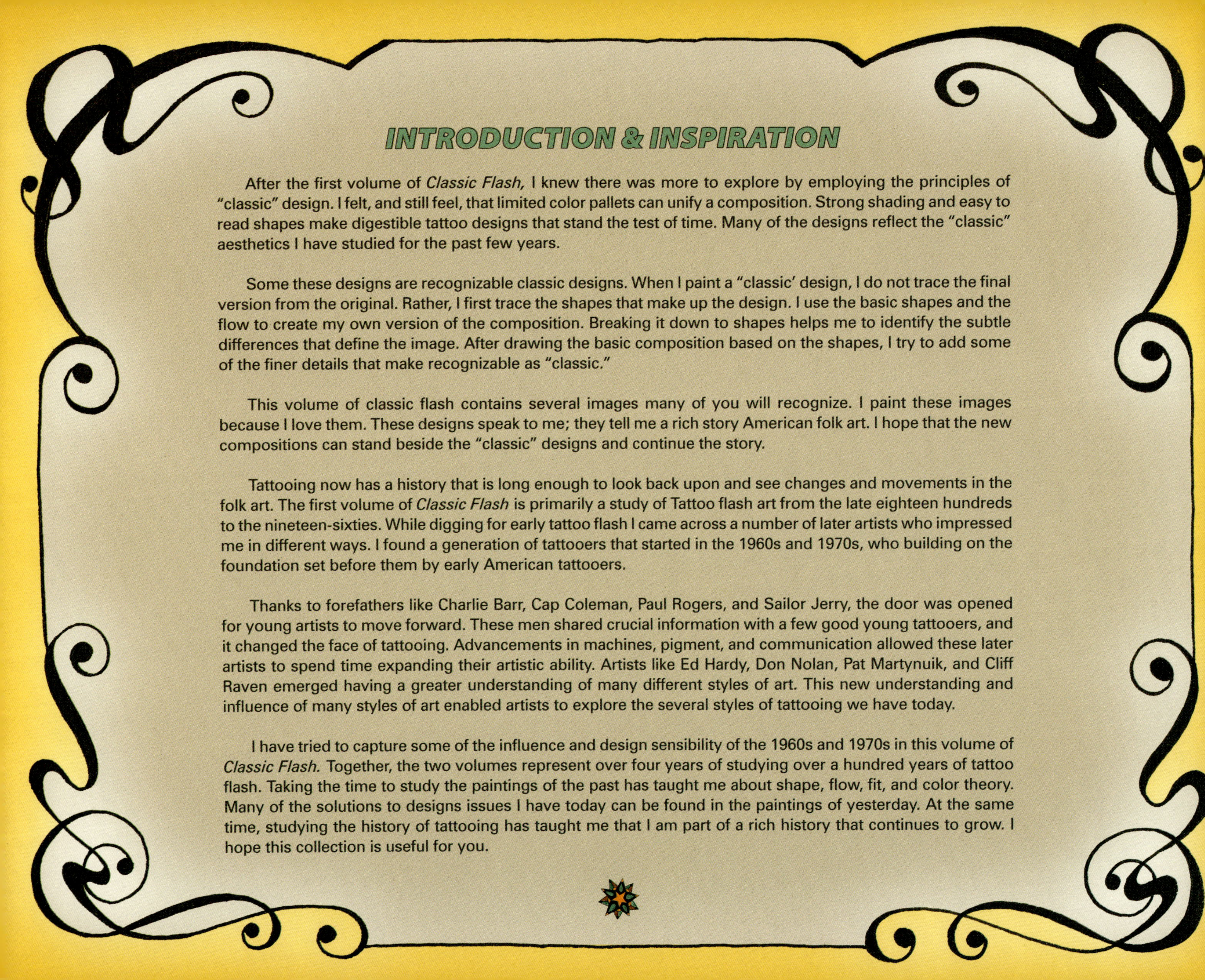

INTRODUCTION & INSPIRATION

After the first volume of *Classic Flash,* I knew there was more to explore by employing the principles of "classic" design. I felt, and still feel, that limited color pallets can unify a composition. Strong shading and easy to read shapes make digestible tattoo designs that stand the test of time. Many of the designs reflect the "classic" aesthetics I have studied for the past few years.

Some these designs are recognizable classic designs. When I paint a "classic' design, I do not trace the final version from the original. Rather, I first trace the shapes that make up the design. I use the basic shapes and the flow to create my own version of the composition. Breaking it down to shapes helps me to identify the subtle differences that define the image. After drawing the basic composition based on the shapes, I try to add some of the finer details that make recognizable as "classic."

This volume of classic flash contains several images many of you will recognize. I paint these images because I love them. These designs speak to me; they tell me a rich story American folk art. I hope that the new compositions can stand beside the "classic" designs and continue the story.

Tattooing now has a history that is long enough to look back upon and see changes and movements in the folk art. The first volume of *Classic Flash* is primarily a study of Tattoo flash art from the late eighteen hundreds to the nineteen-sixties. While digging for early tattoo flash I came across a number of later artists who impressed me in different ways. I found a generation of tattooers that started in the 1960s and 1970s, who building on the foundation set before them by early American tattooers.

Thanks to forefathers like Charlie Barr, Cap Coleman, Paul Rogers, and Sailor Jerry, the door was opened for young artists to move forward. These men shared crucial information with a few good young tattooers, and it changed the face of tattooing. Advancements in machines, pigment, and communication allowed these later artists to spend time expanding their artistic ability. Artists like Ed Hardy, Don Nolan, Pat Martynuik, and Cliff Raven emerged having a greater understanding of many different styles of art. This new understanding and influence of many styles of art enabled artists to explore the several styles of tattooing we have today.

I have tried to capture some of the influence and design sensibility of the 1960s and 1970s in this volume of *Classic Flash.* Together, the two volumes represent over four years of studying over a hundred years of tattoo flash. Taking the time to study the paintings of the past has taught me about shape, flow, fit, and color theory. Many of the solutions to designs issues I have today can be found in the paintings of yesterday. At the same time, studying the history of tattooing has taught me that I am part of a rich history that continues to grow. I hope this collection is useful for you.

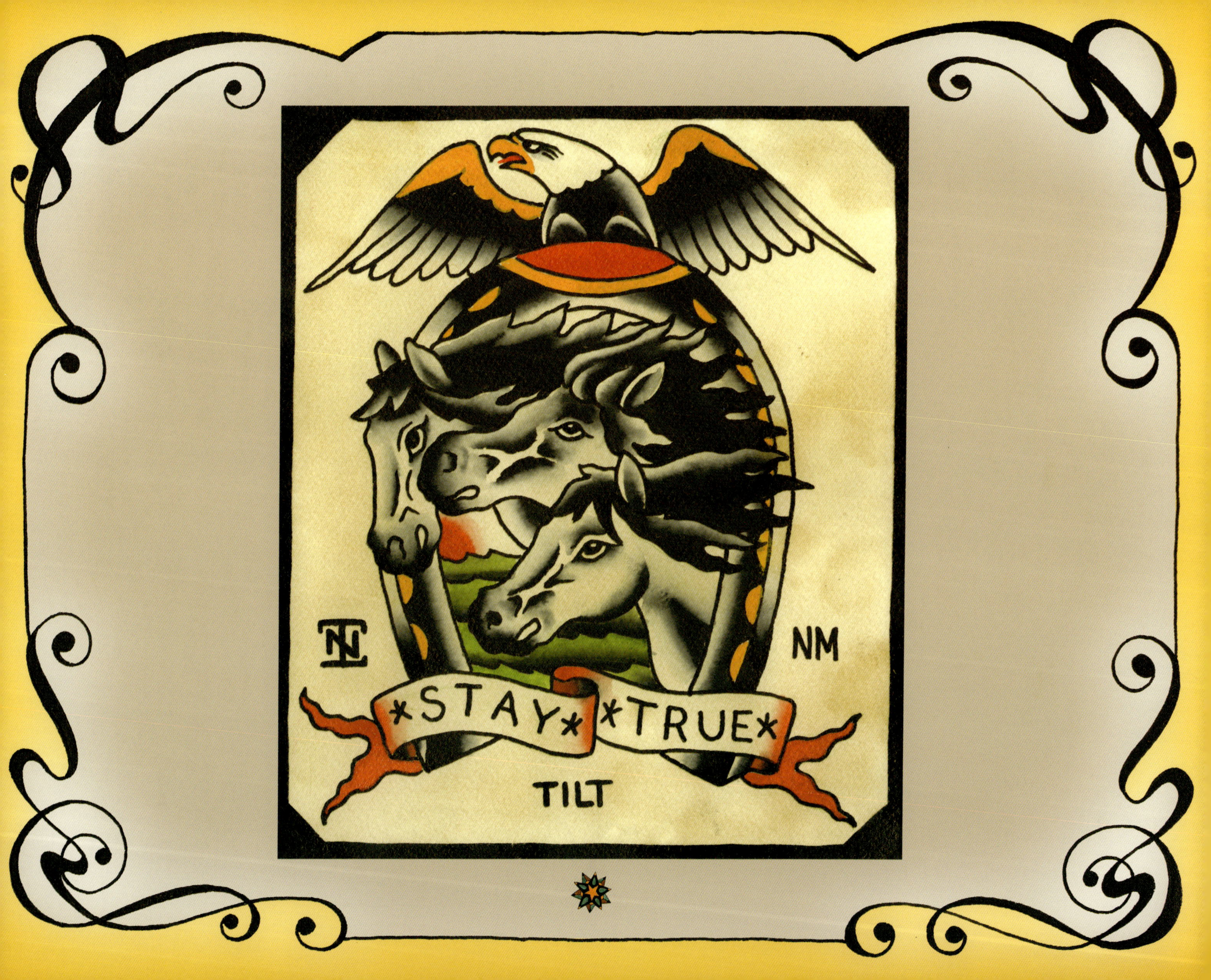

NM
STAY *TRUE*
TILT

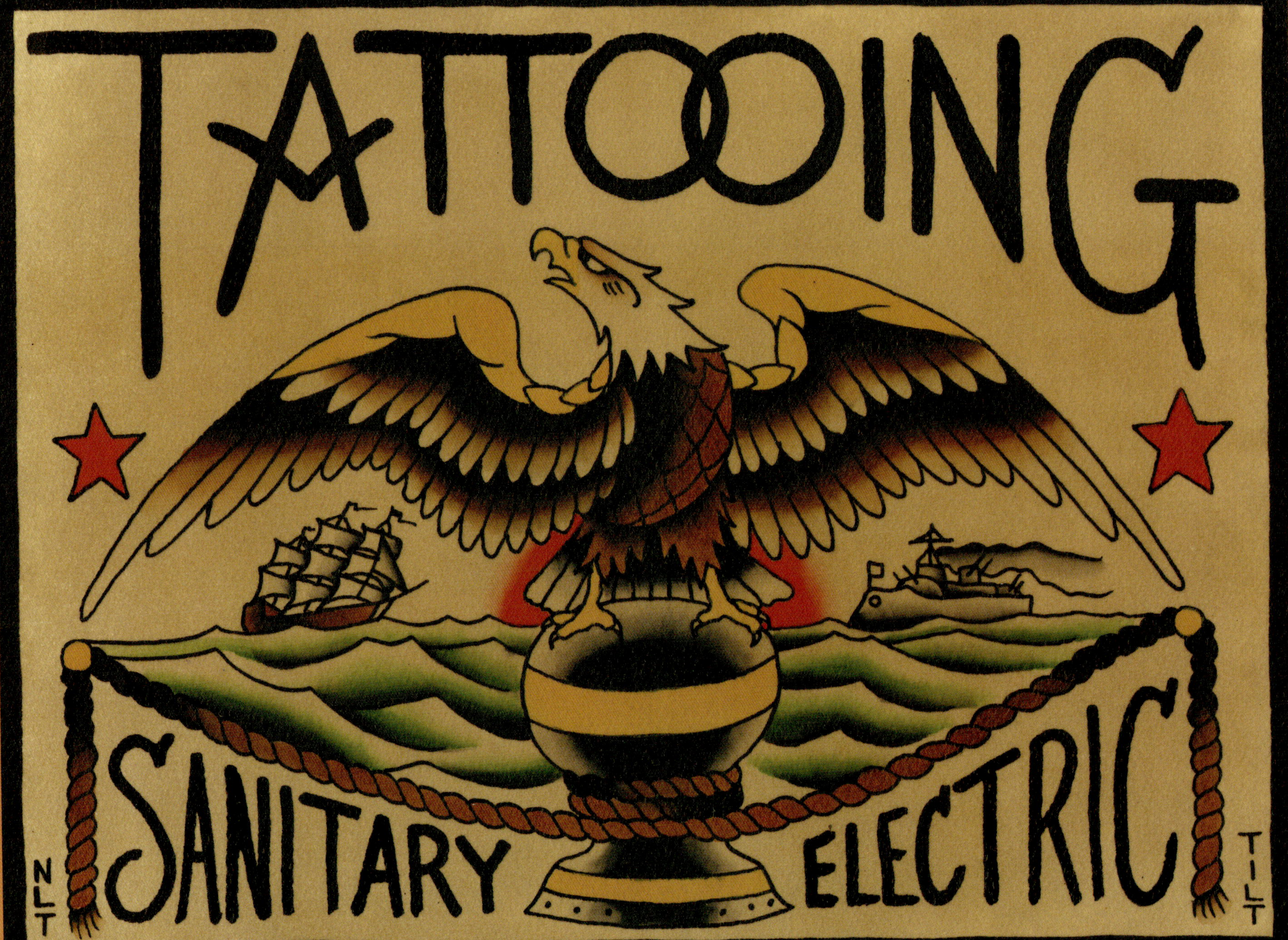
TATTOOING
SANITARY
ELECTRIC
NLT
TILT

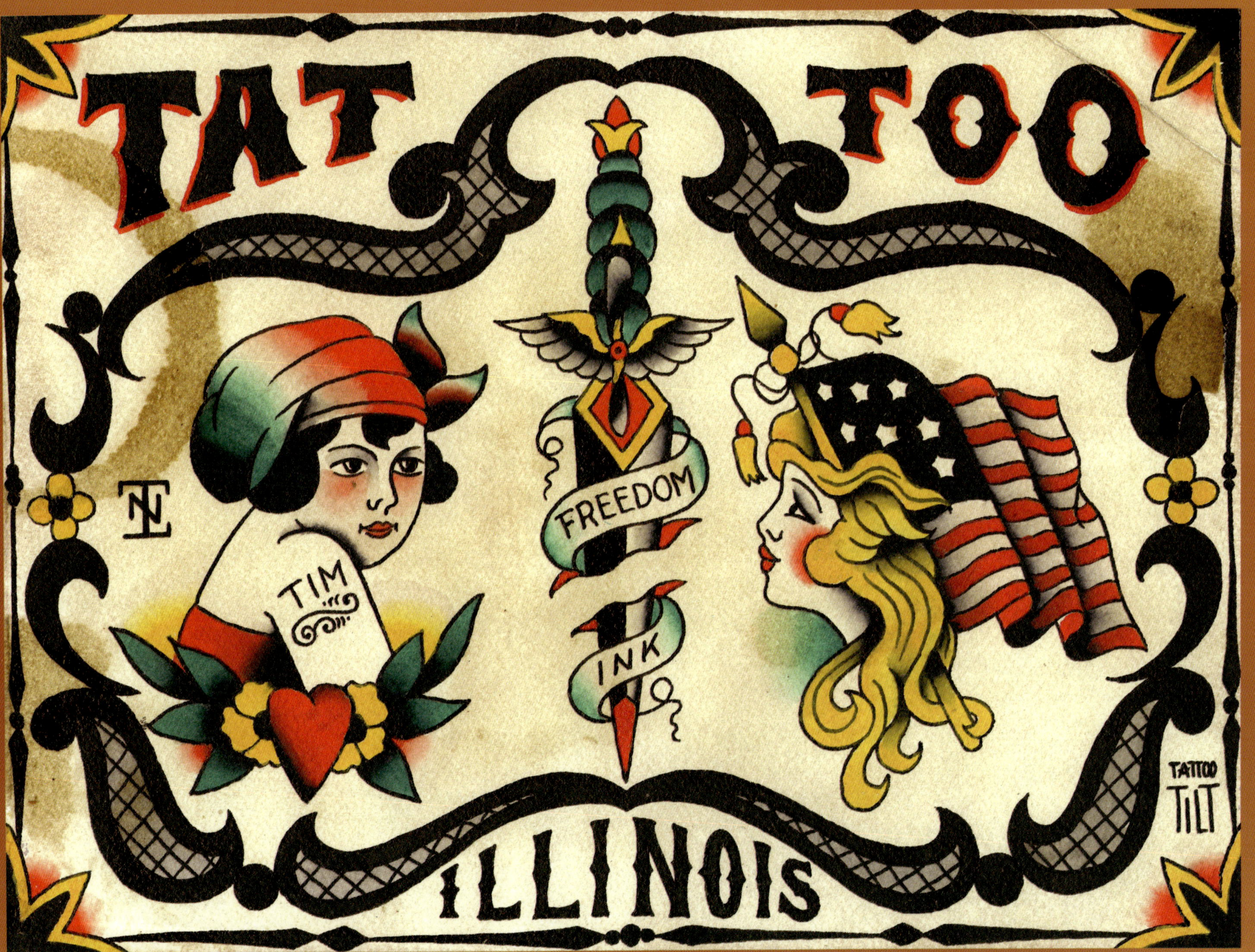
TAT
TOO
FREEDOM
INK
TIM
ILLINOIS
TATTOO
TILT

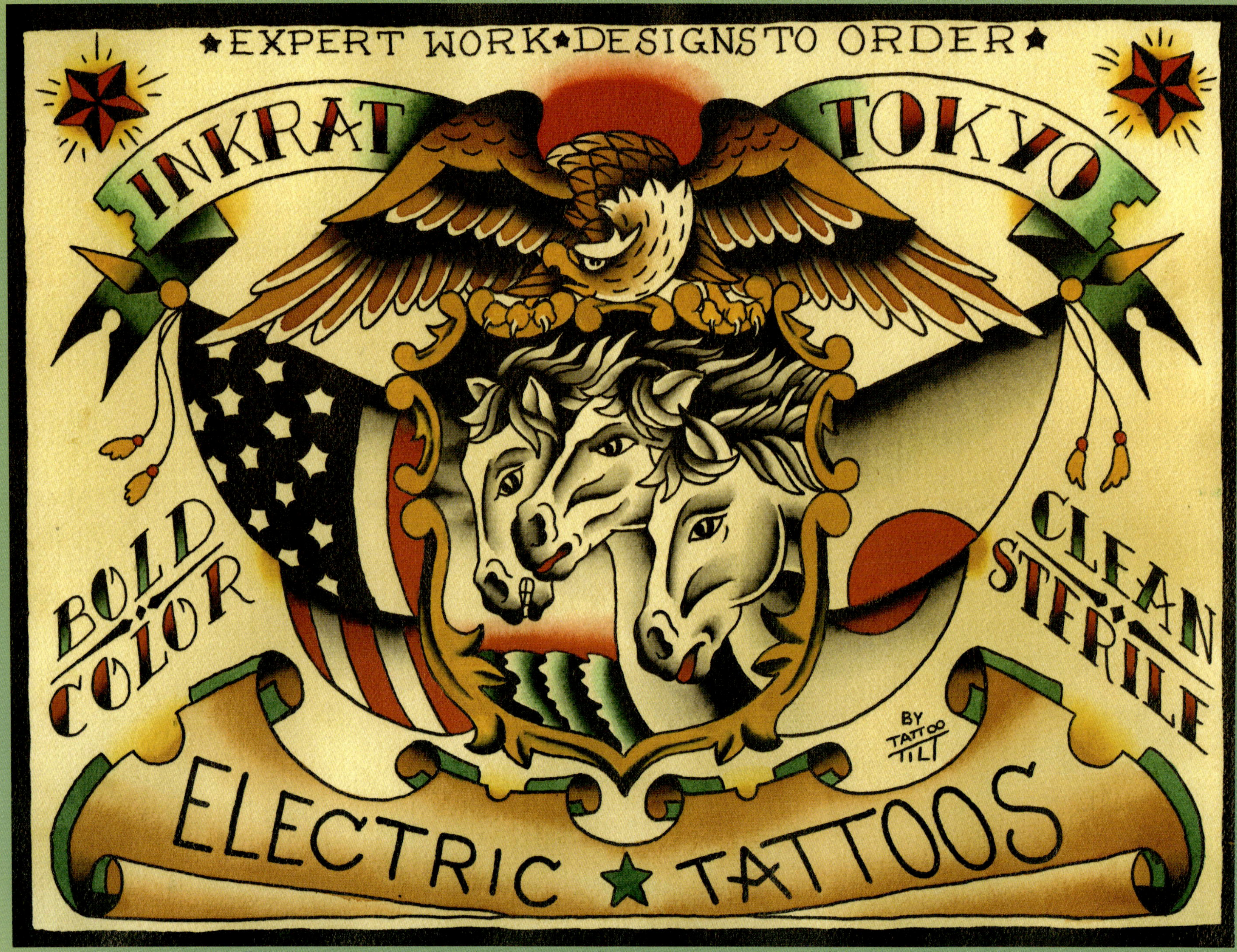
EXPERT WORK DESIGNS TO ORDER
INKRAT
TOKYO
BOLD COLOR
CLEAN STERILE
BY TATTOO TILT
ELECTRIC TATTOOS

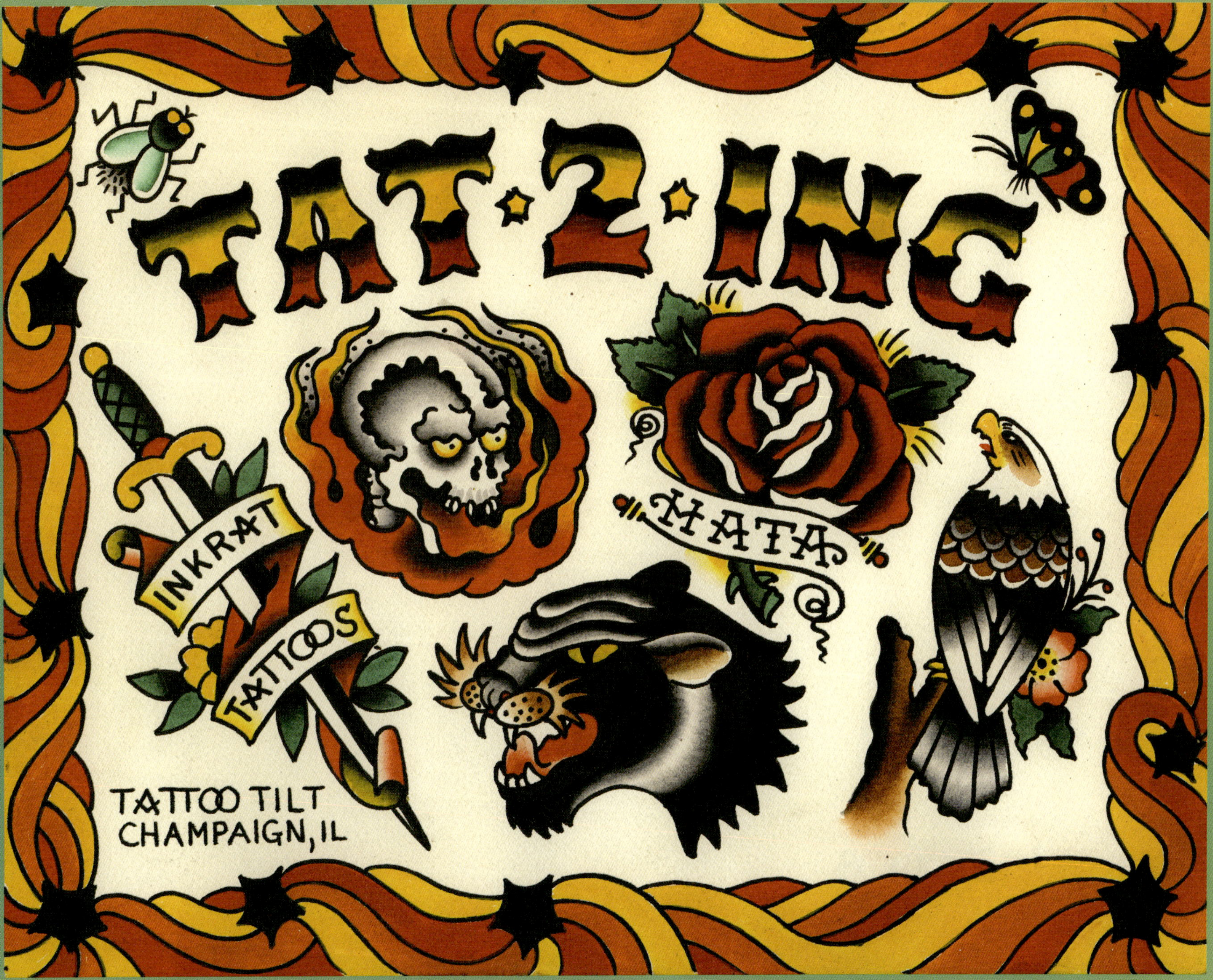

TAT·2·ING

INKRAT

TATTOOS

MATA

TATTOO TILT
CHAMPAIGN, IL

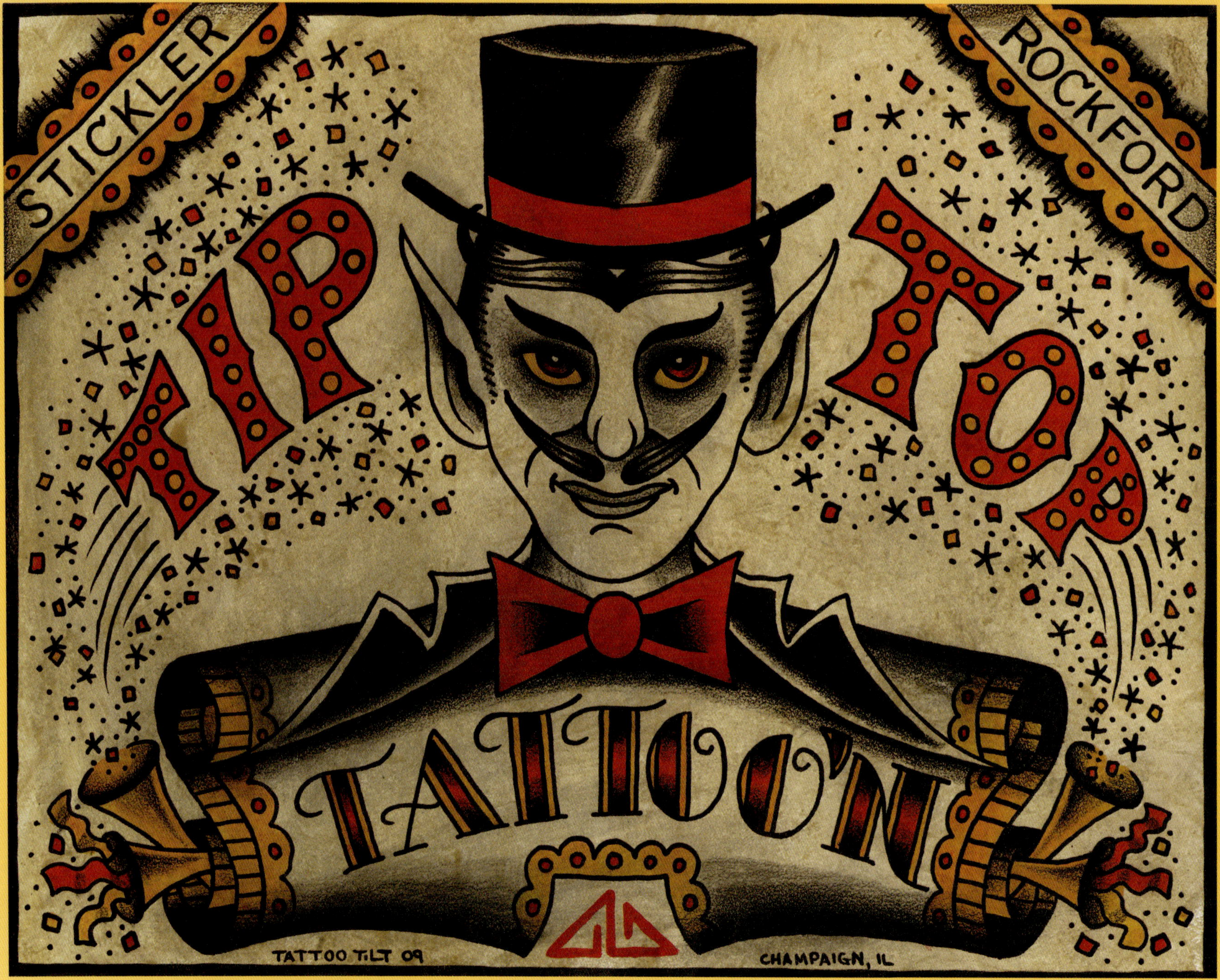

STICKLER
ROCKFORD
TIP TOP
TATTOO'N
TATTOO TILT 09
CHAMPAIGN, IL

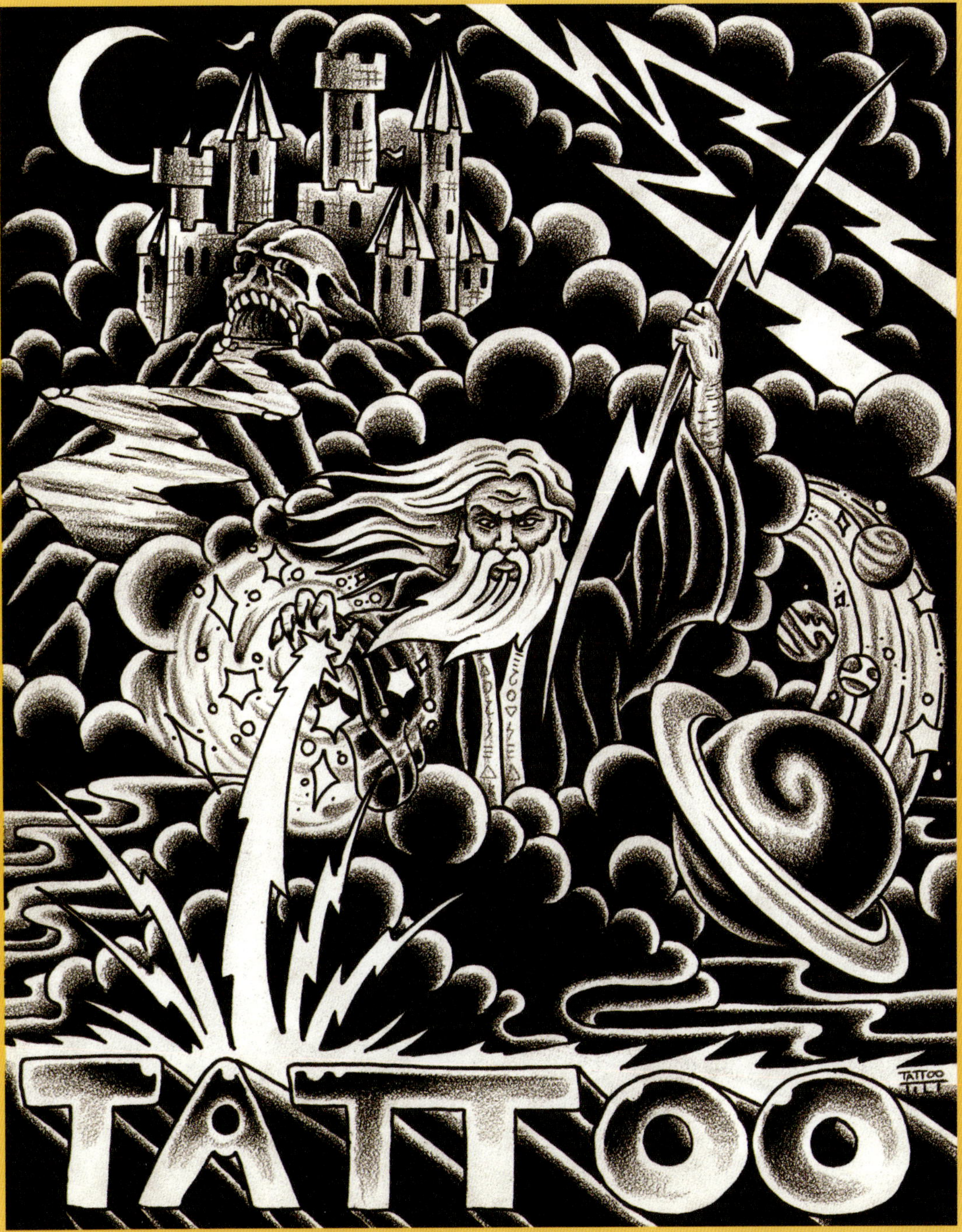

TATTOO

TATTOO TILT

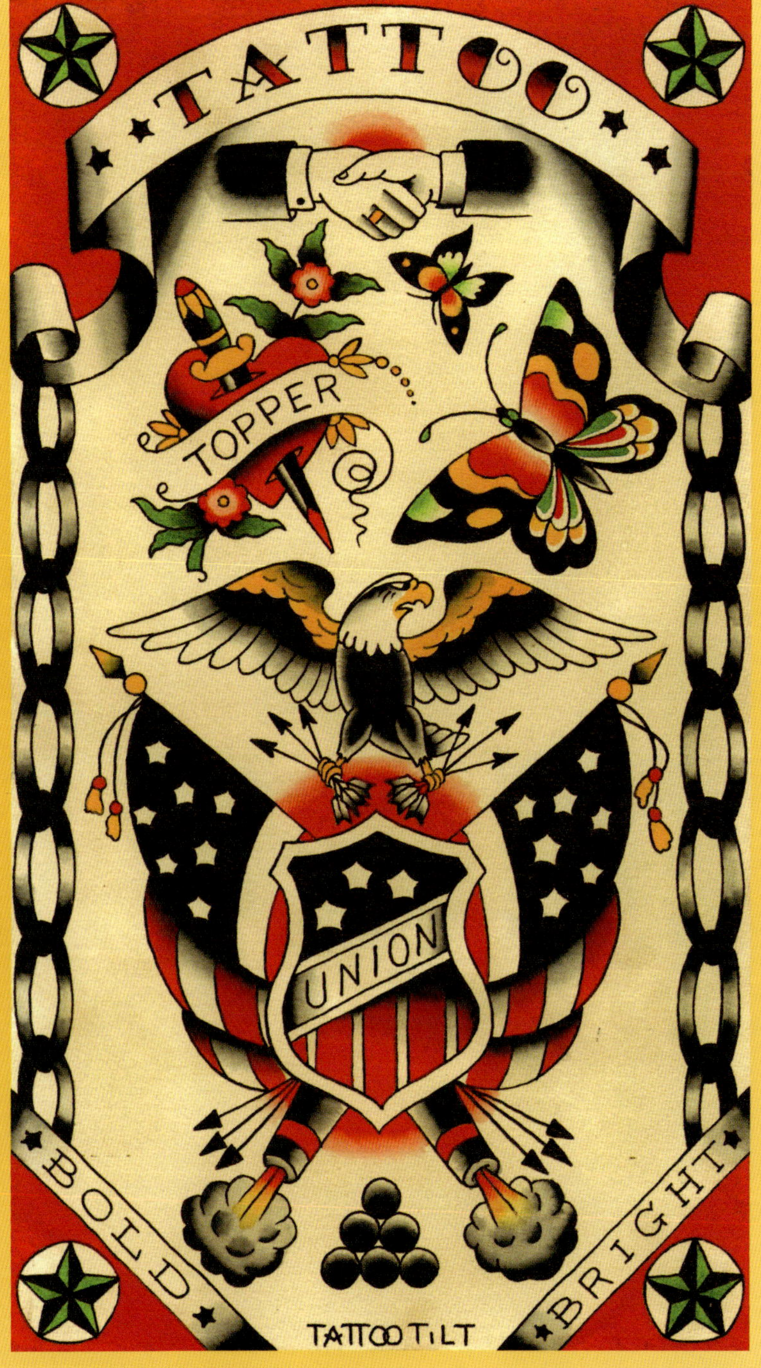

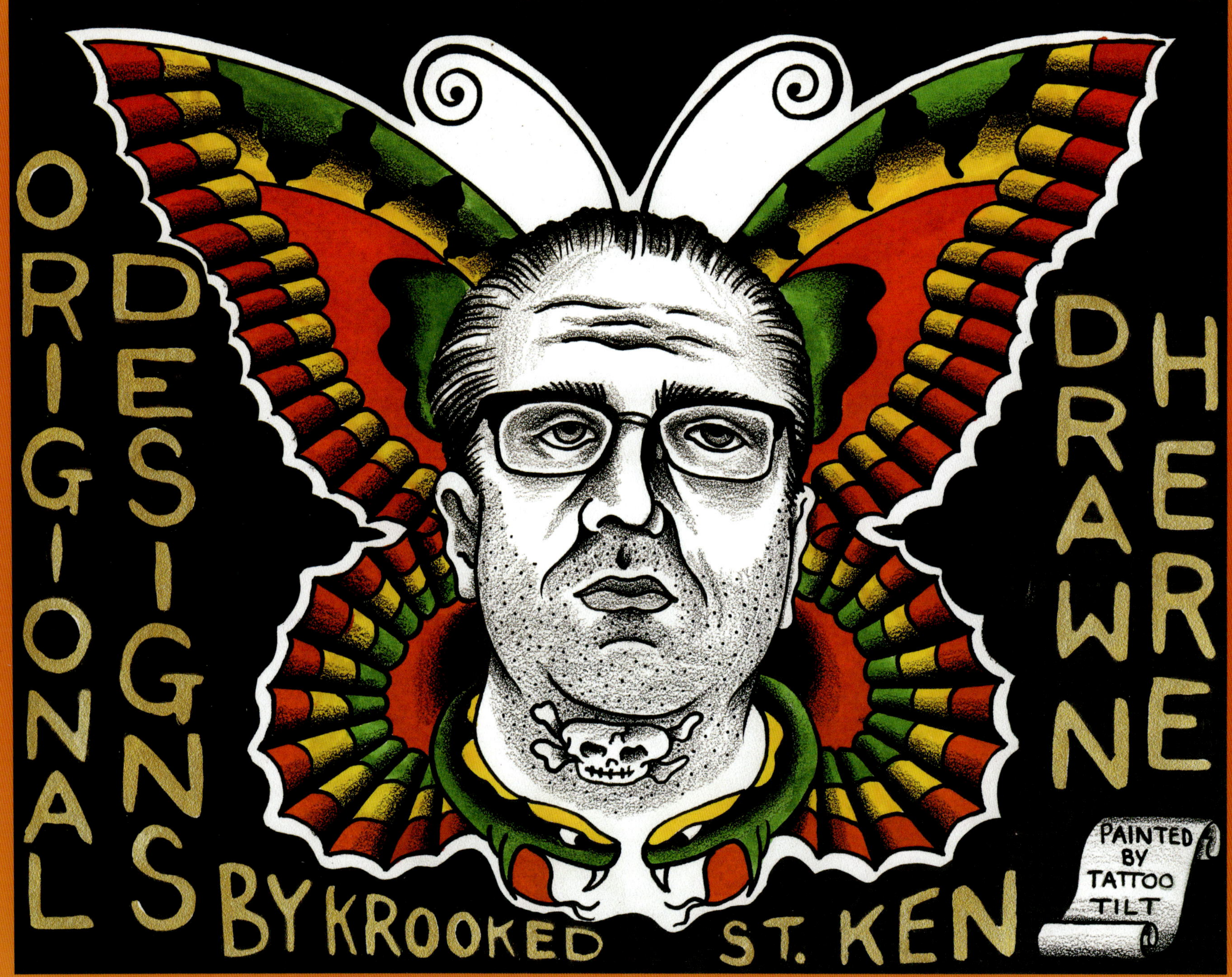
ORIGIONAL
DESIGNS
DRAWN
HERE
BY KROOKED
ST. KEN
PAINTED BY TATTOO TILT

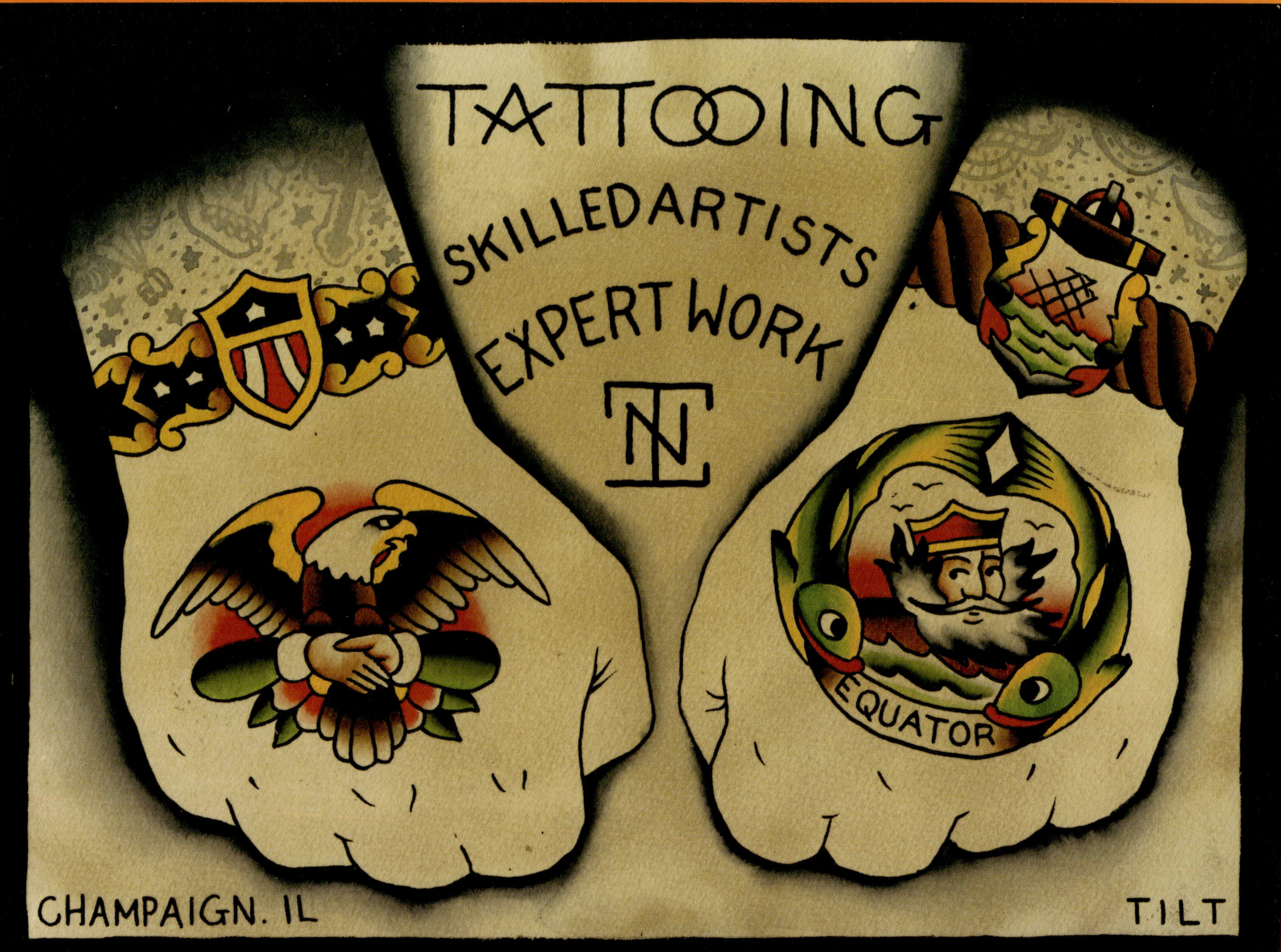
TATTOOING
SKILLED ARTISTS
EXPERT WORK
EQUATOR
CHAMPAIGN. IL
TILT

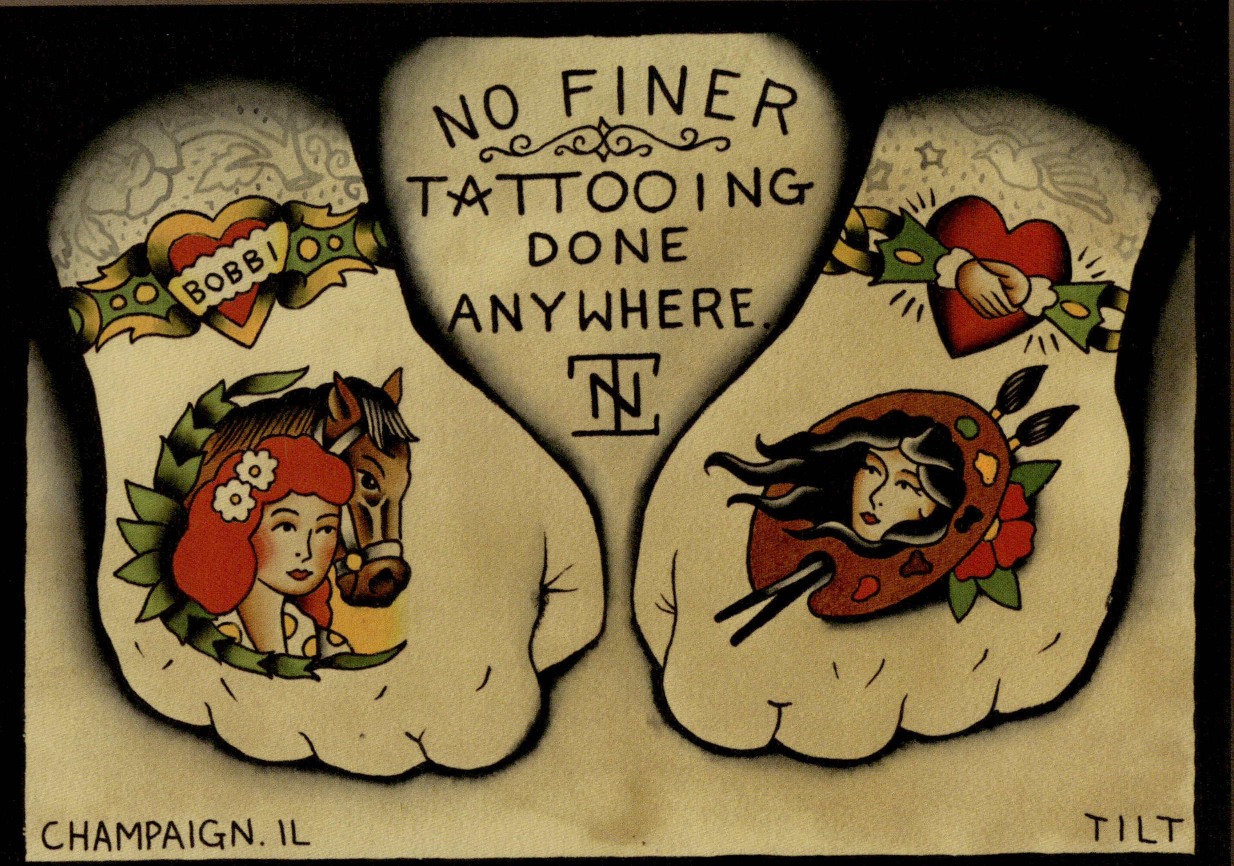
NO FINER
TATTOOING
DONE
ANYWHERE.
BOBBI
CHAMPAIGN. IL
TILT

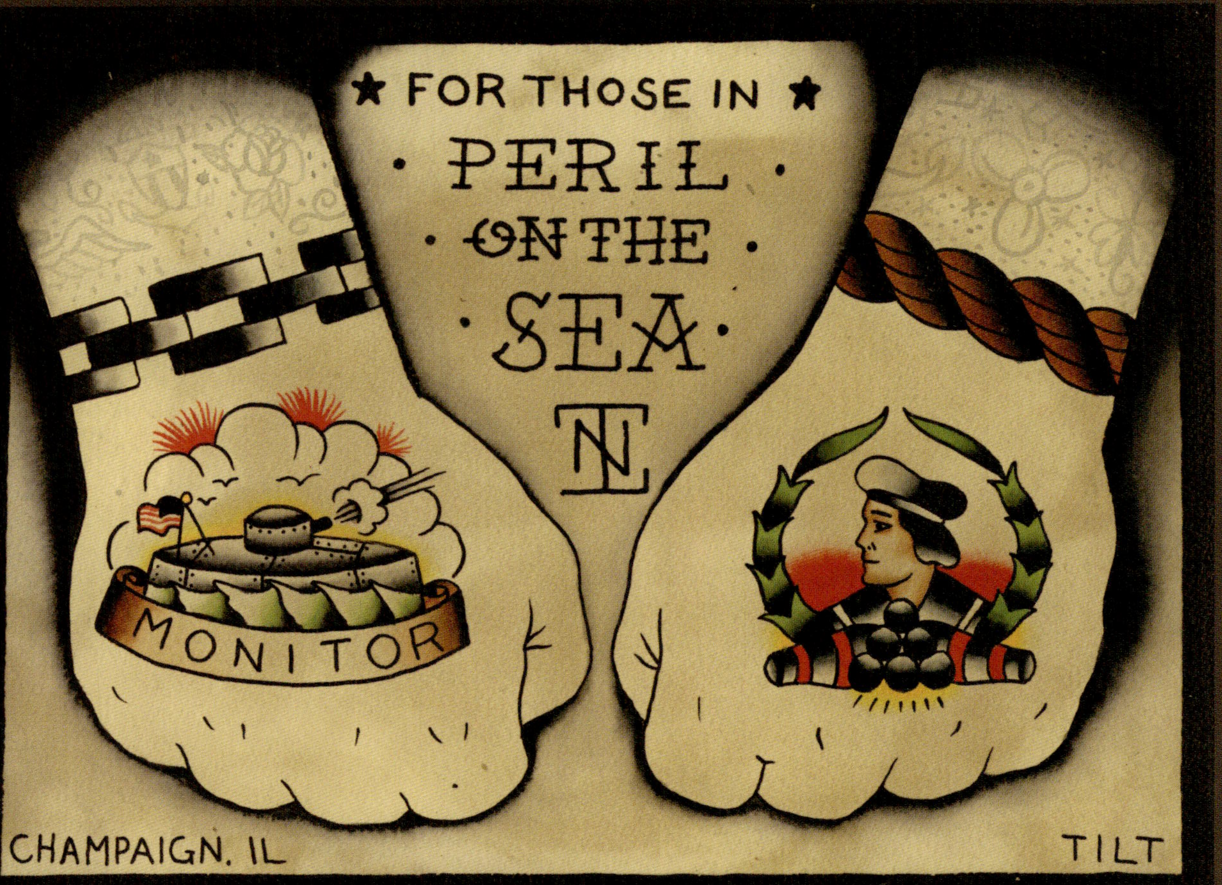
FOR THOSE IN
PERIL
ON THE
SEA
MONITOR
CHAMPAIGN. IL
TILT

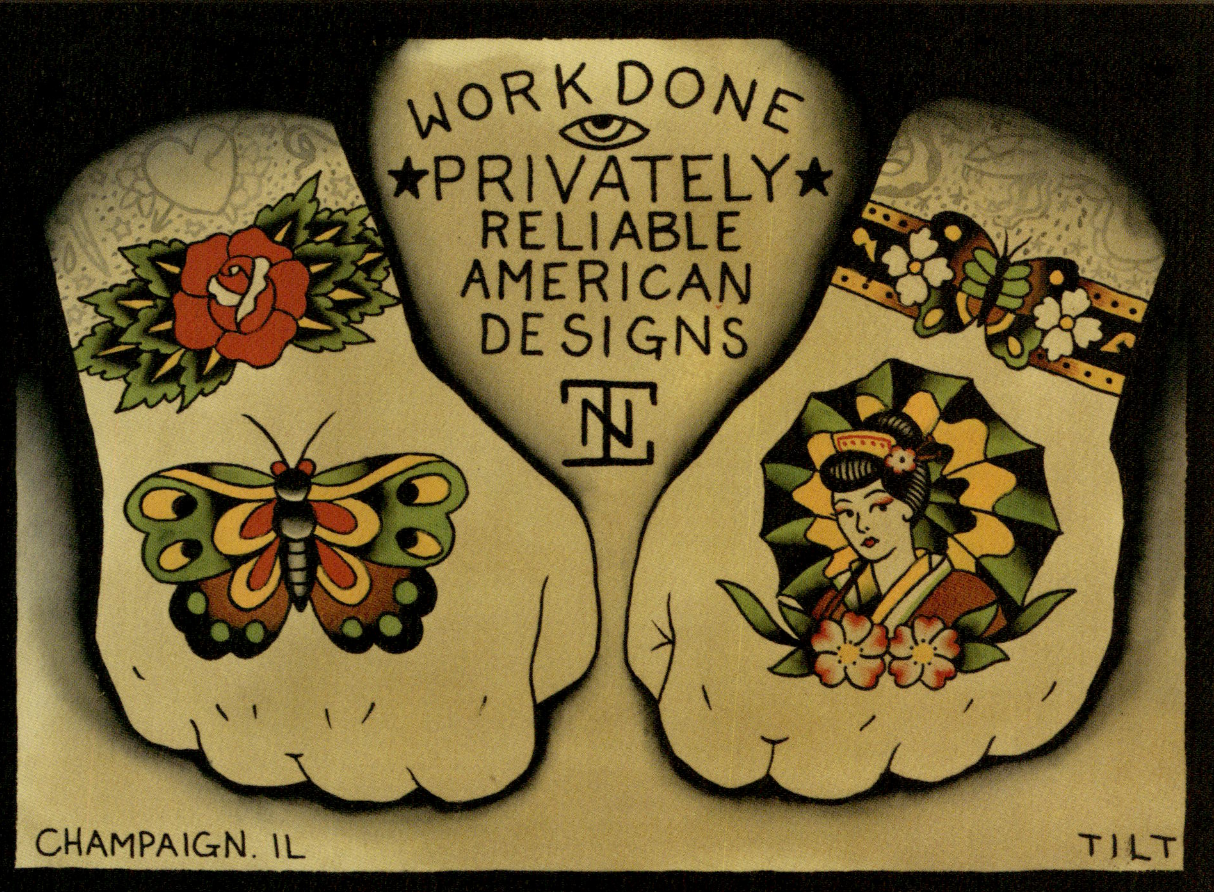
WORK DONE
★PRIVATELY★
RELIABLE
AMERICAN
DESIGNS
CHAMPAIGN. IL
TILT

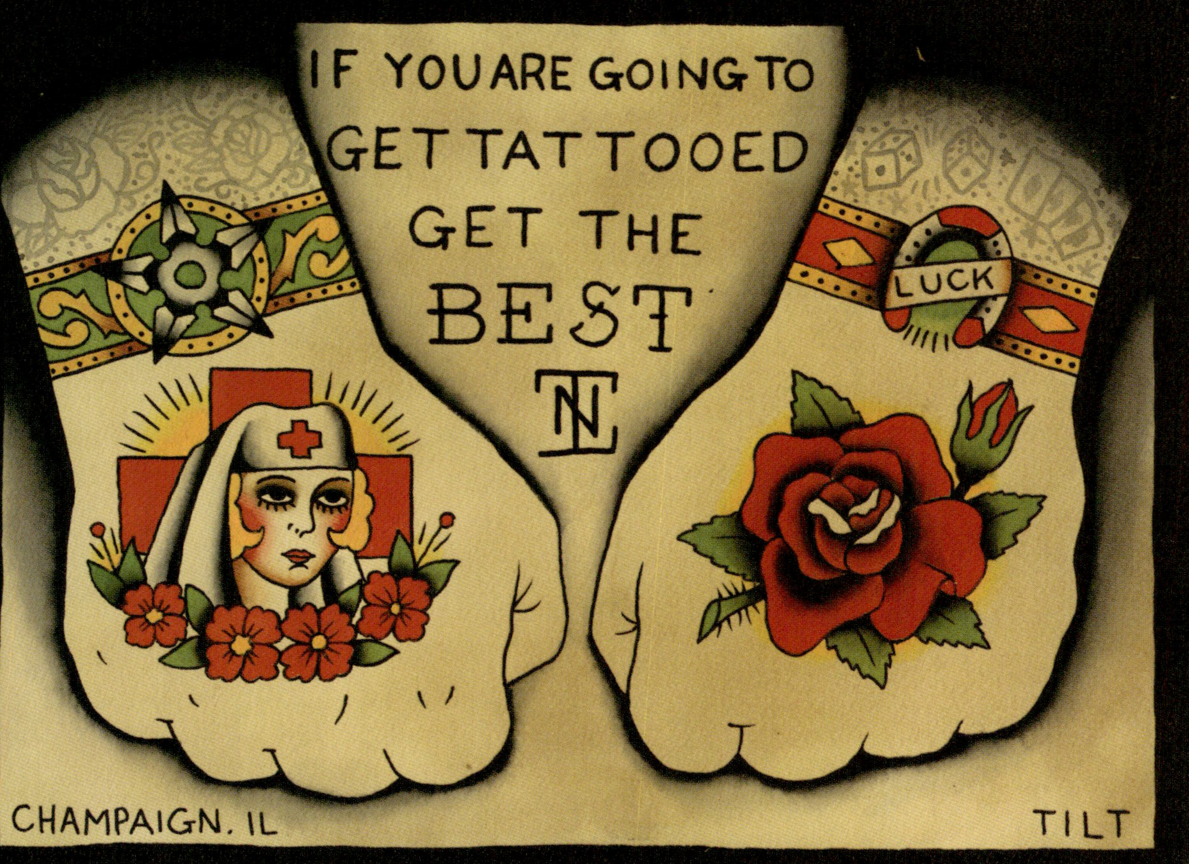
IF YOU ARE GOING TO
GET TATTOOED
GET THE
BEST
LUCK
CHAMPAIGN. IL
TILT

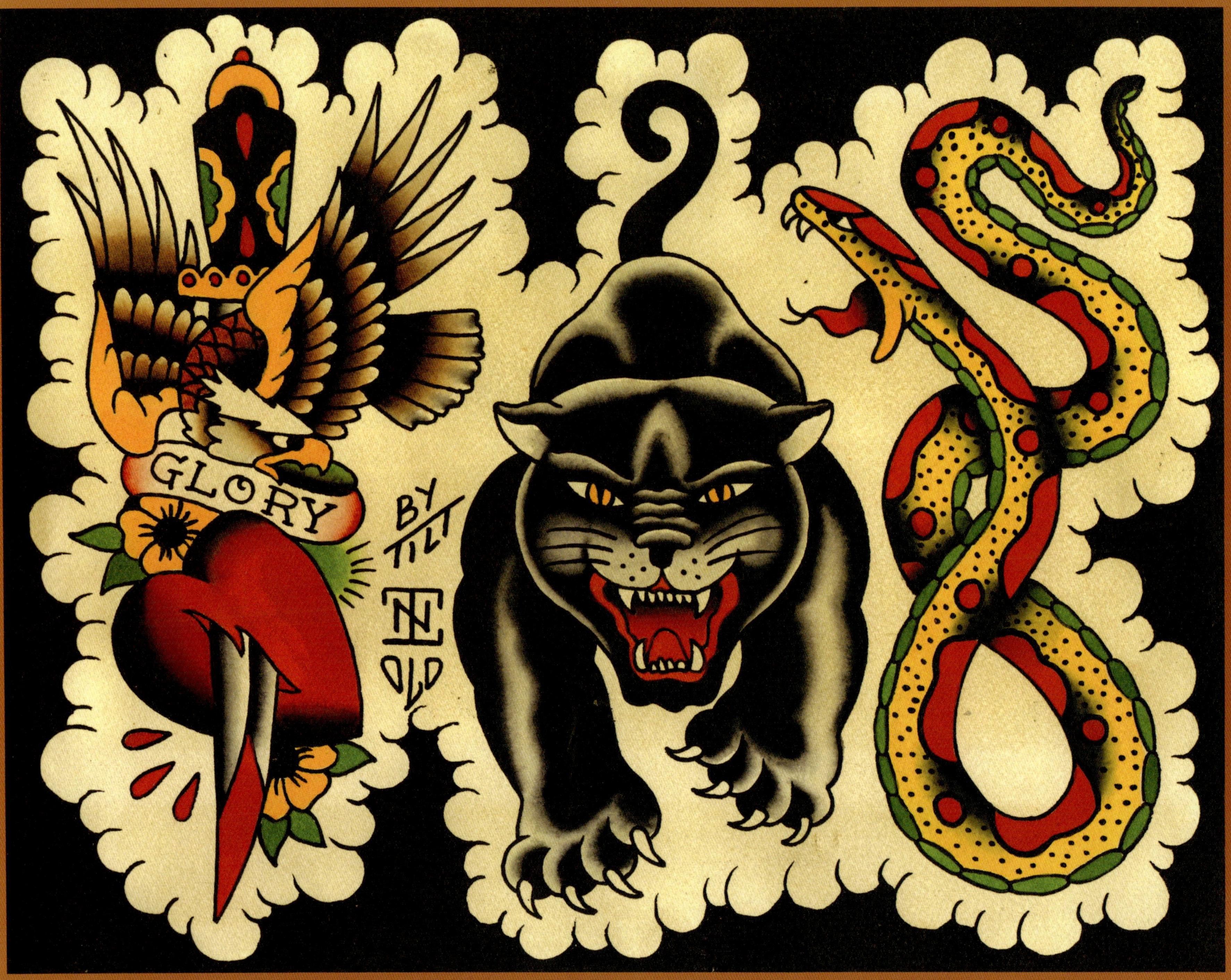
GLORY
BY TILT
OLD

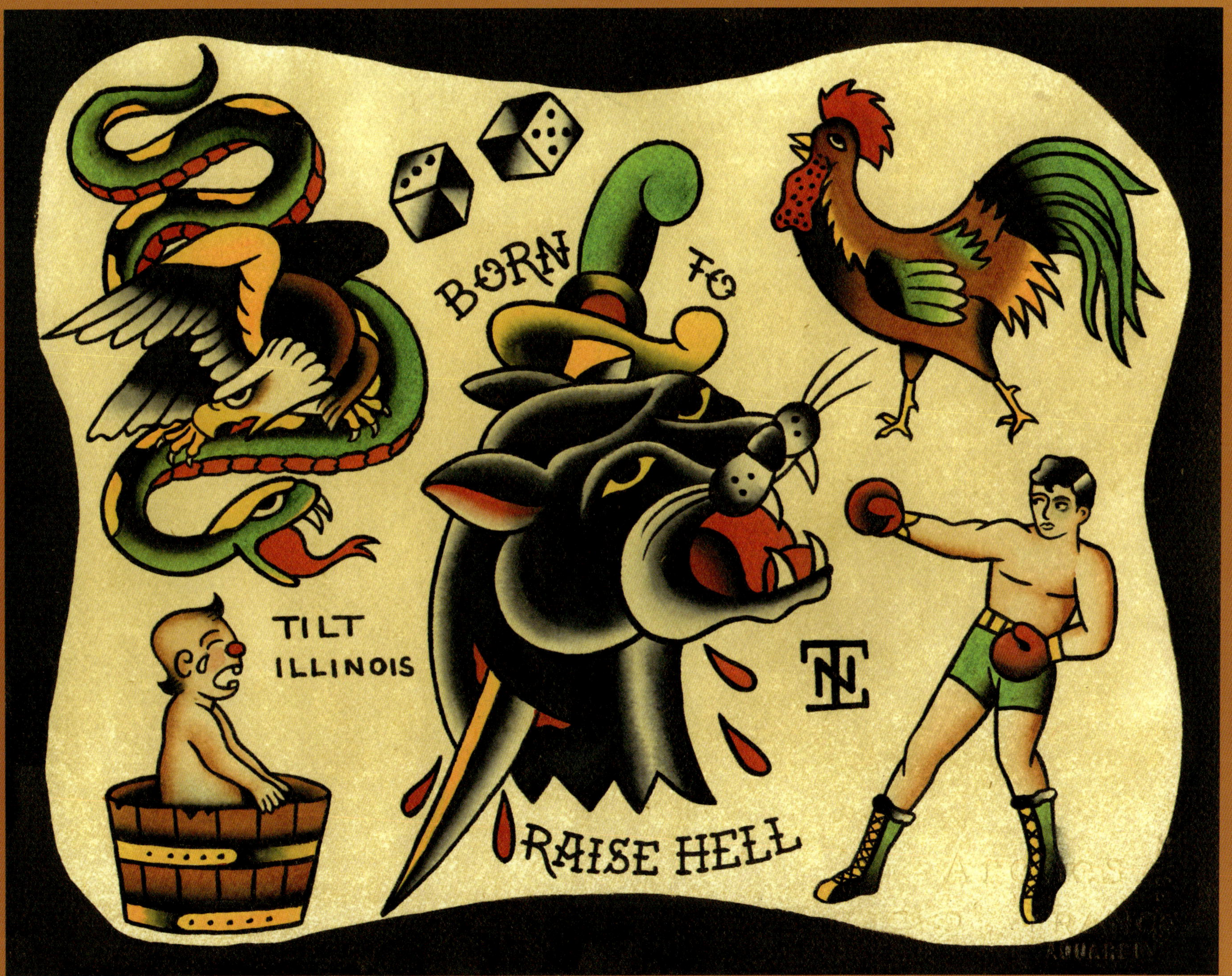
BORN TO
TILT
ILLINOIS
RAISE HELL

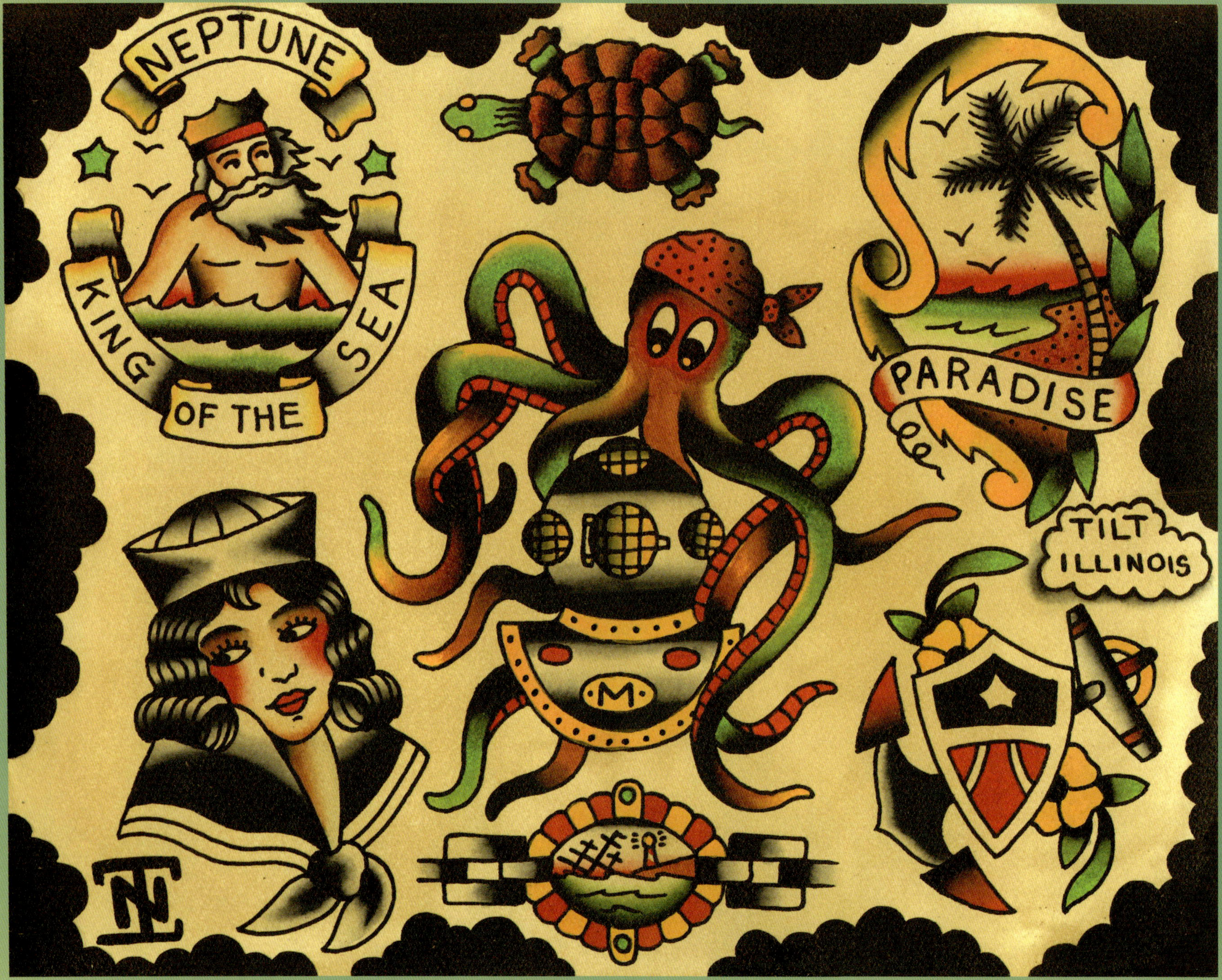

NEPTUNE
KING OF THE SEA

PARADISE

TILT
ILLINOIS

M

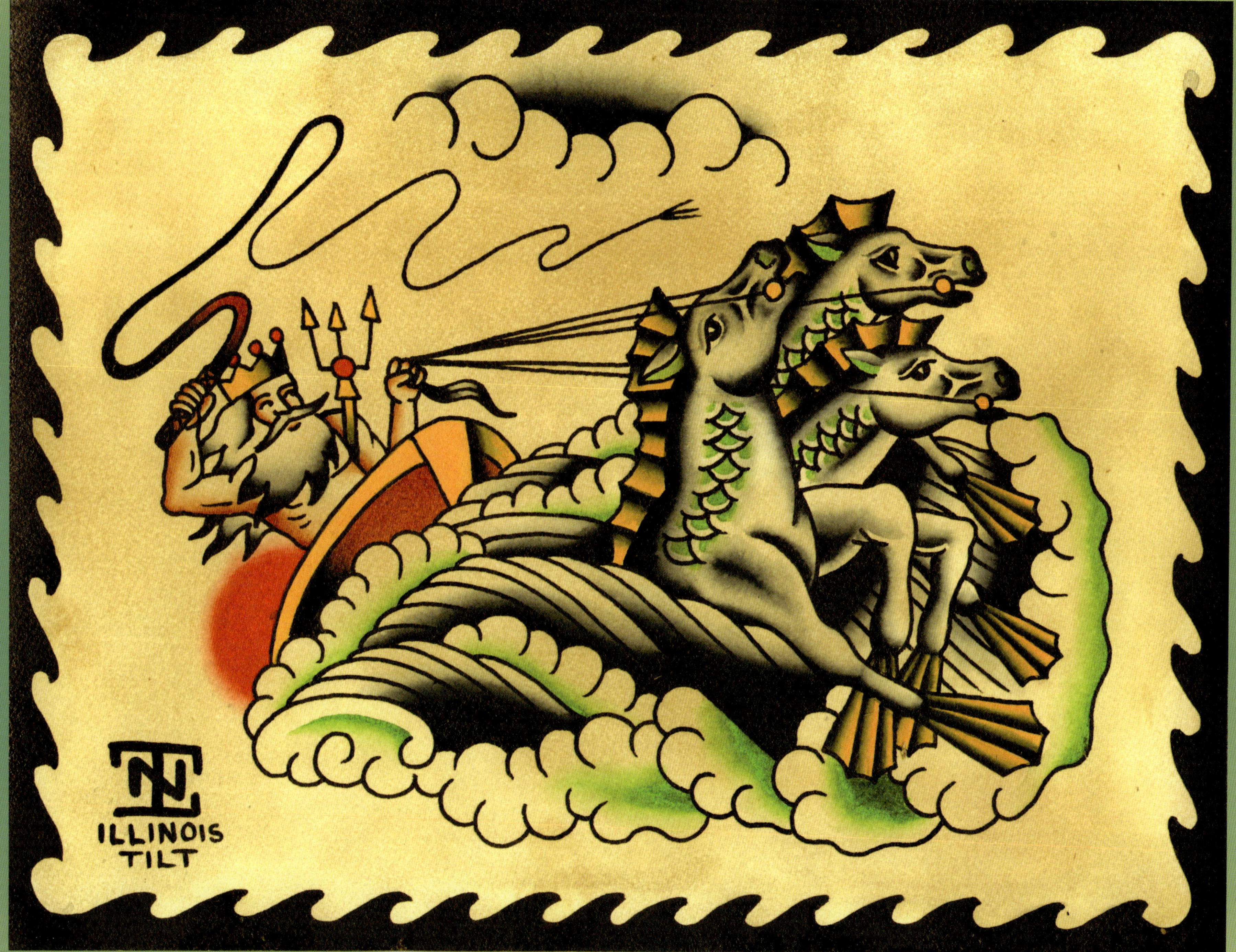
ILLINOIS
TILT

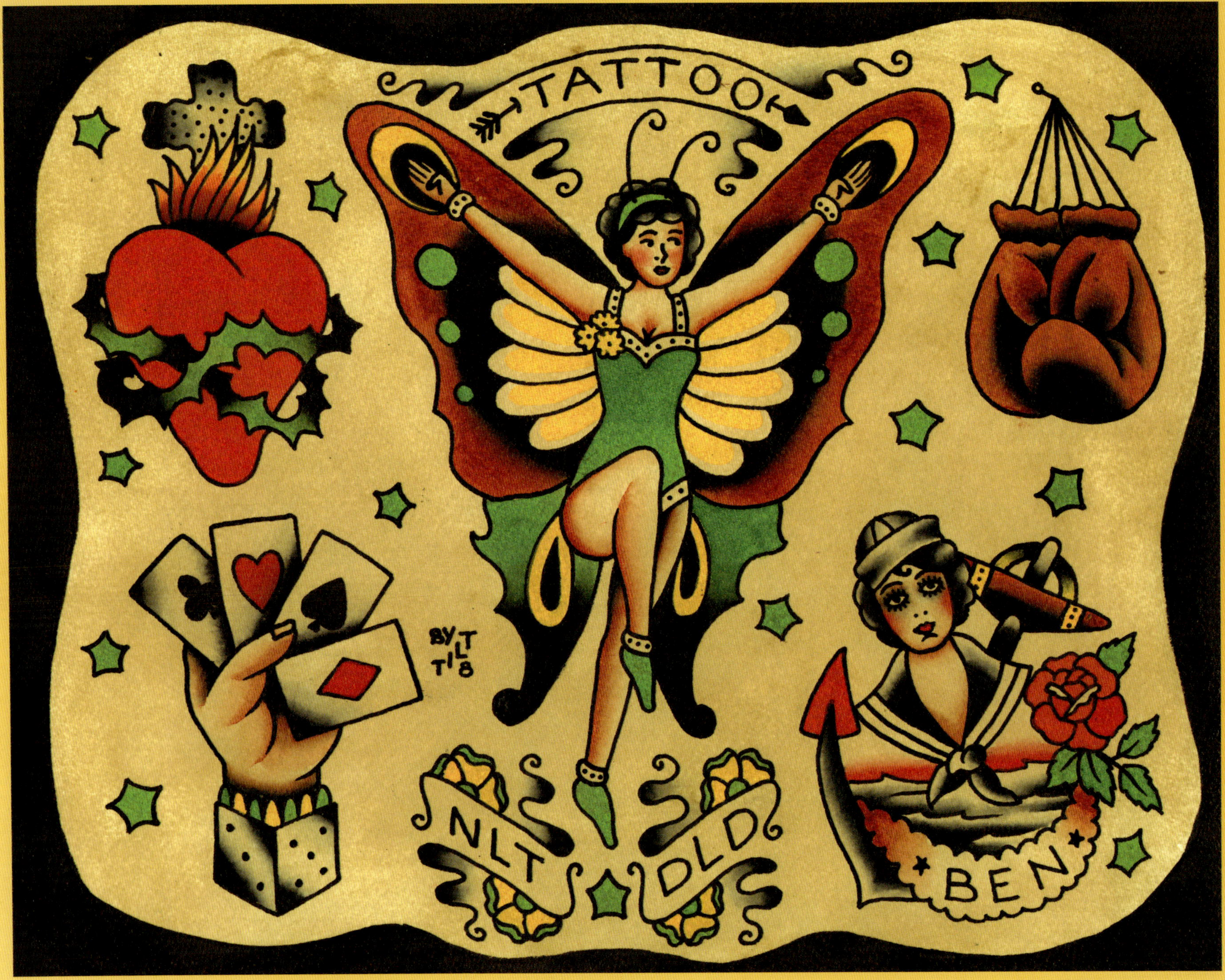

TATTOO
BY TLT T'18
NLT
DLD
BEN

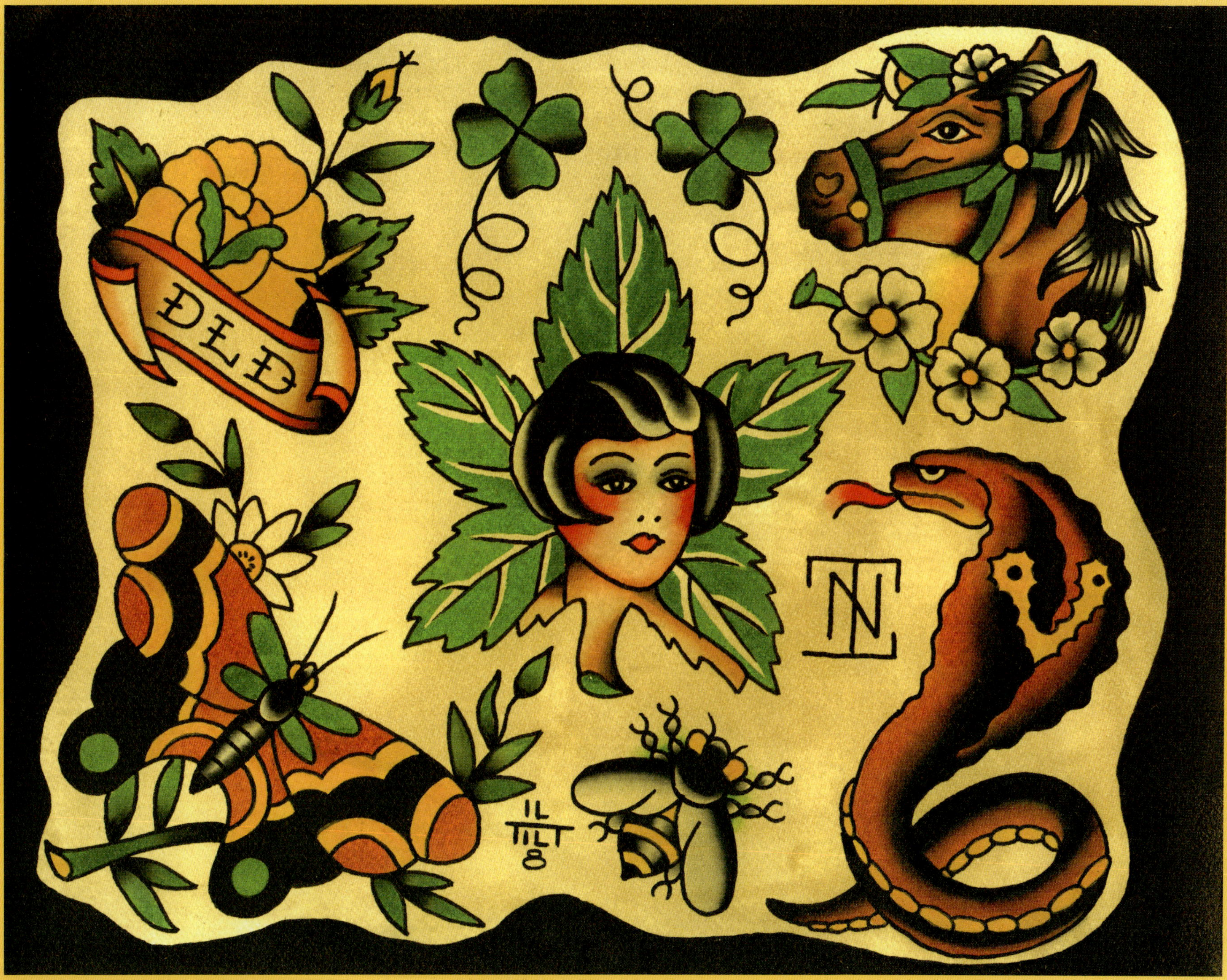

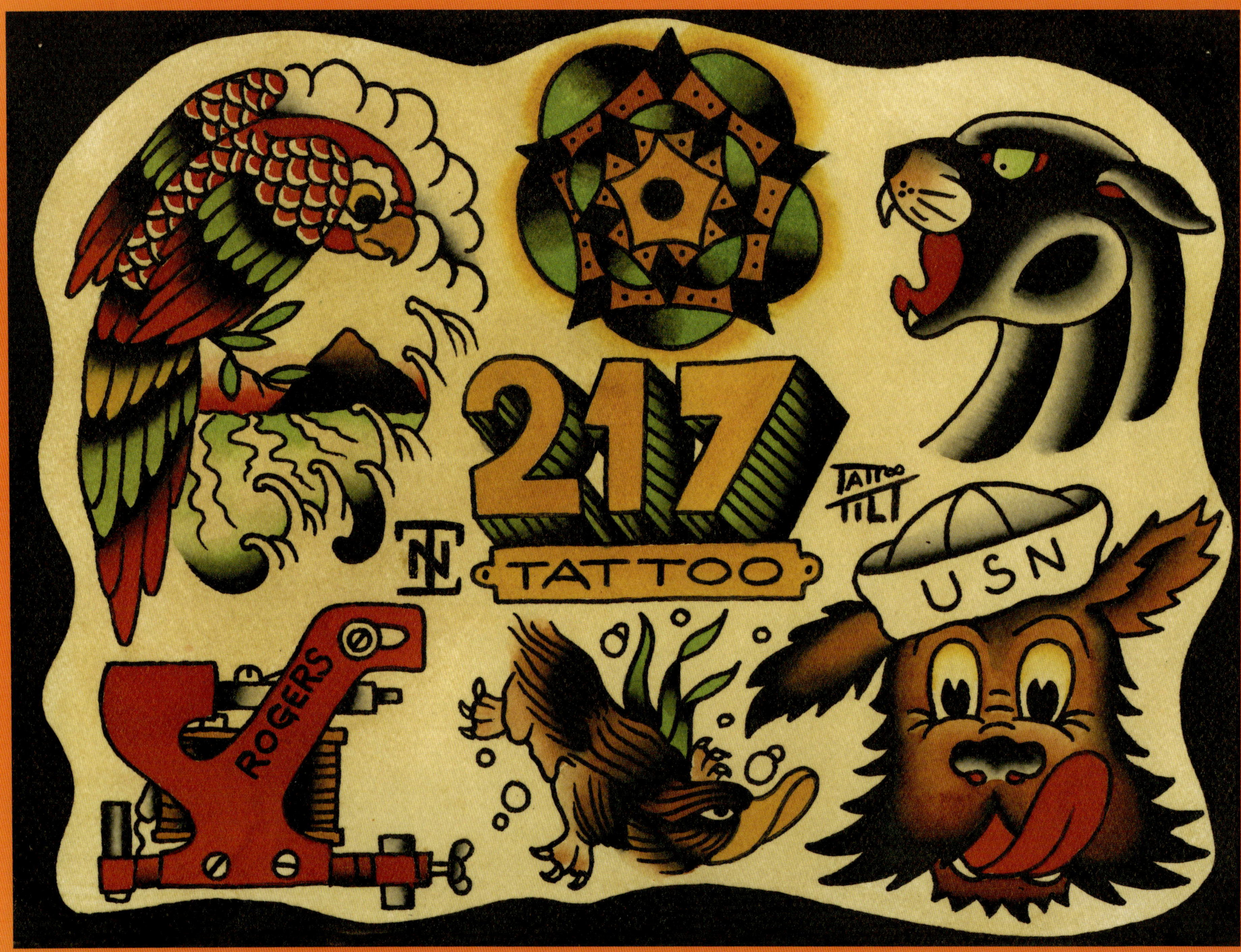

217
TATTOO
TATTOO TILT
USN
ROGERS

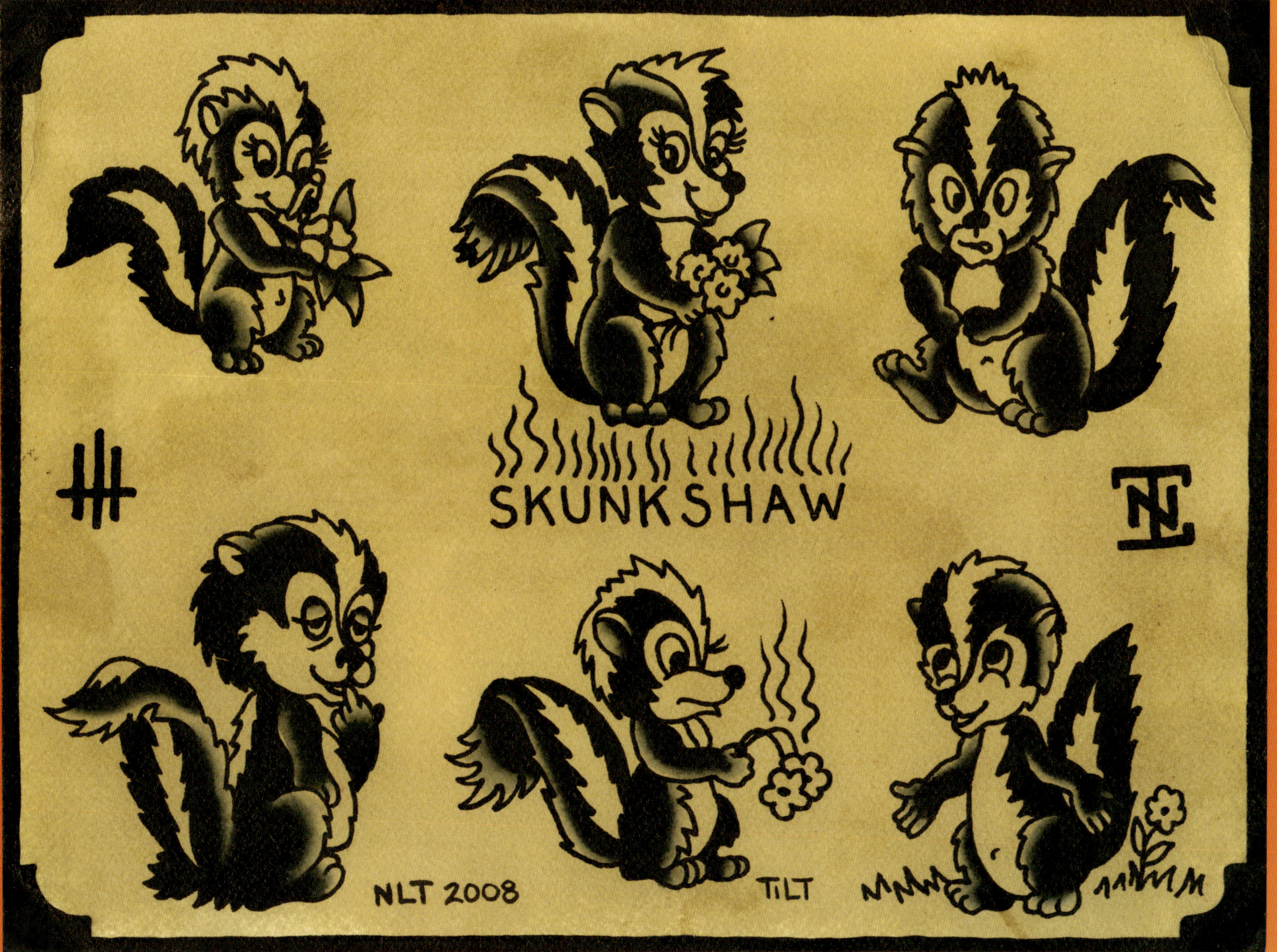
SKUNKSHAW
NLT 2008
TILT

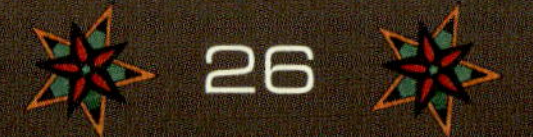

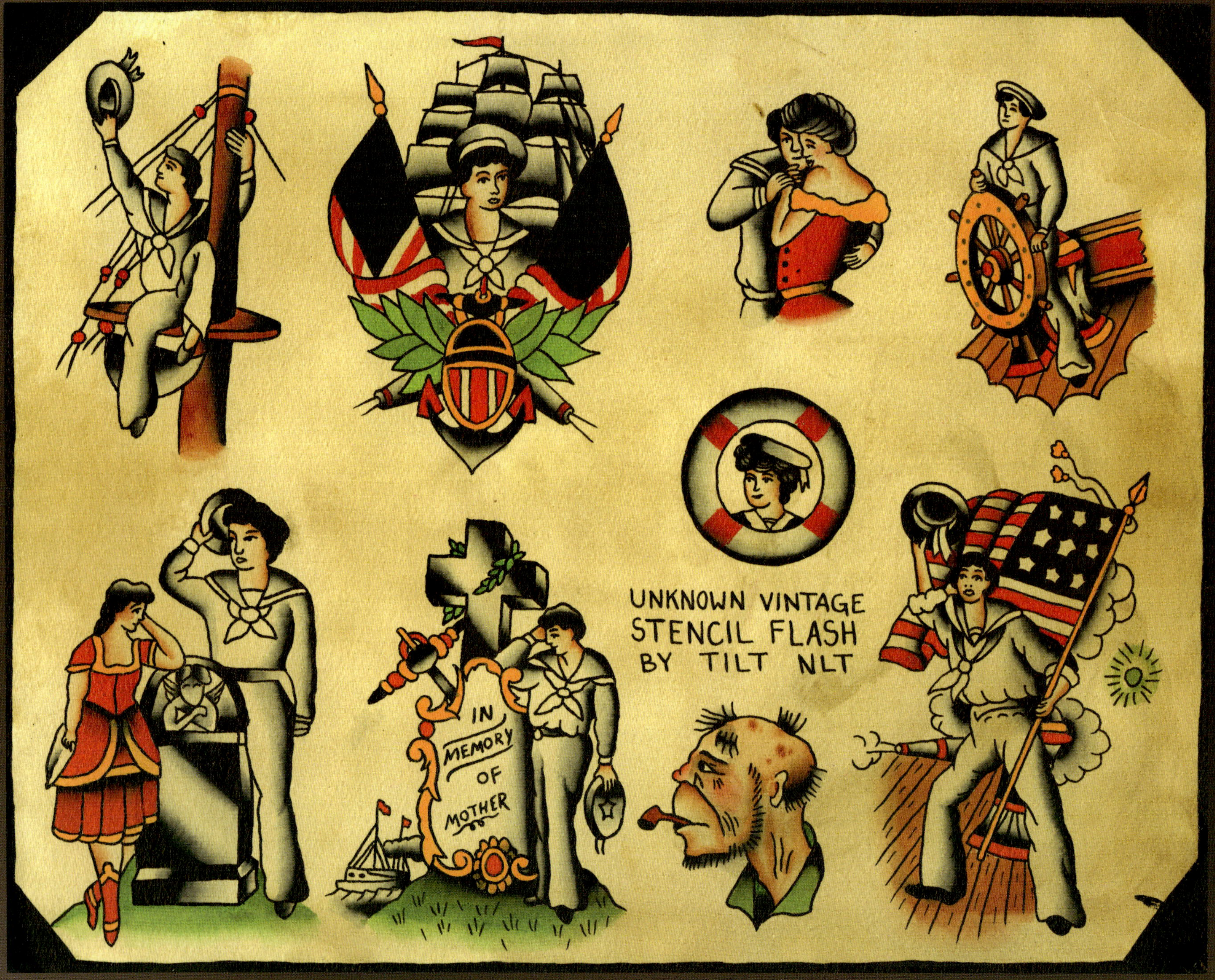

IN MEMORY OF MOTHER

UNKNOWN VINTAGE
STENCIL FLASH
BY TILT NLT

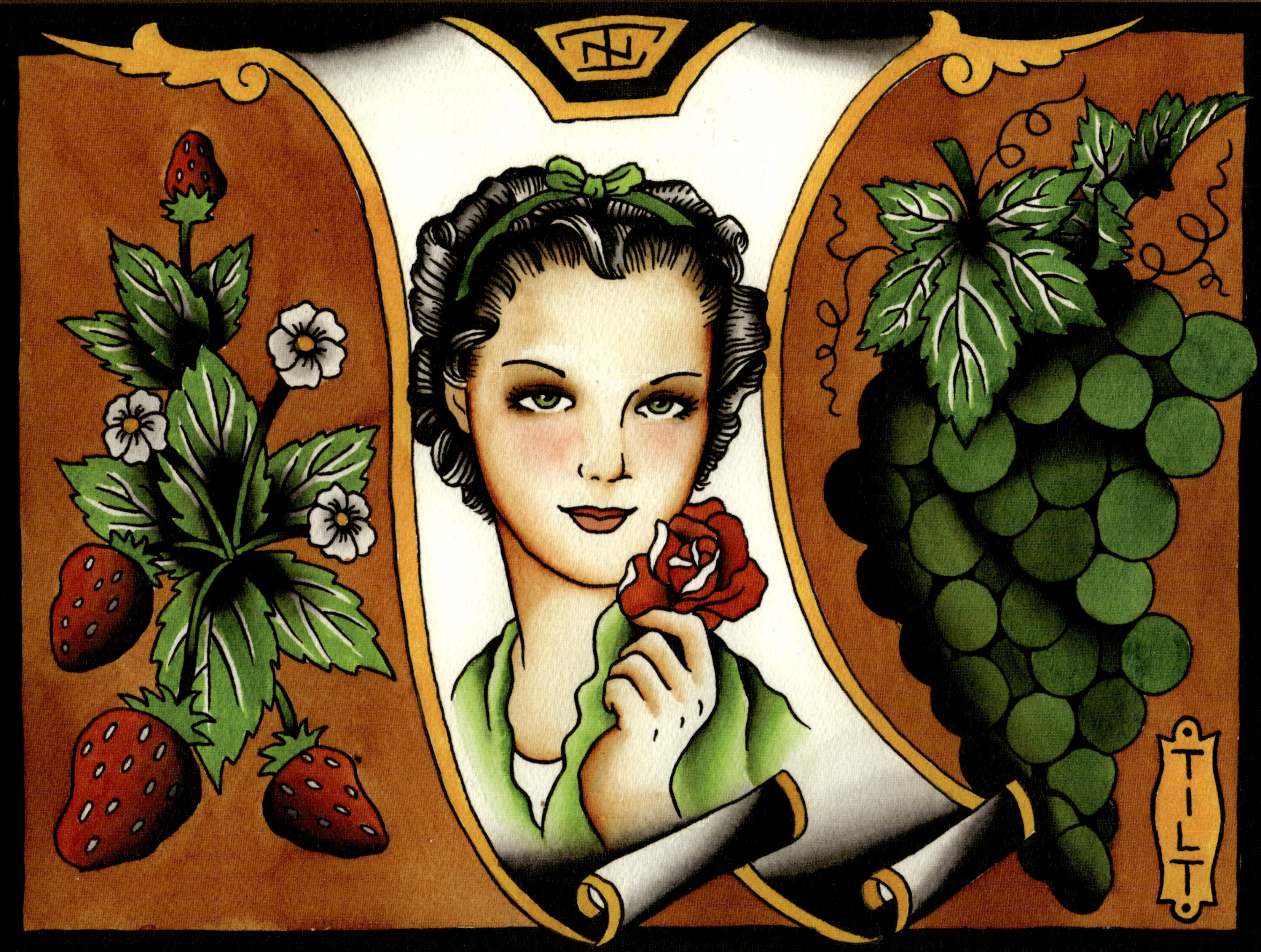
TILT

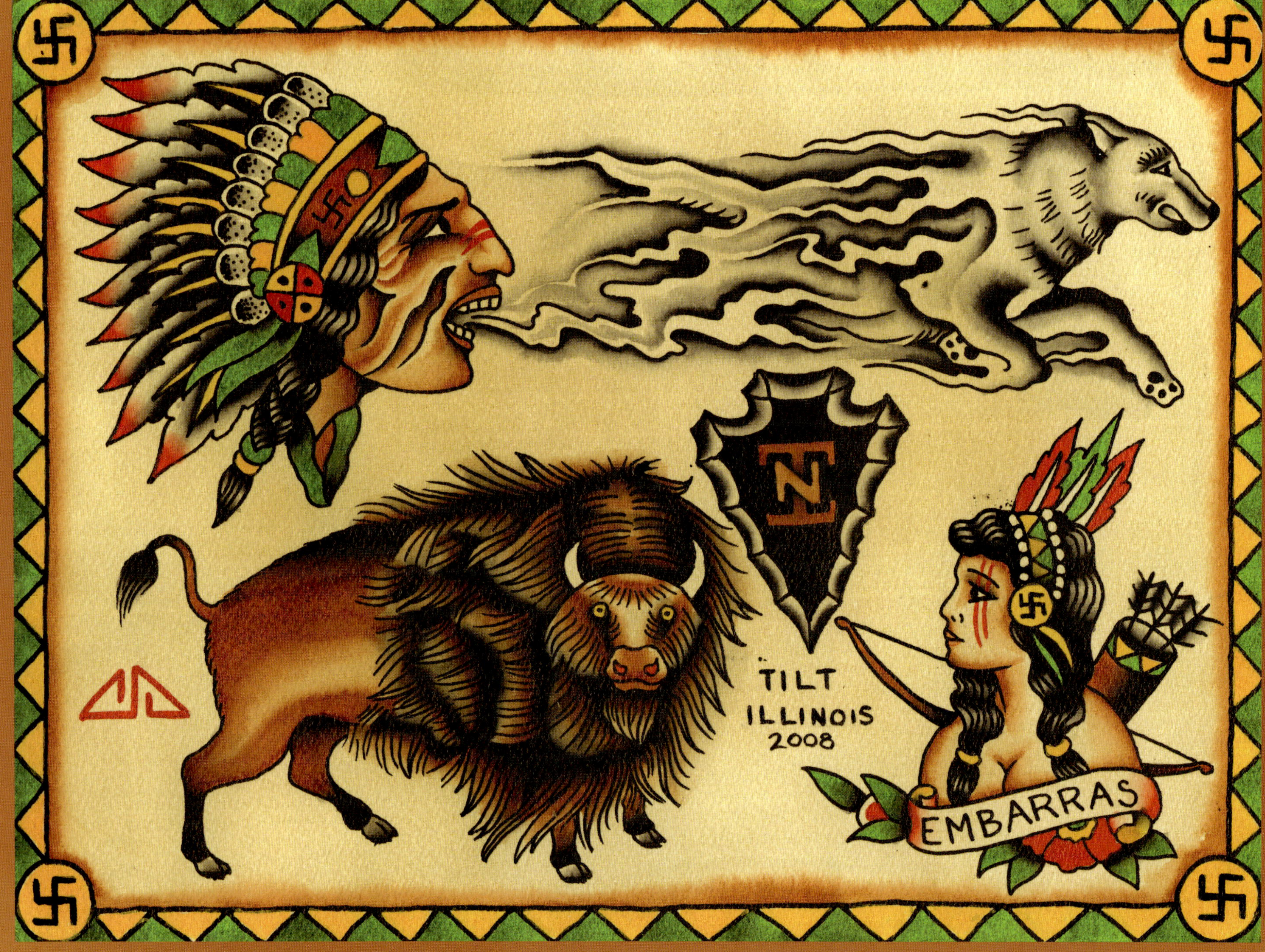
N
TILT
ILLINOIS
2008
EMBARRAS

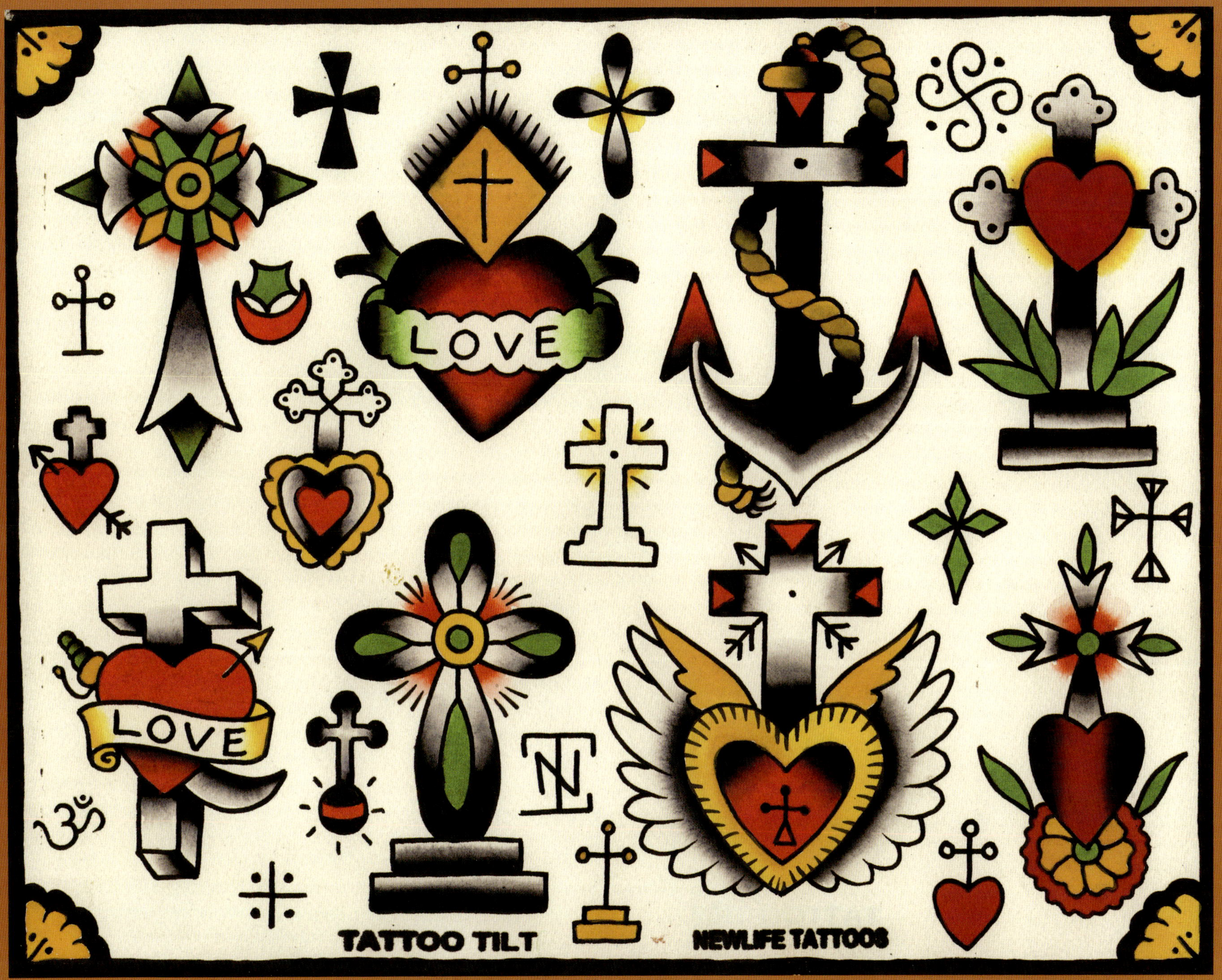
LOVE
LOVE
TATTOO TILT
NEWLIFE TATTOOS

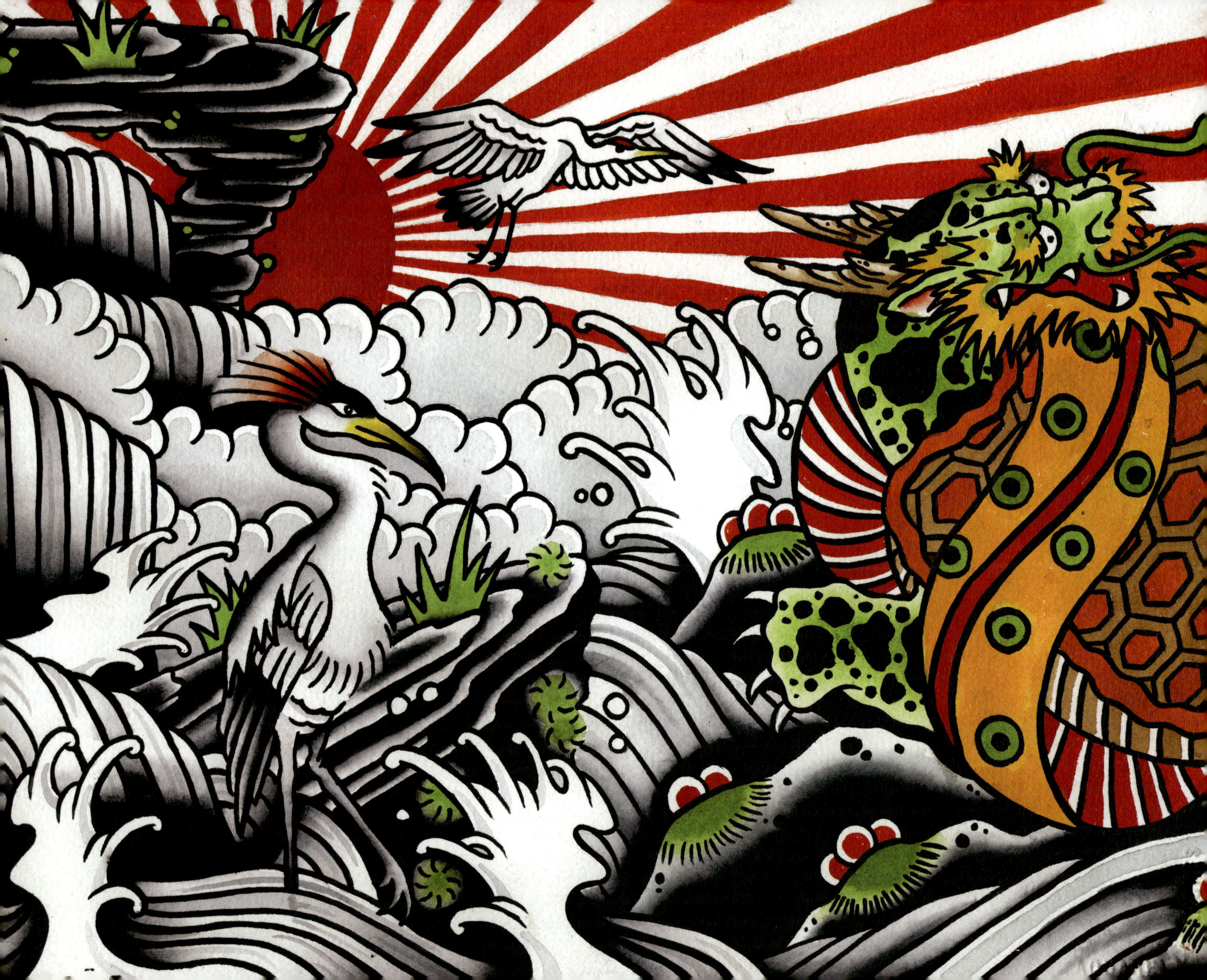

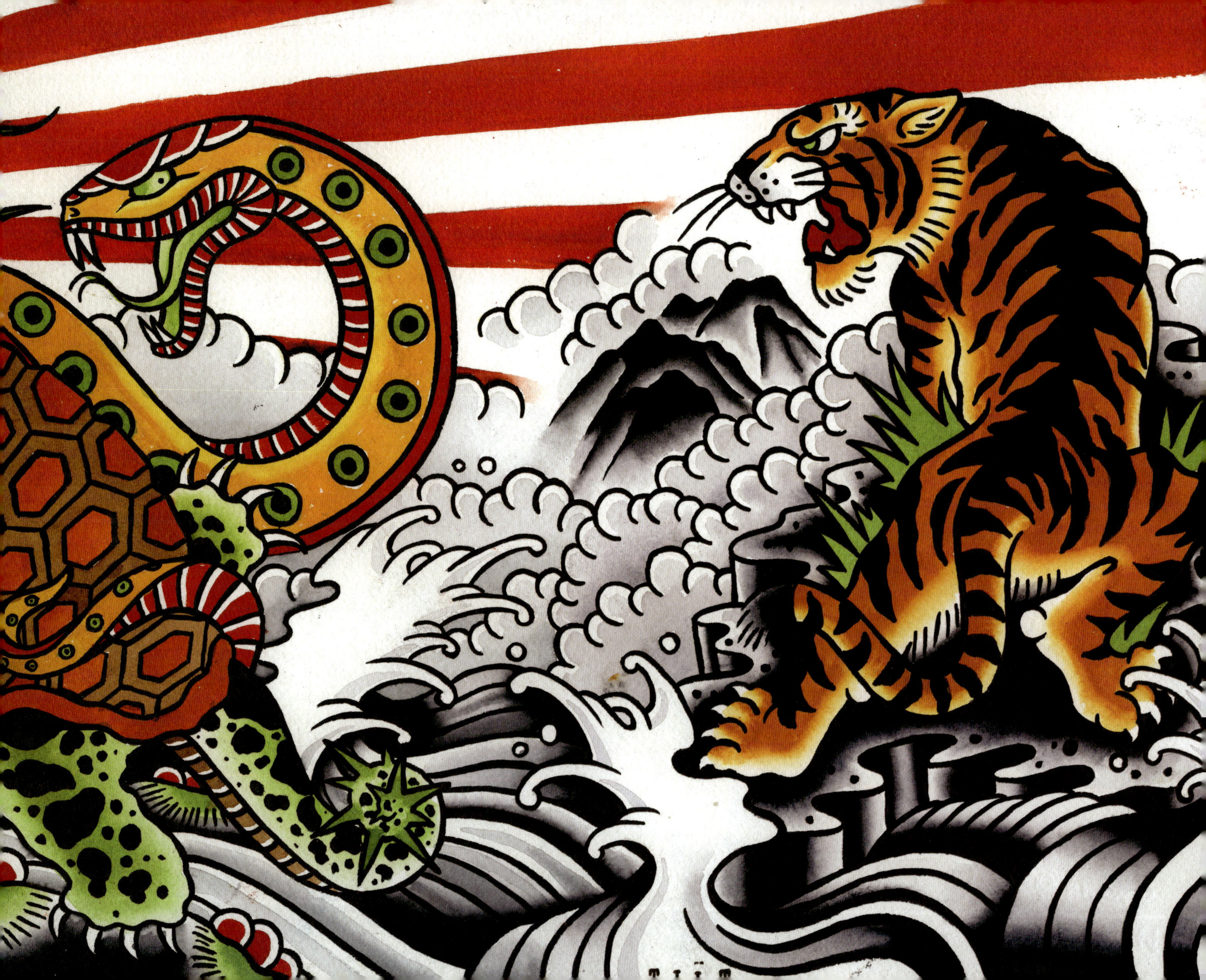

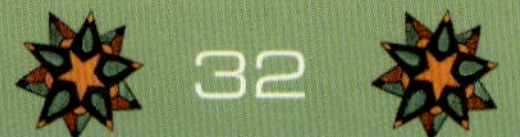

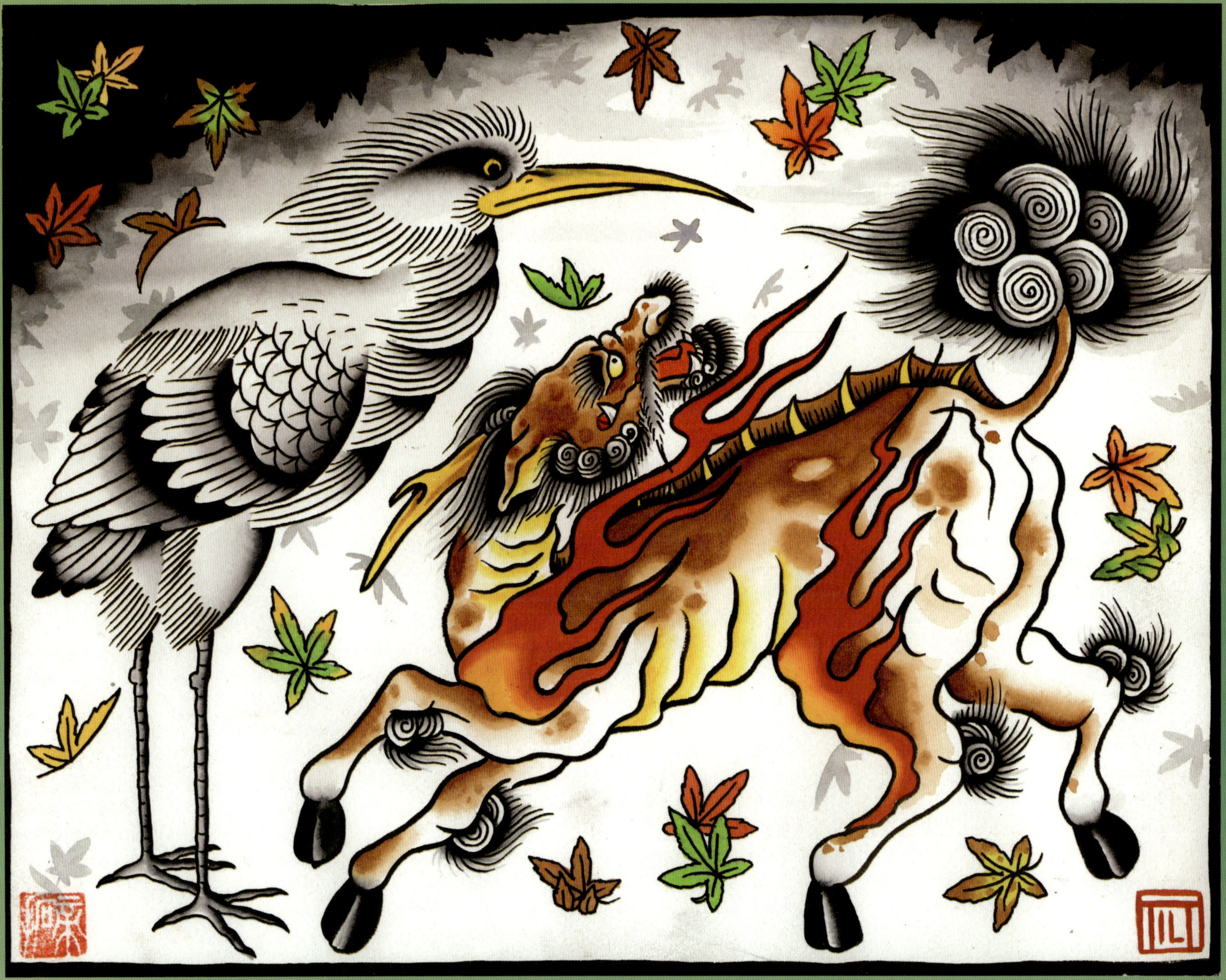

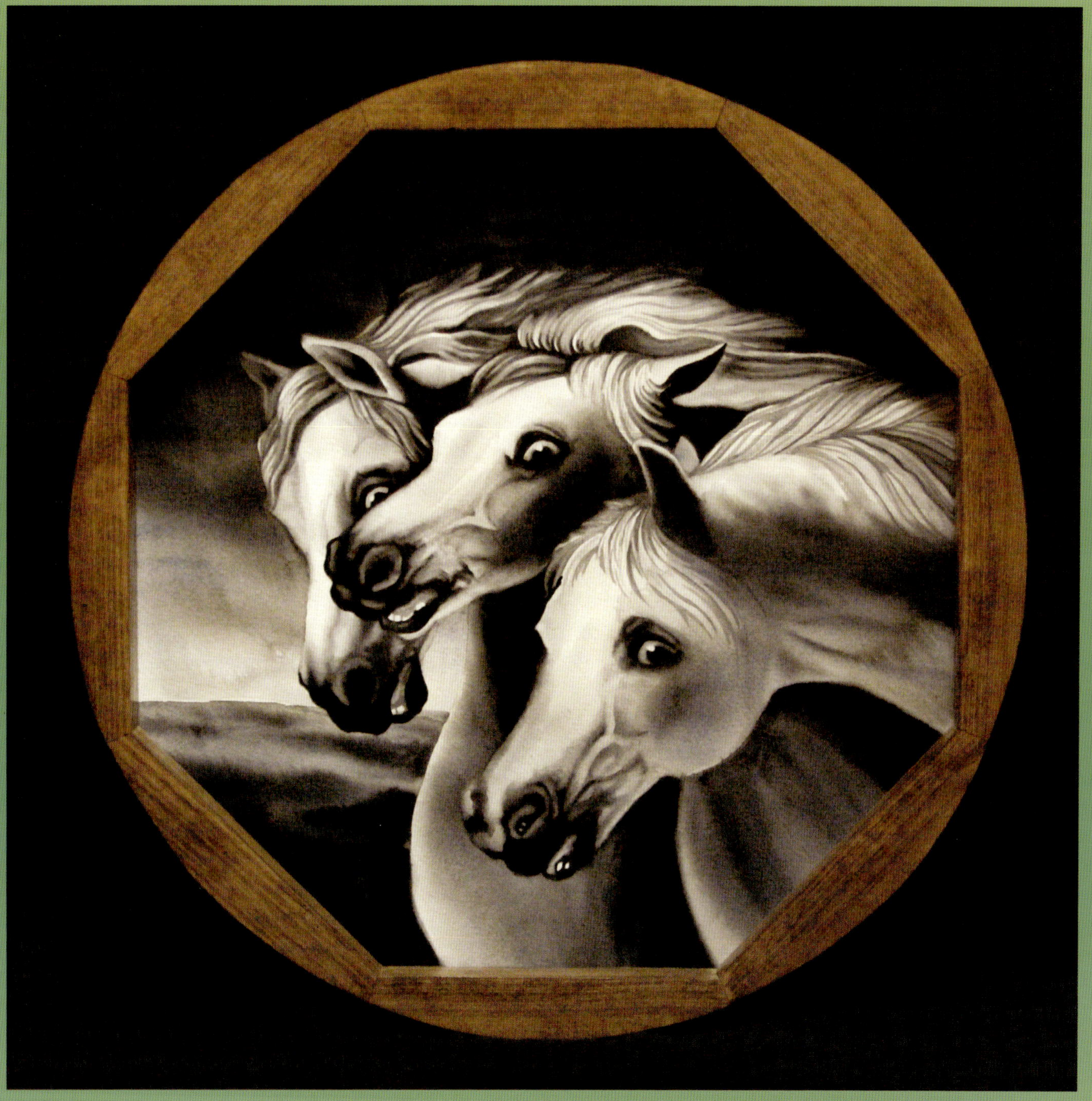

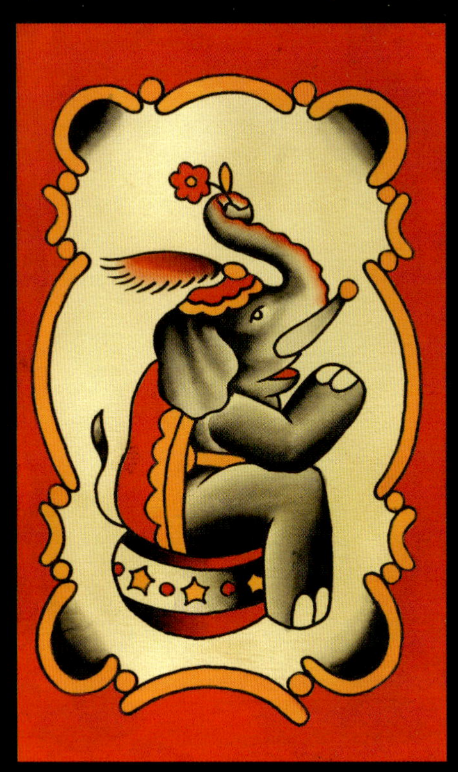

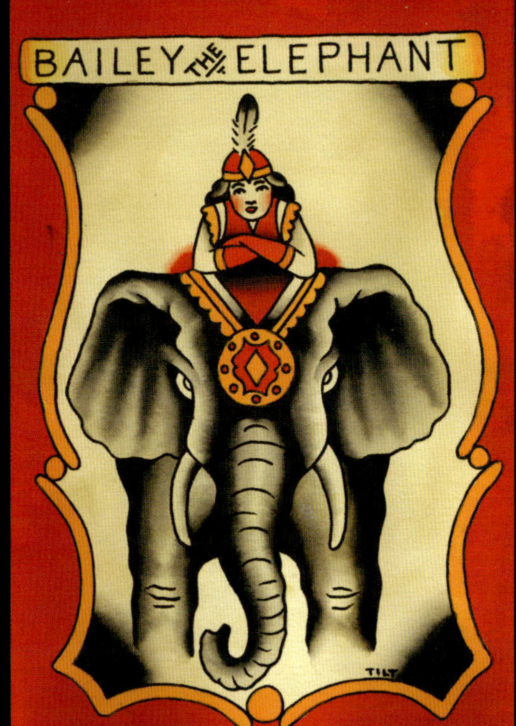

BAILEY THE ELEPHANT
TILT

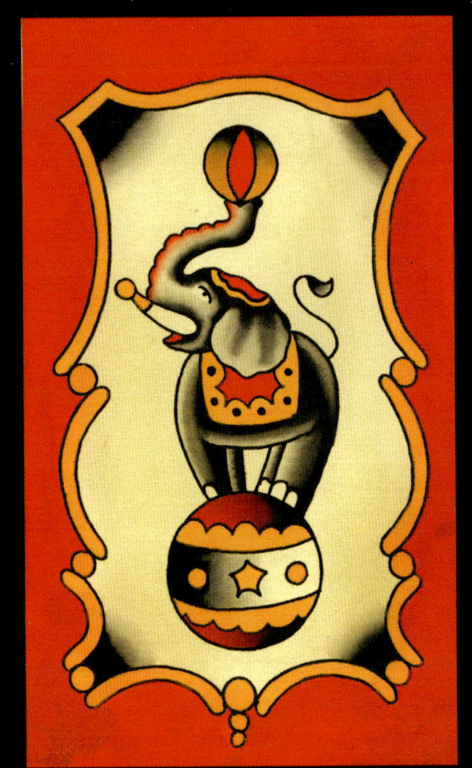

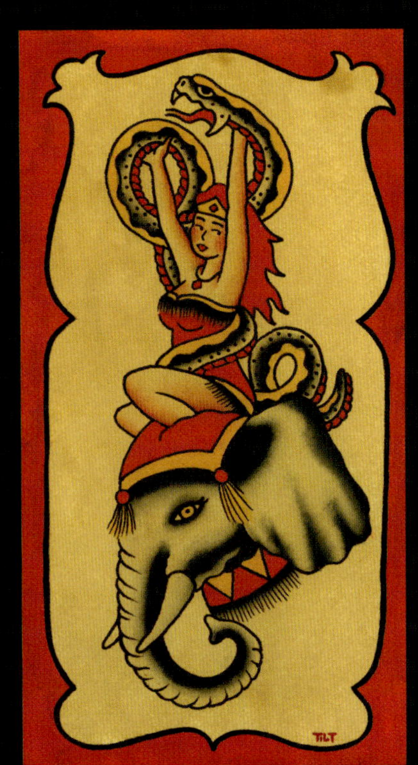

TILT

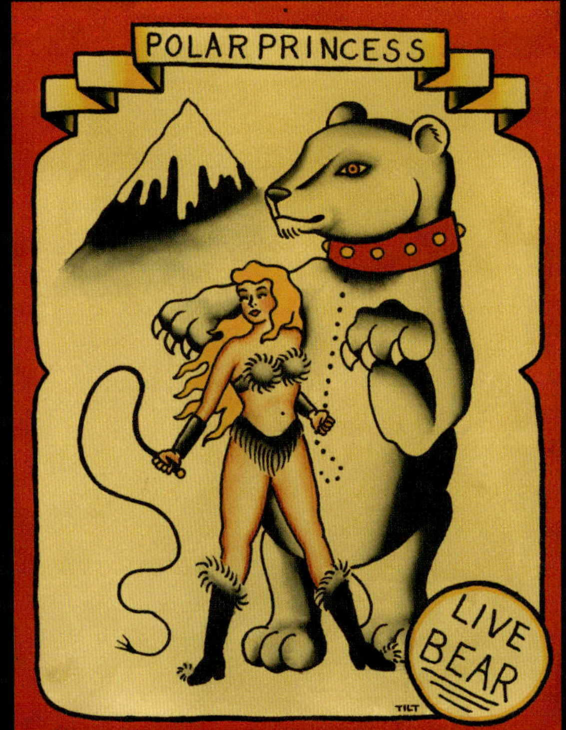

POLAR PRINCESS
LIVE BEAR
TILT

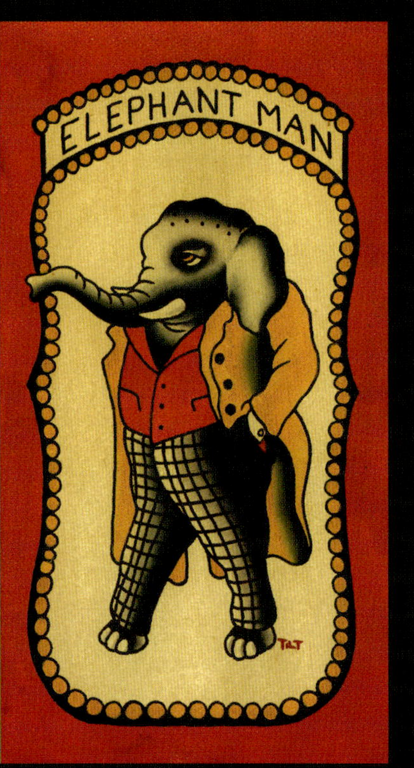

ELEPHANT MAN
TILT

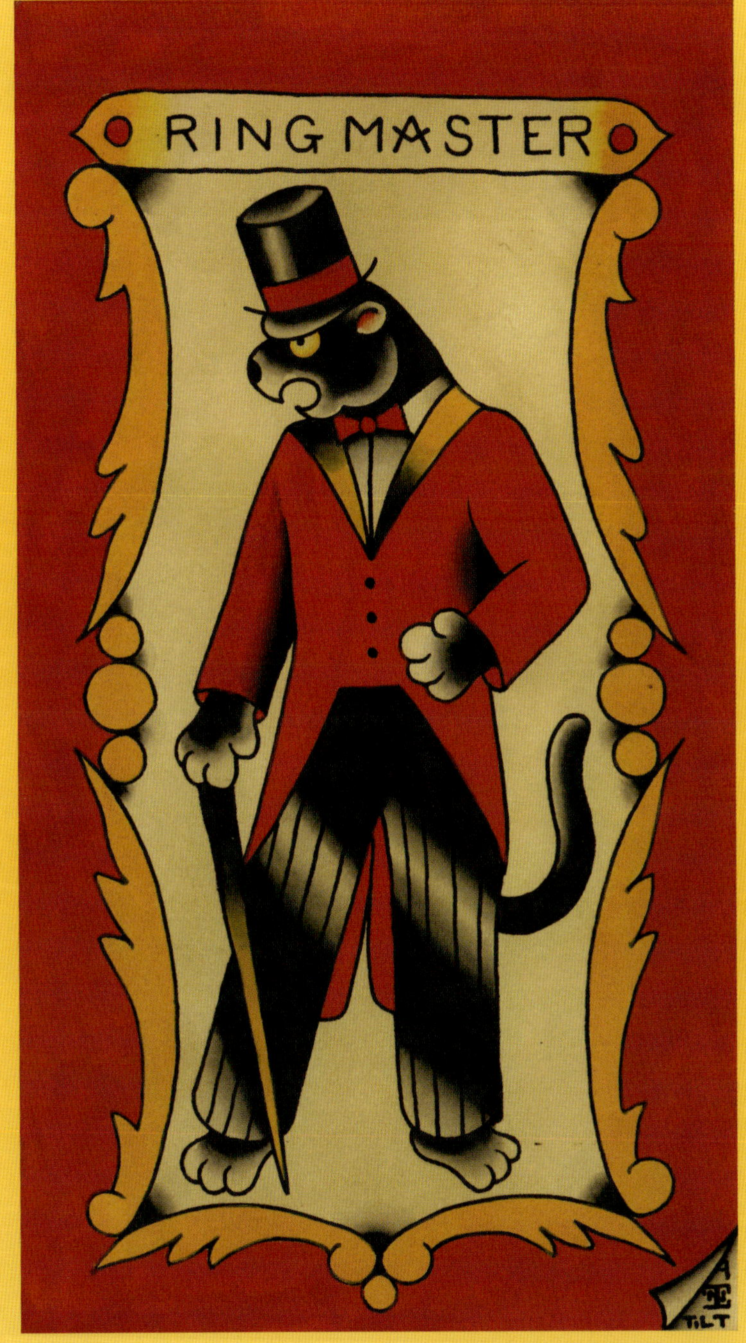

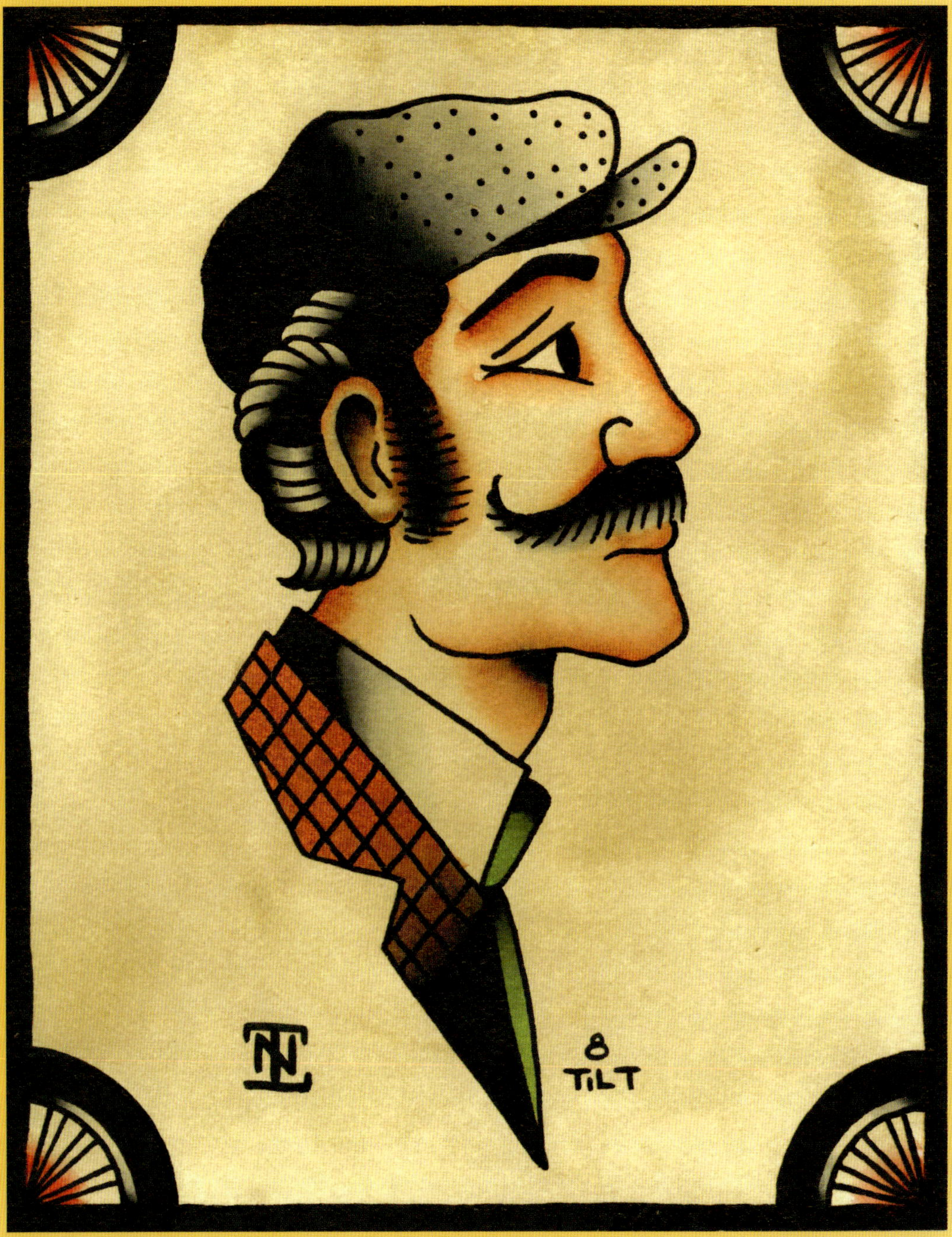

8
TiLT

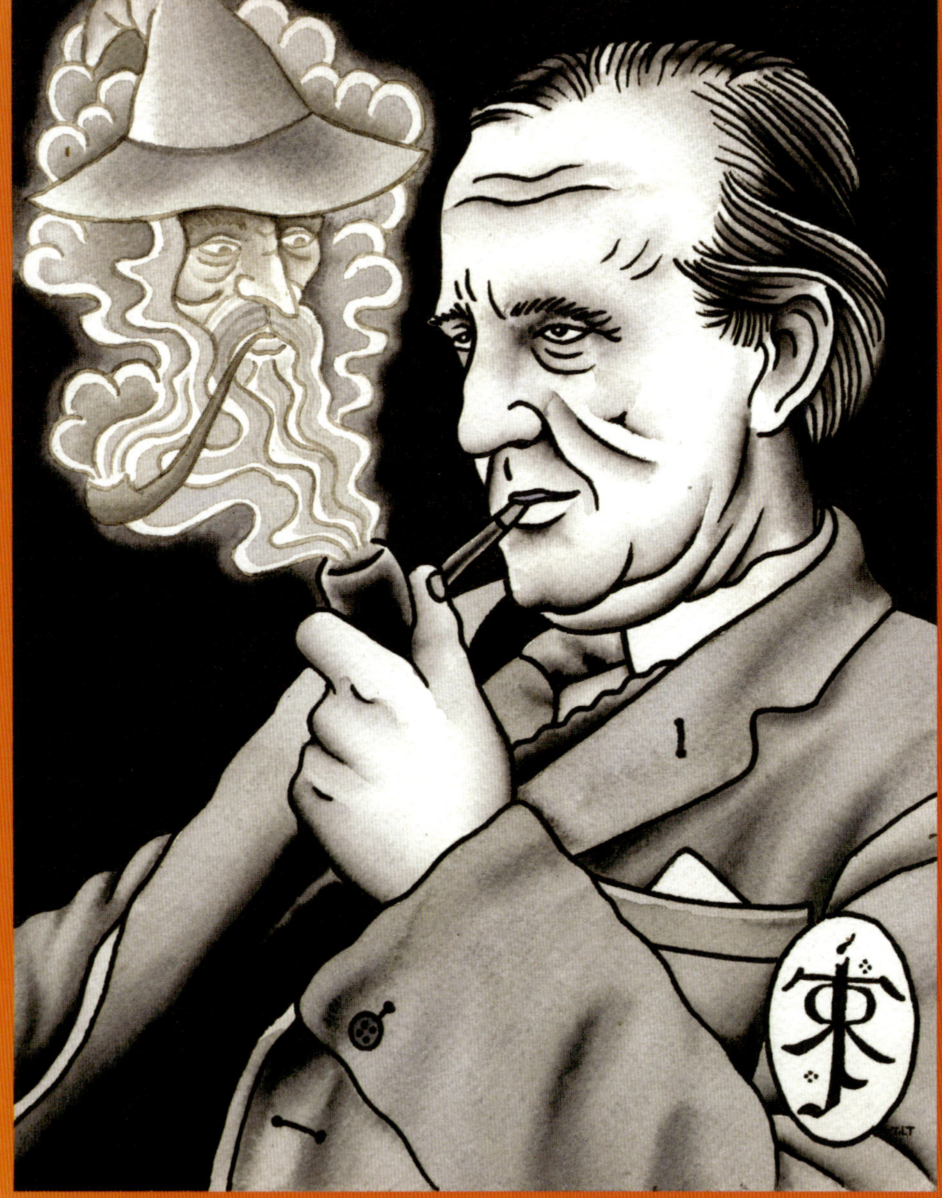

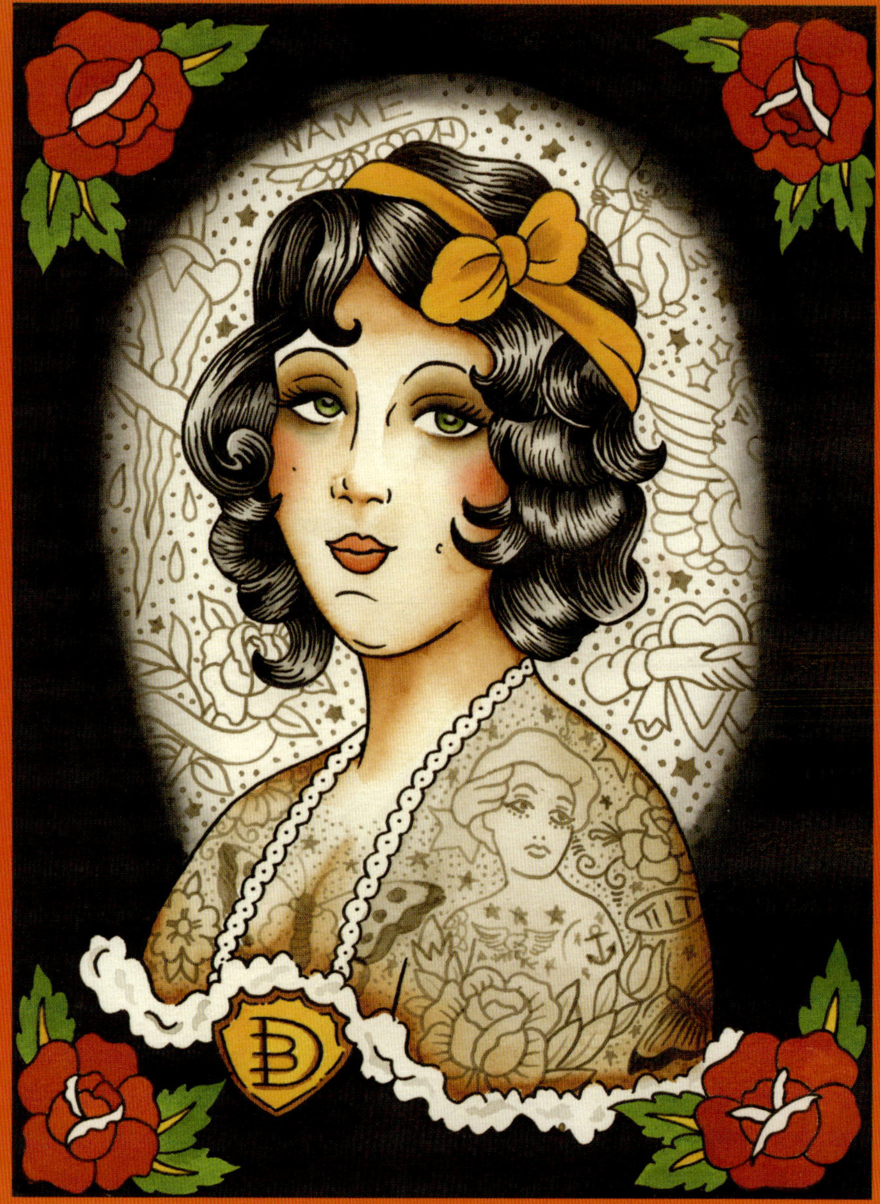
NAME
TILT

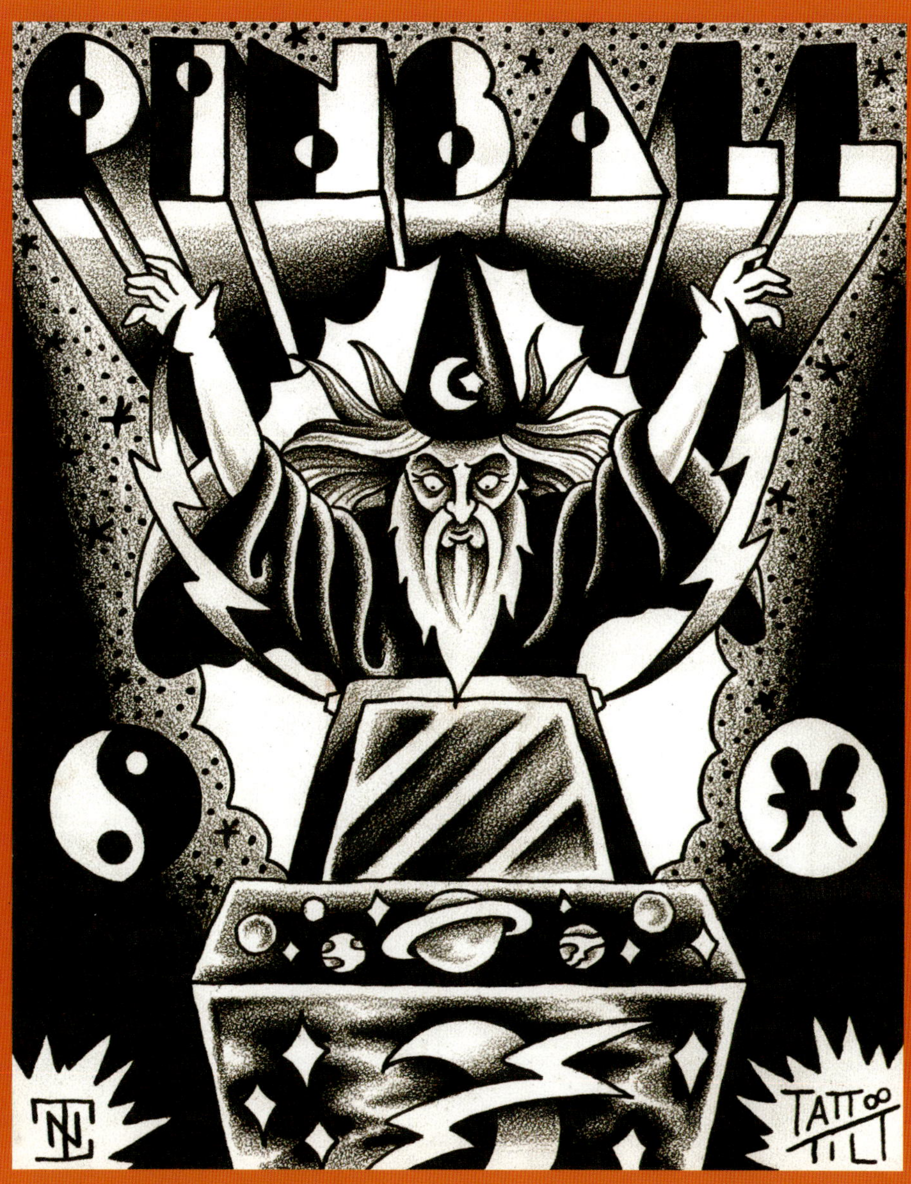
PINBALL
TATTOO
TILT

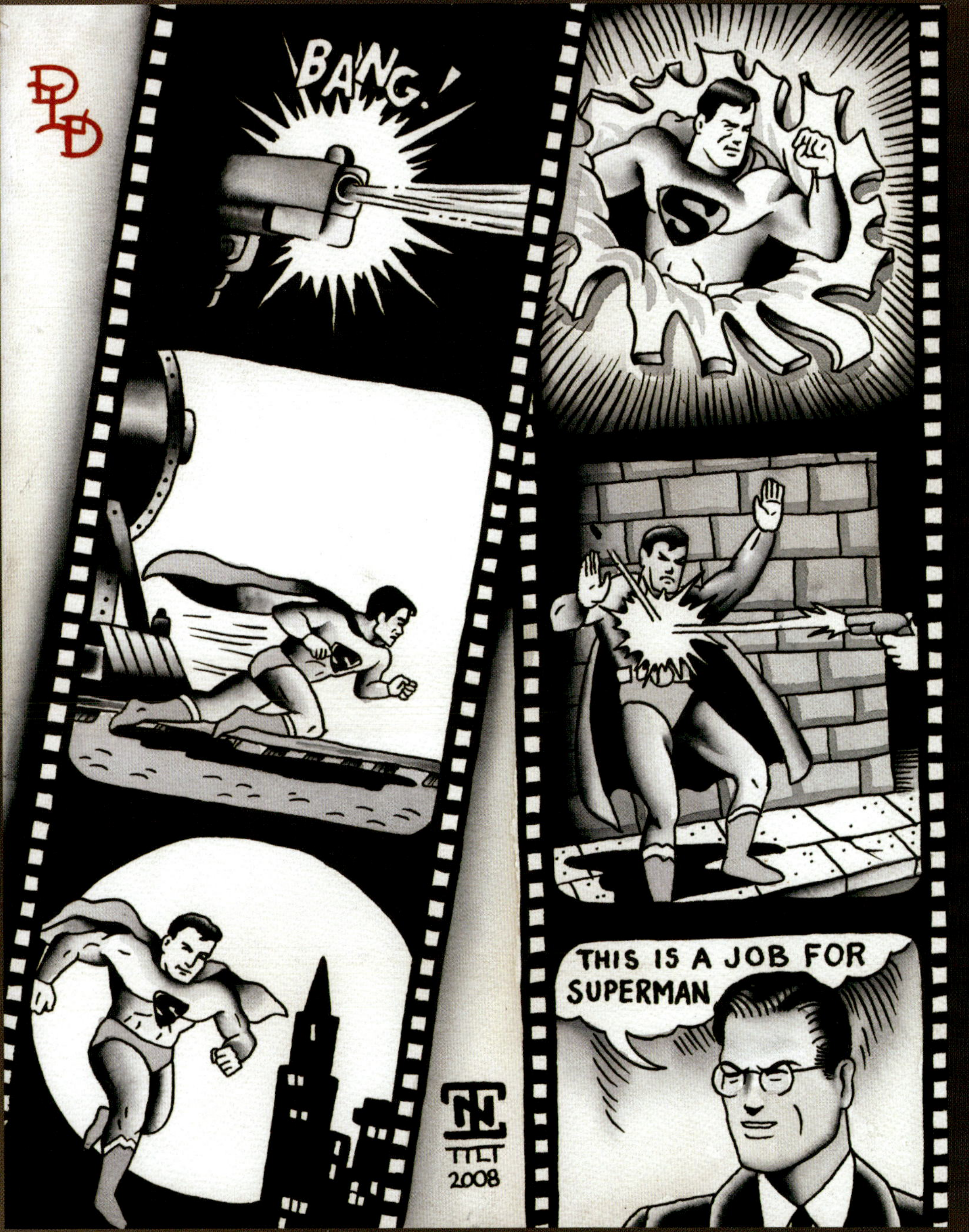

BANG.!
THIS IS A JOB FOR SUPERMAN
TILT
2008

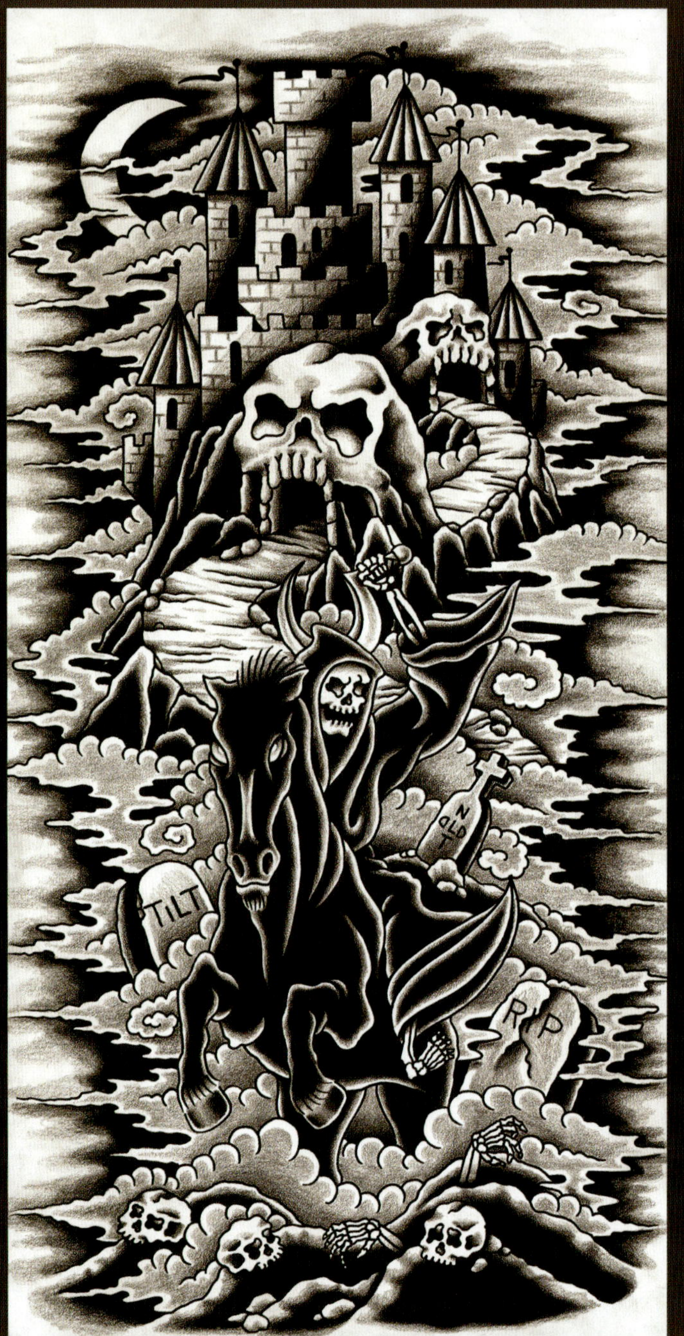
TILT
RIP

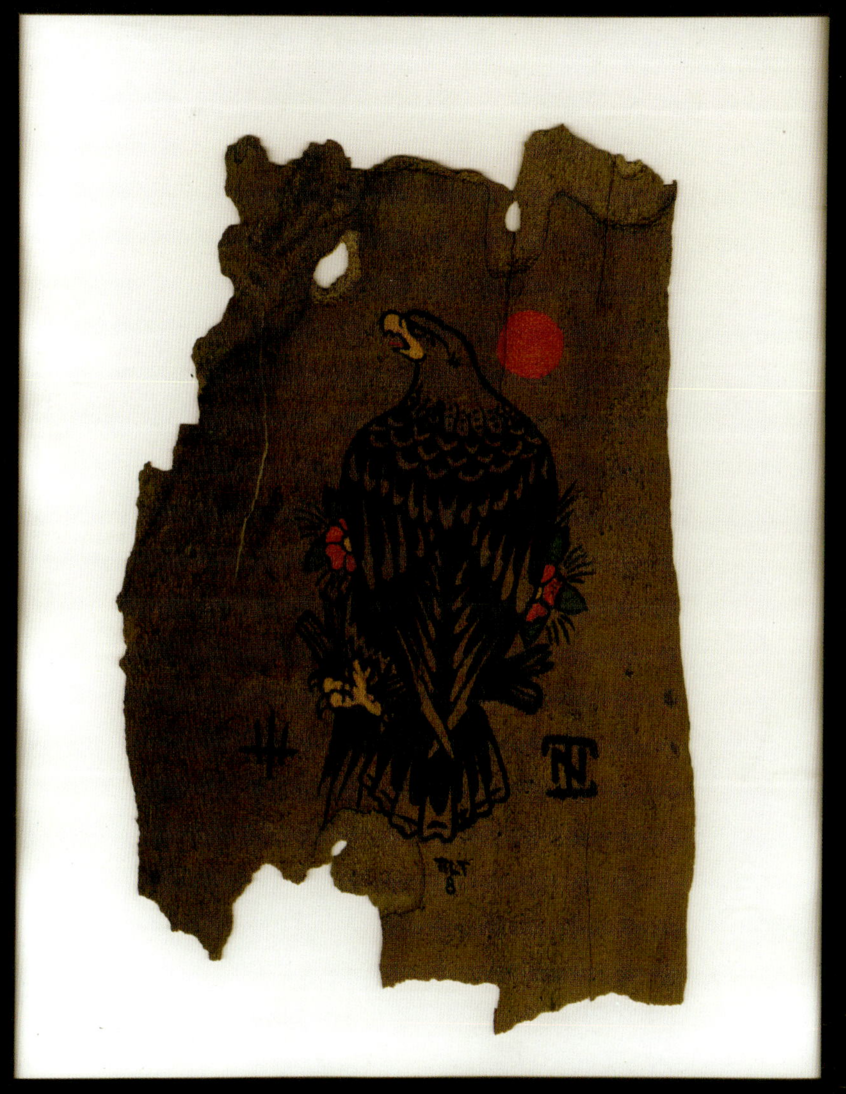

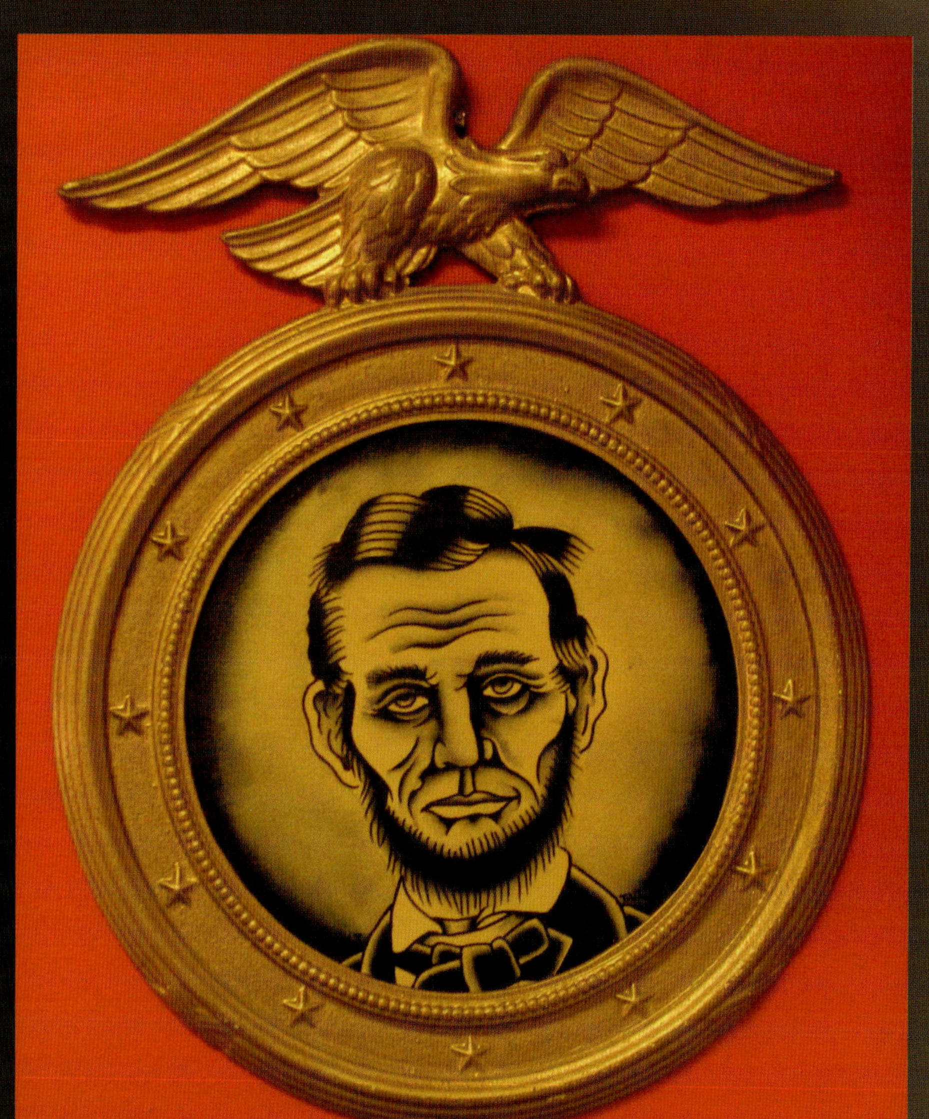

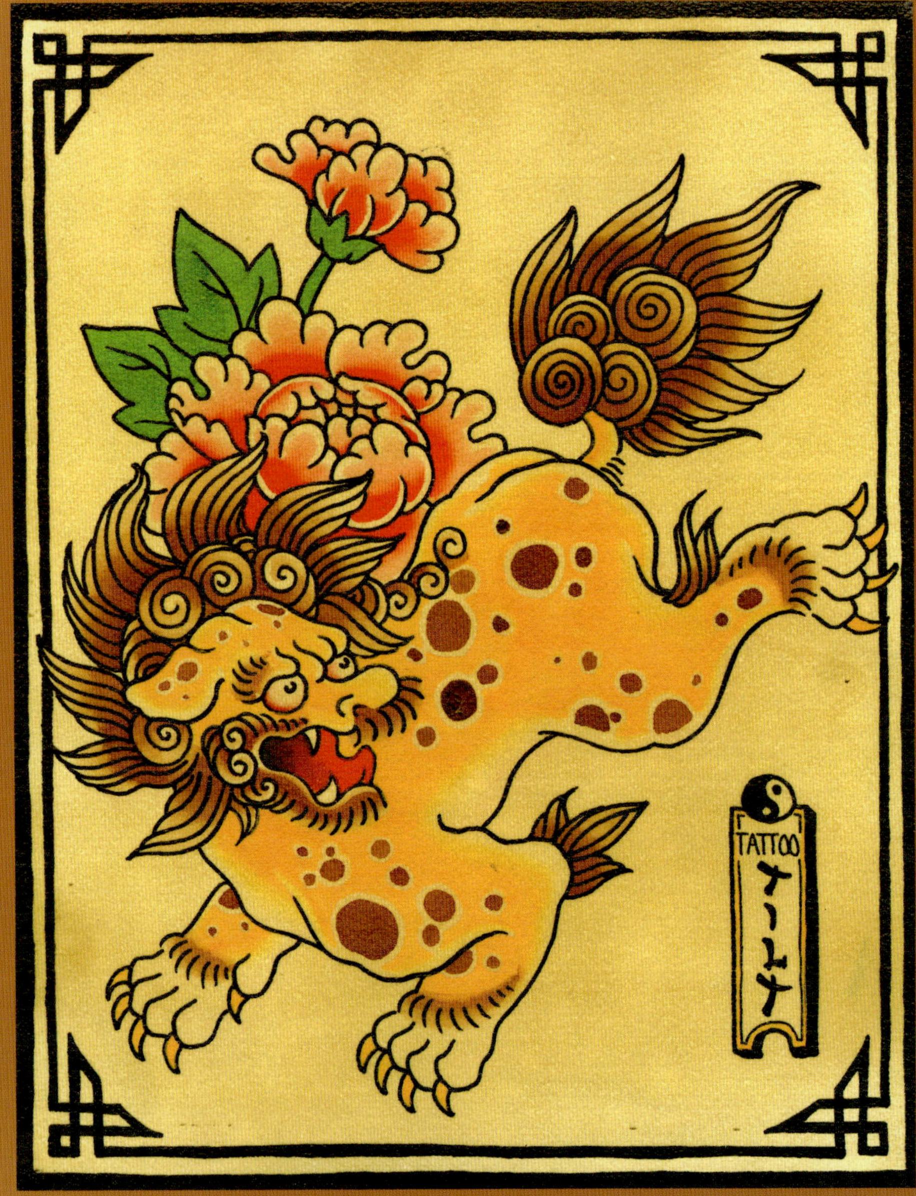
TATTOO

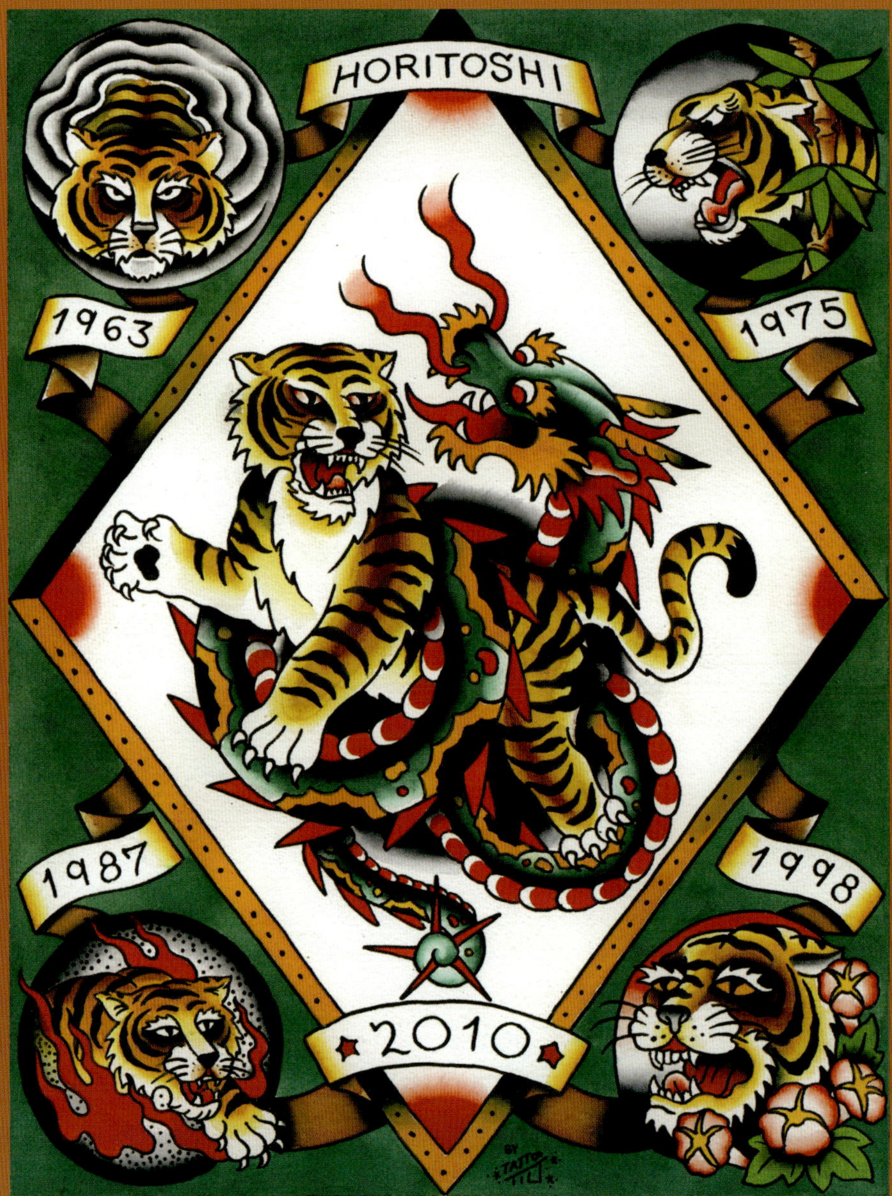
HORITOSHI
1963
1975
1987
1998
2010

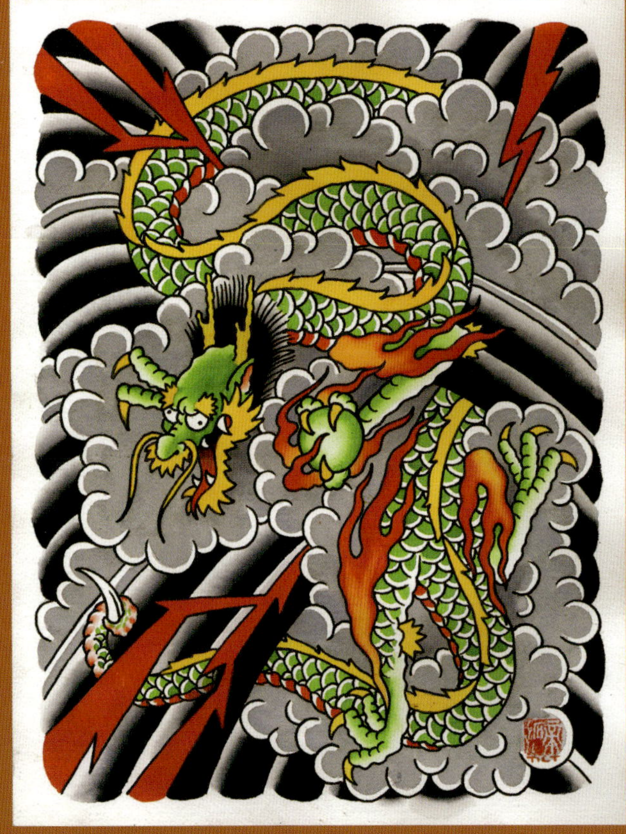

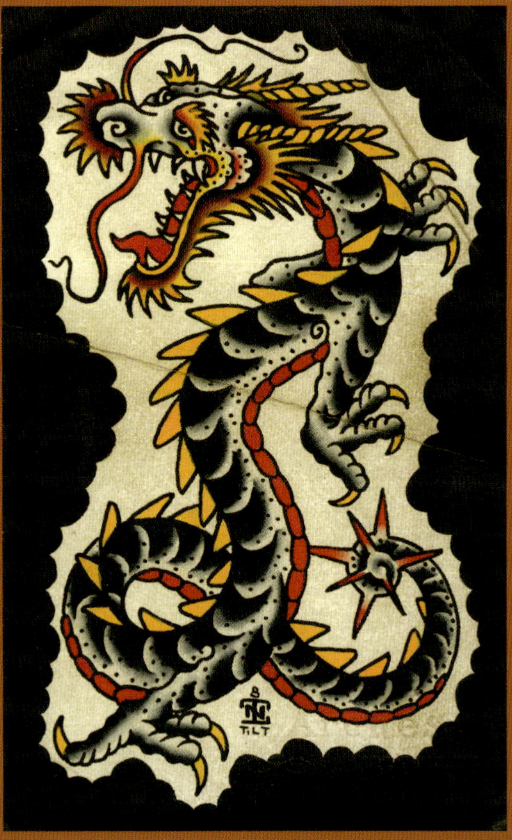

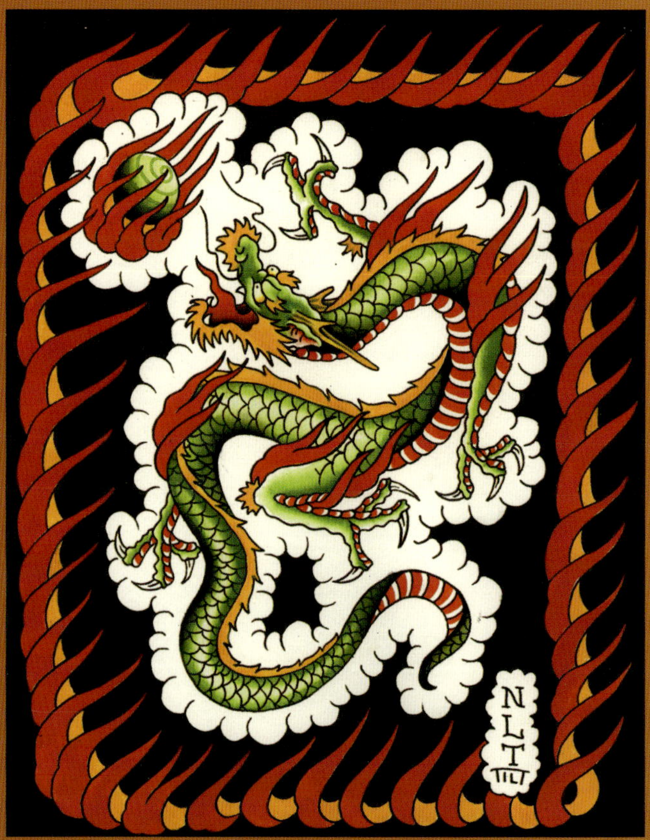
NLT

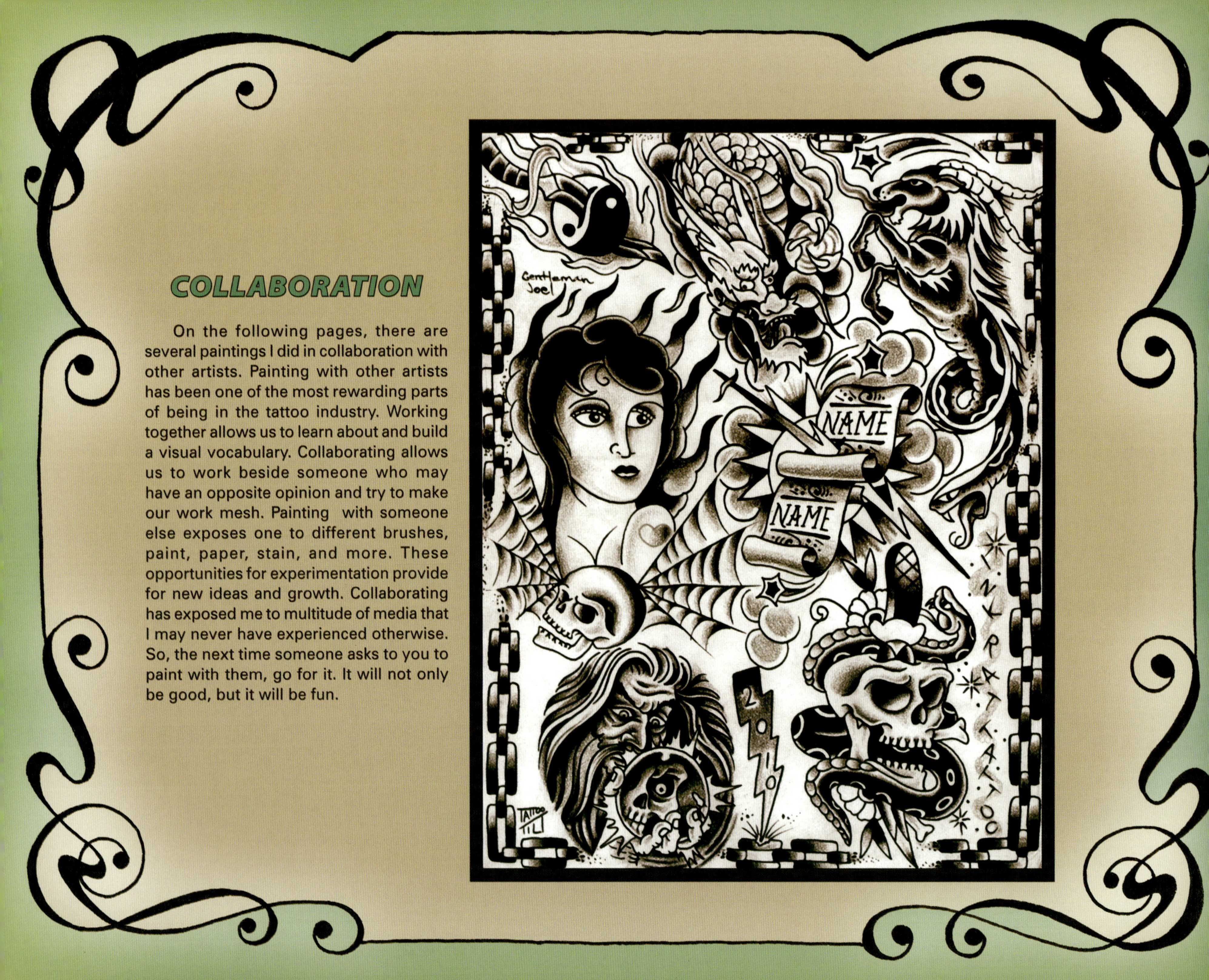

COLLABORATION

On the following pages, there are several paintings I did in collaboration with other artists. Painting with other artists has been one of the most rewarding parts of being in the tattoo industry. Working together allows us to learn about and build a visual vocabulary. Collaborating allows us to work beside someone who may have an opposite opinion and try to make our work mesh. Painting with someone else exposes one to different brushes, paint, paper, stain, and more. These opportunities for experimentation provide for new ideas and growth. Collaborating has exposed me to multitude of media that I may never have experienced otherwise. So, the next time someone asks to you to paint with them, go for it. It will not only be good, but it will be fun.

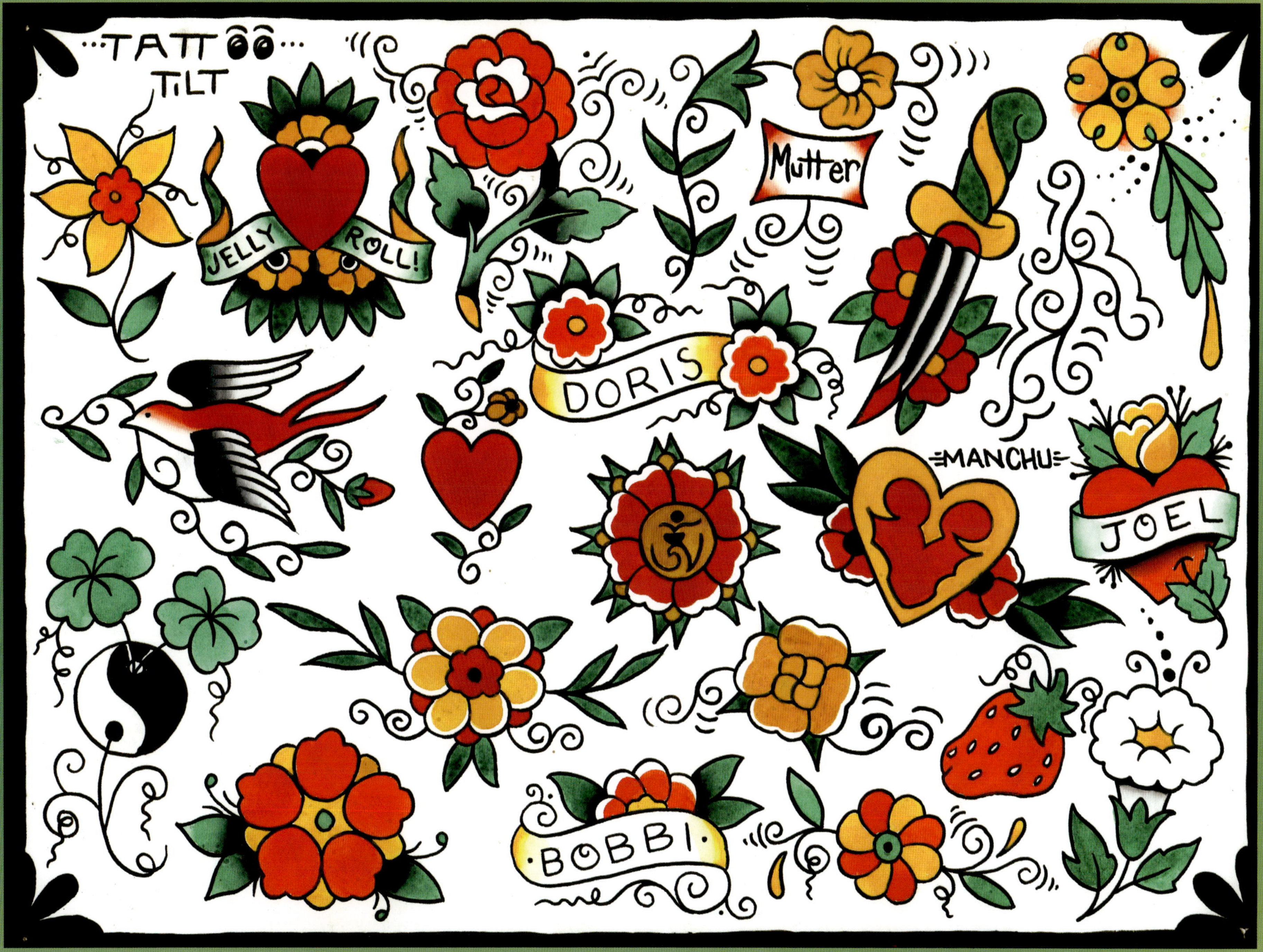

Gentleman Joel and Tilt

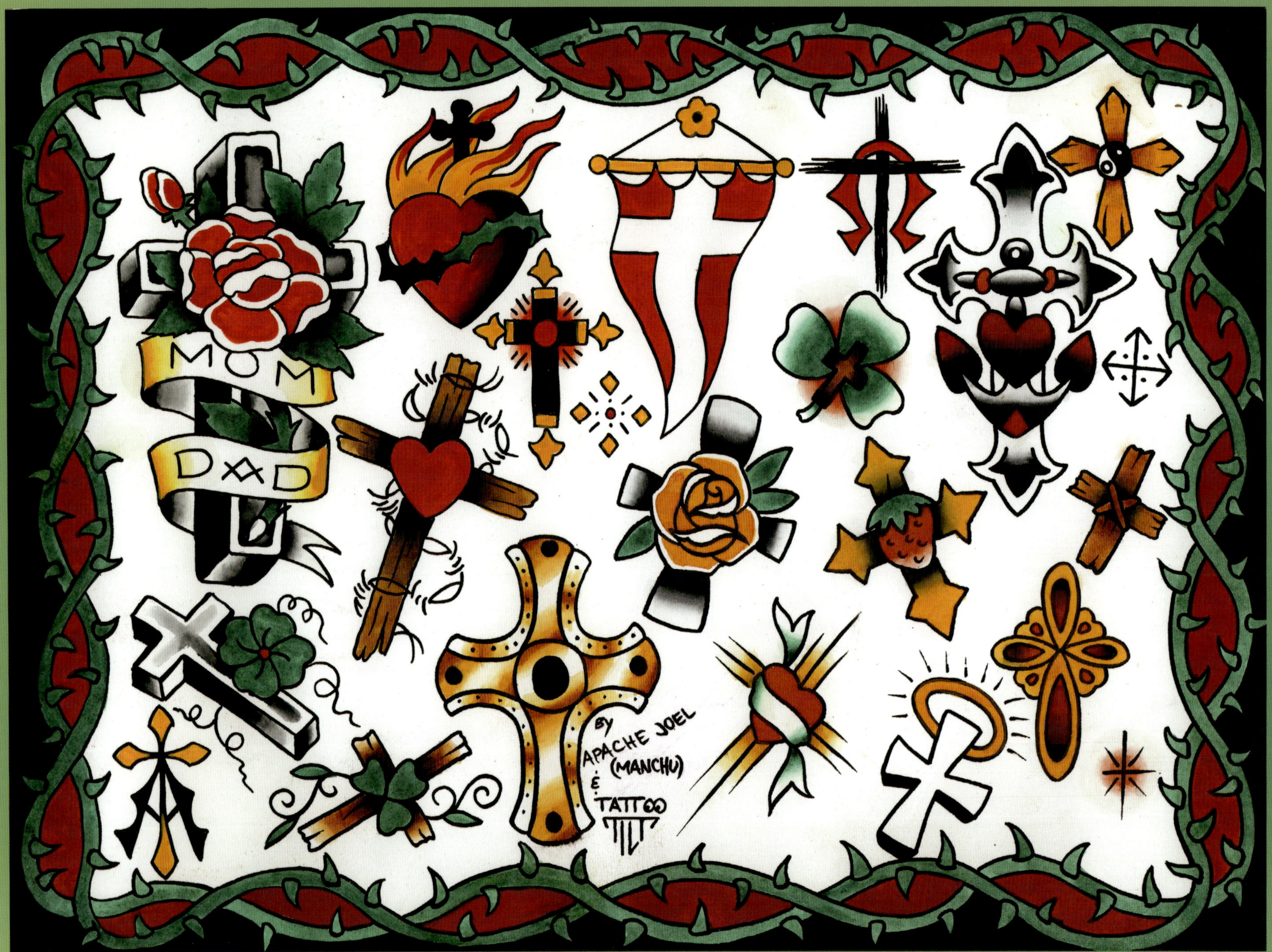

Gentleman Joel and Tilt

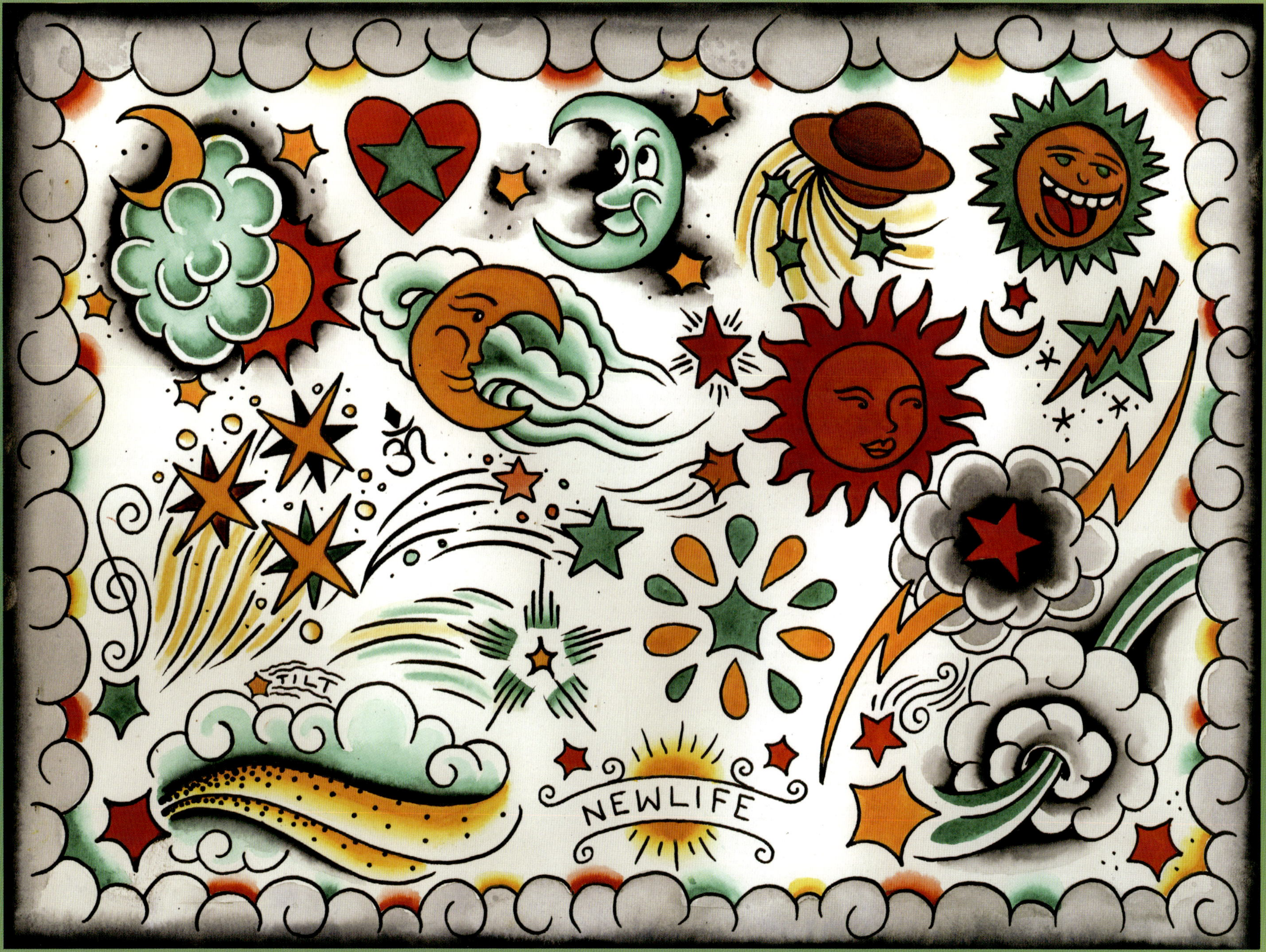

Gentleman Joel and Tilt

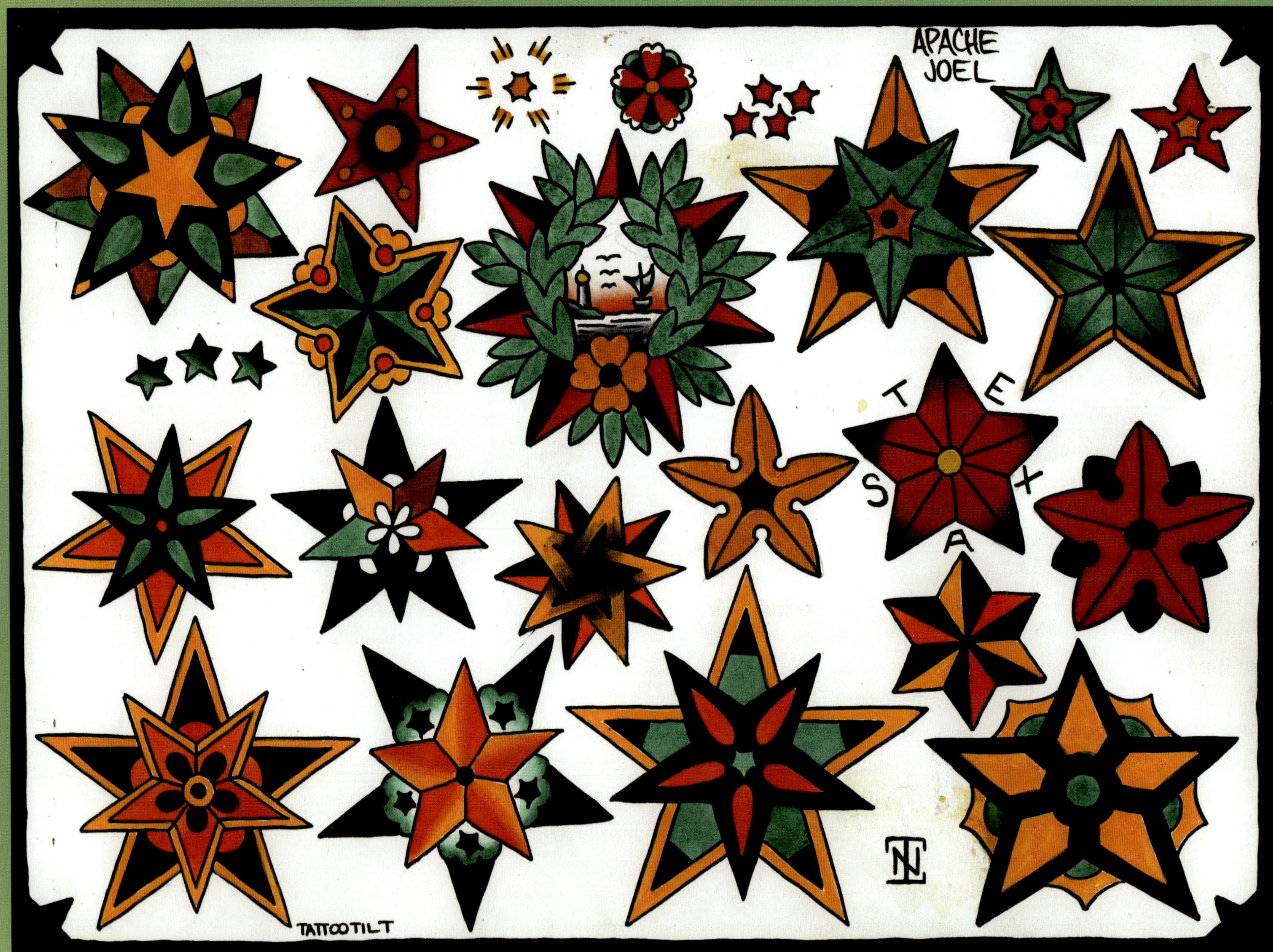

Gentleman Joel and Tilt

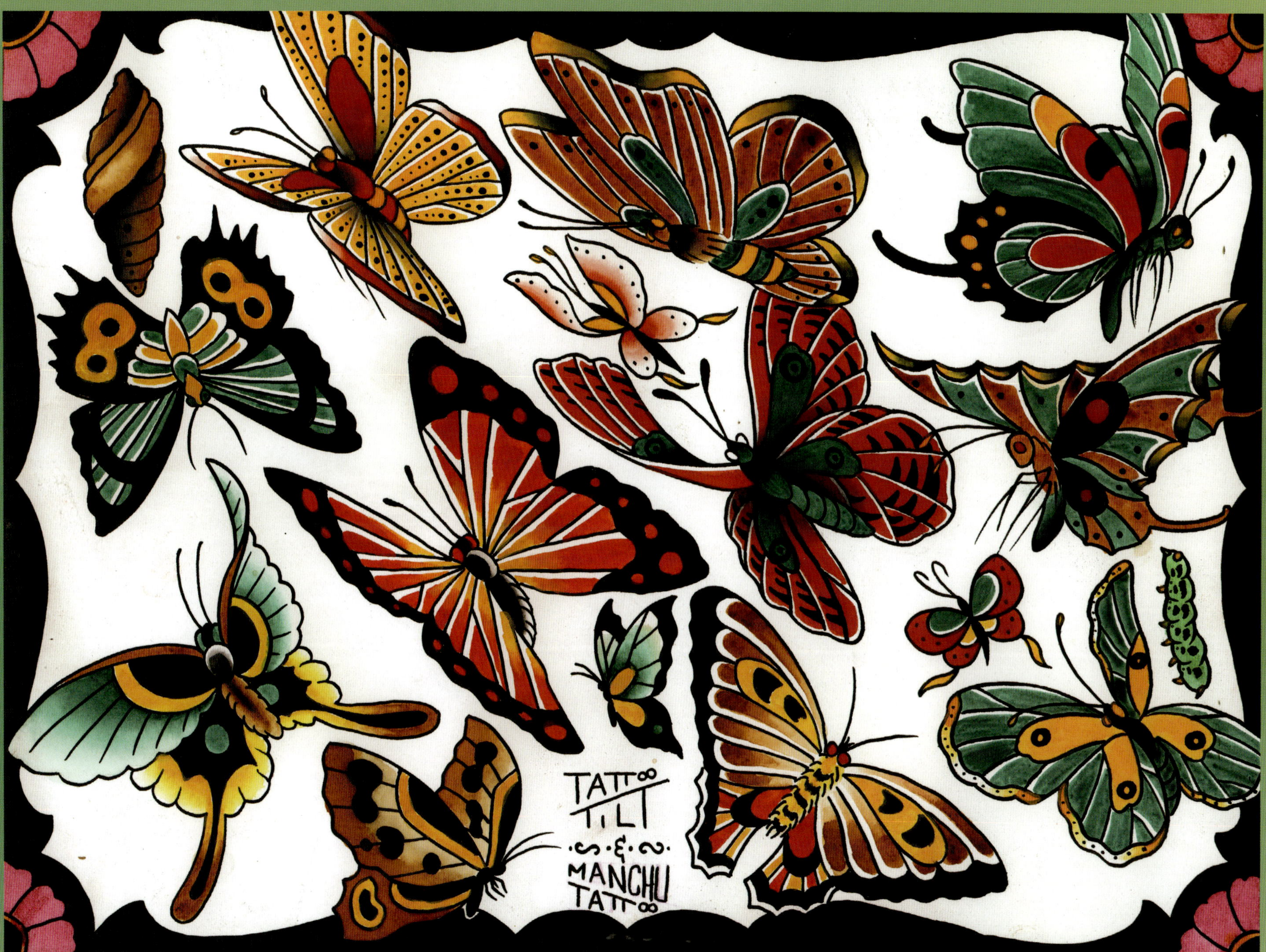

Gentleman Joel and Tilt

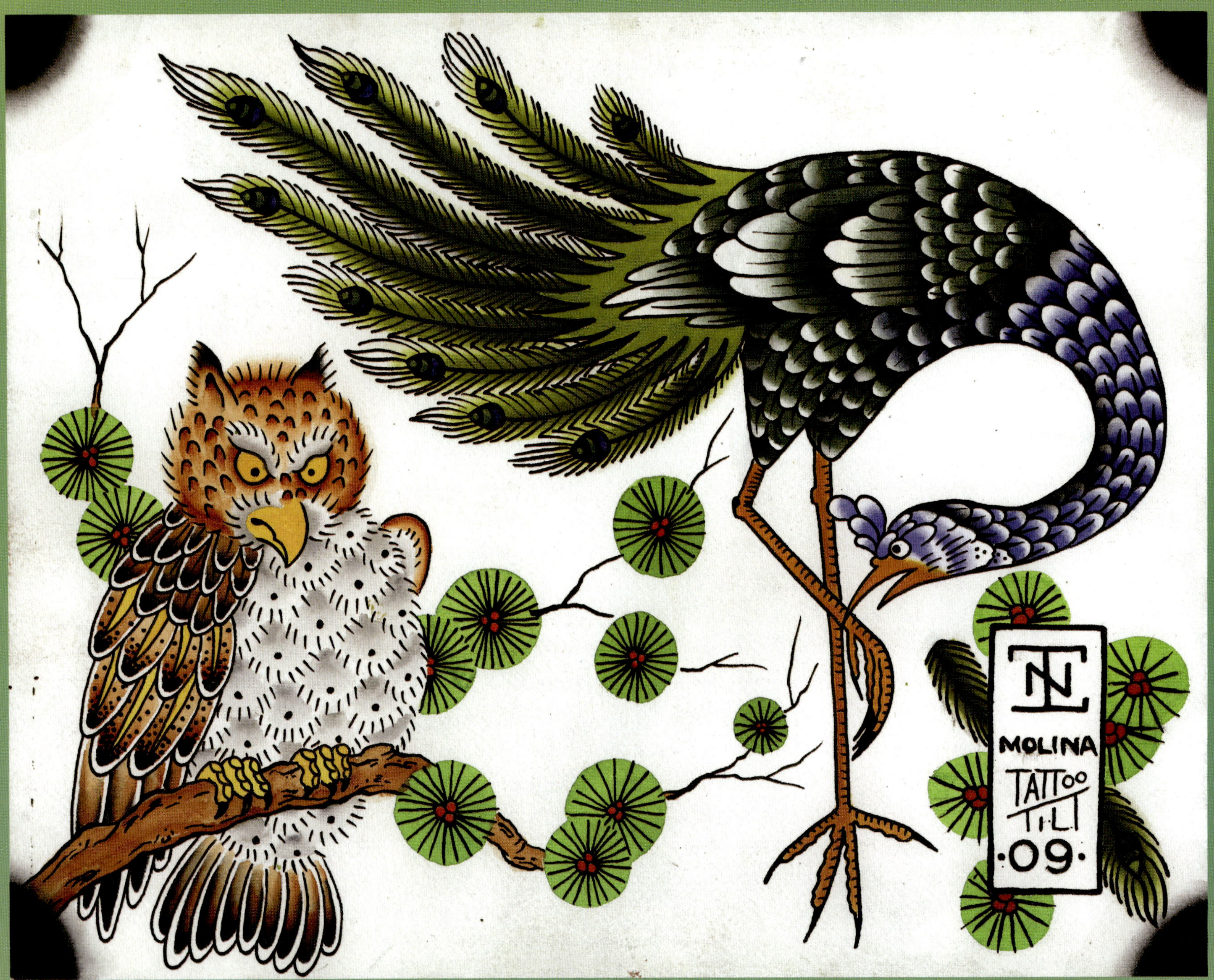

Gentleman Joel and Tilt

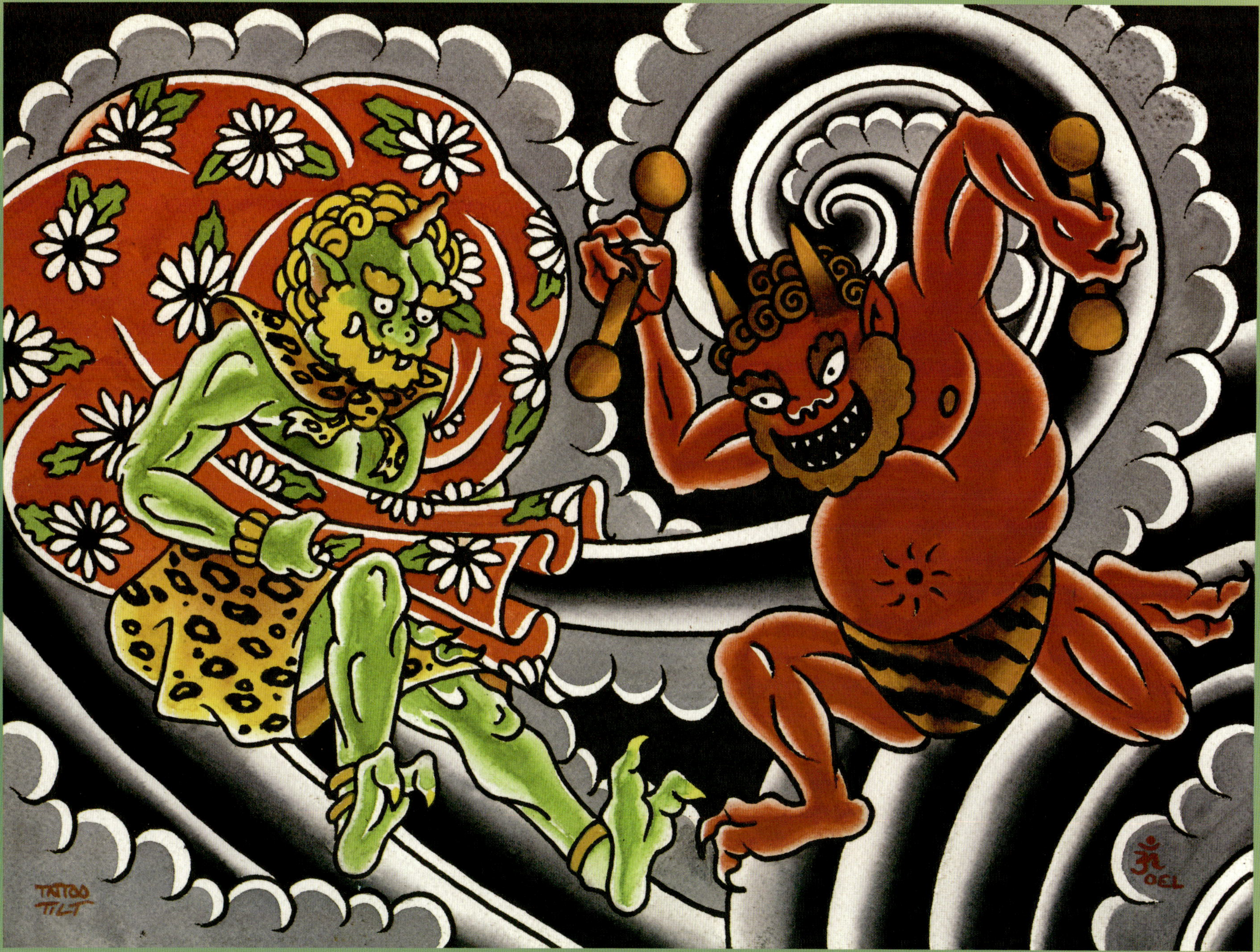

Gentleman Joel and Tilt

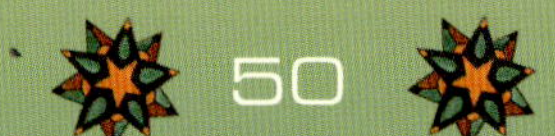

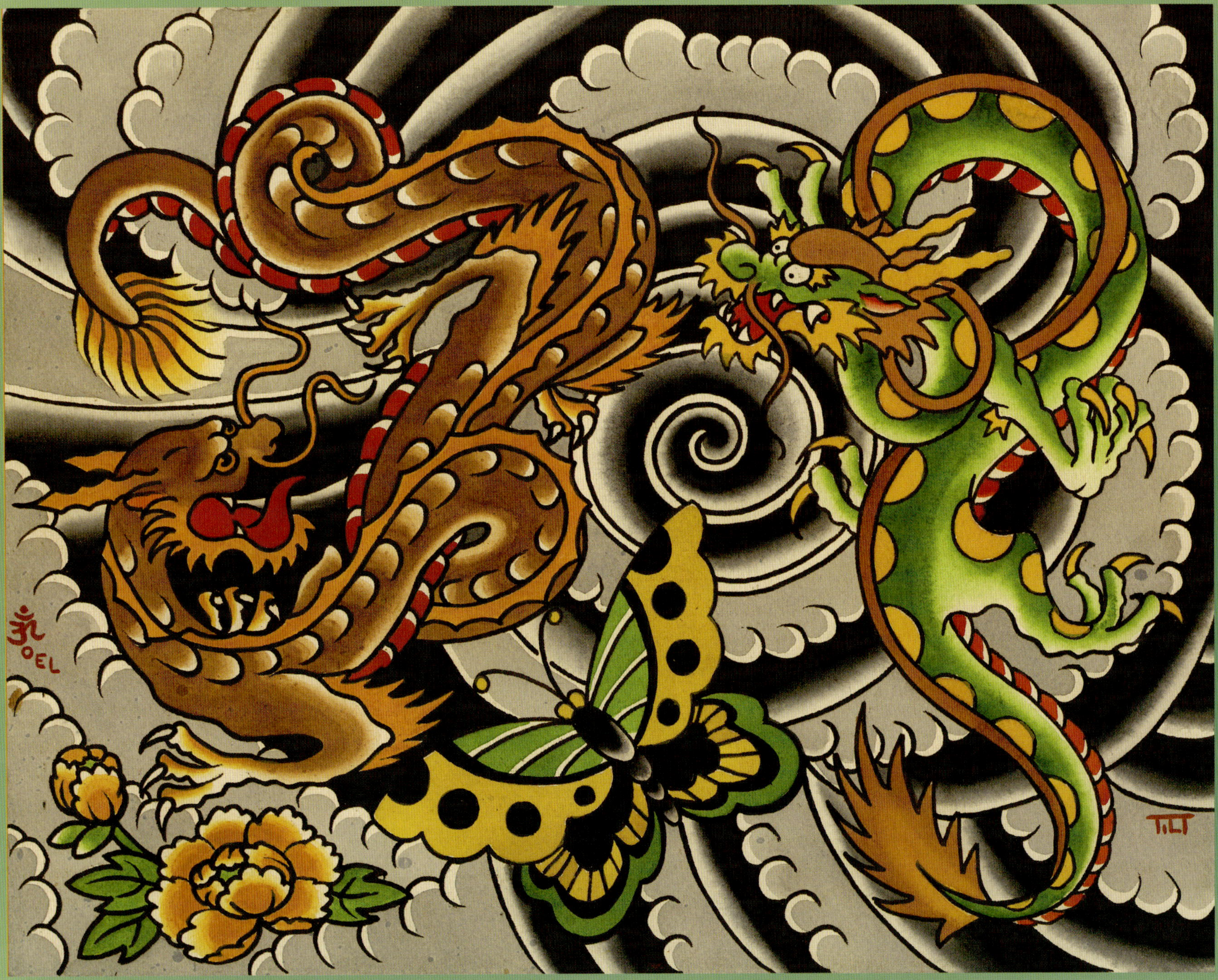

Gentleman Joel and Tilt

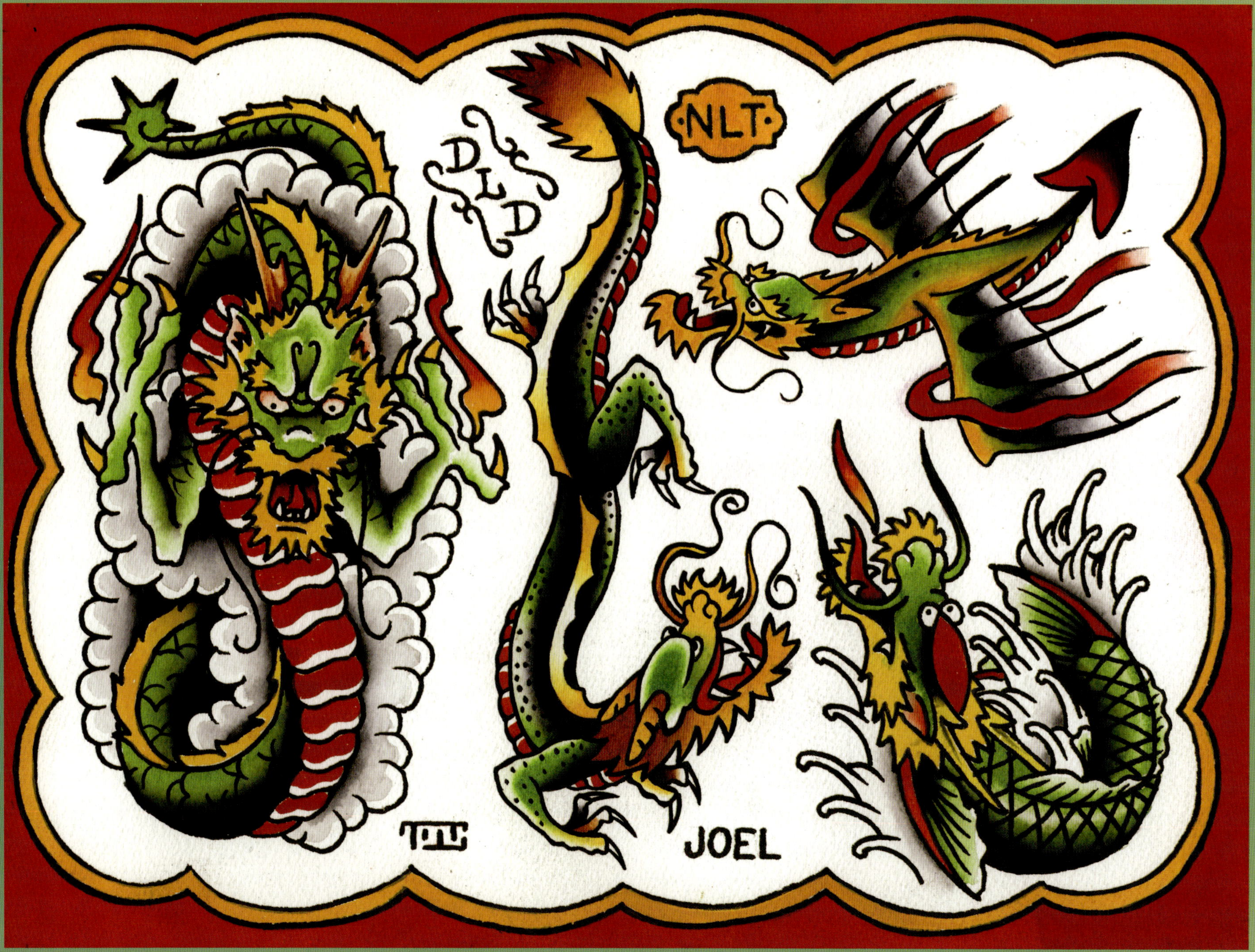

Gentleman Joel and Tilt

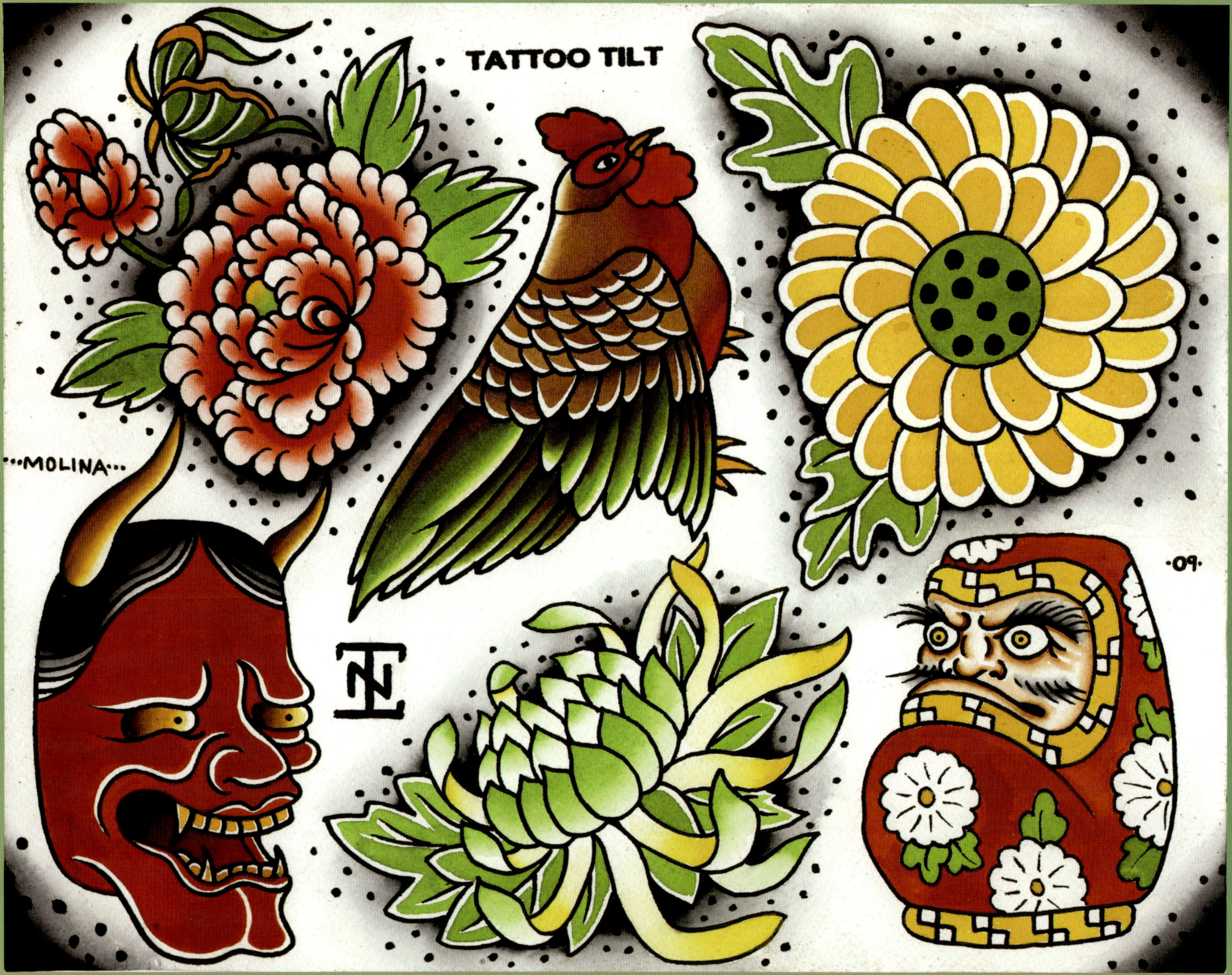

Gentleman Joel and Tilt

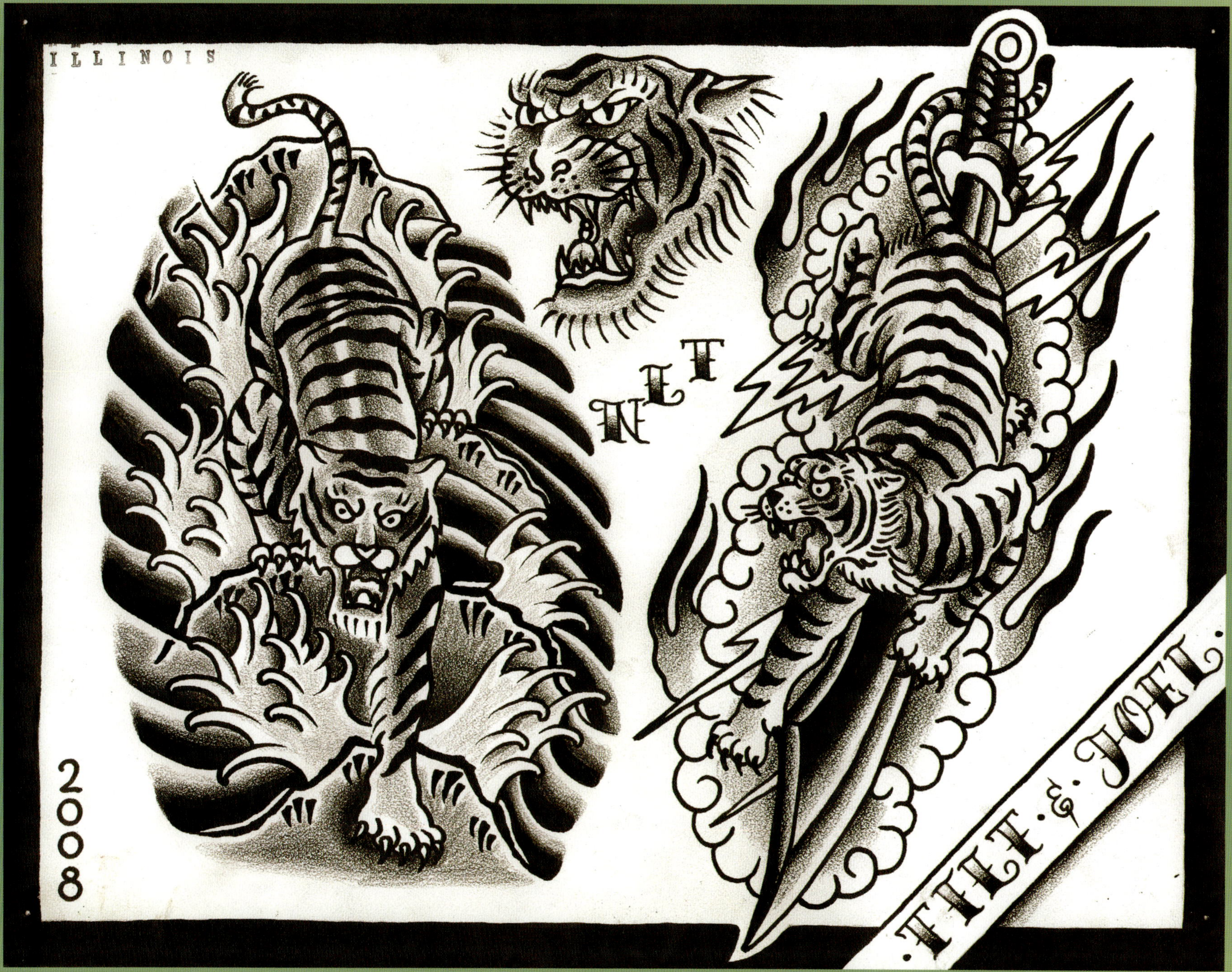

Gentleman Joel and Tilt

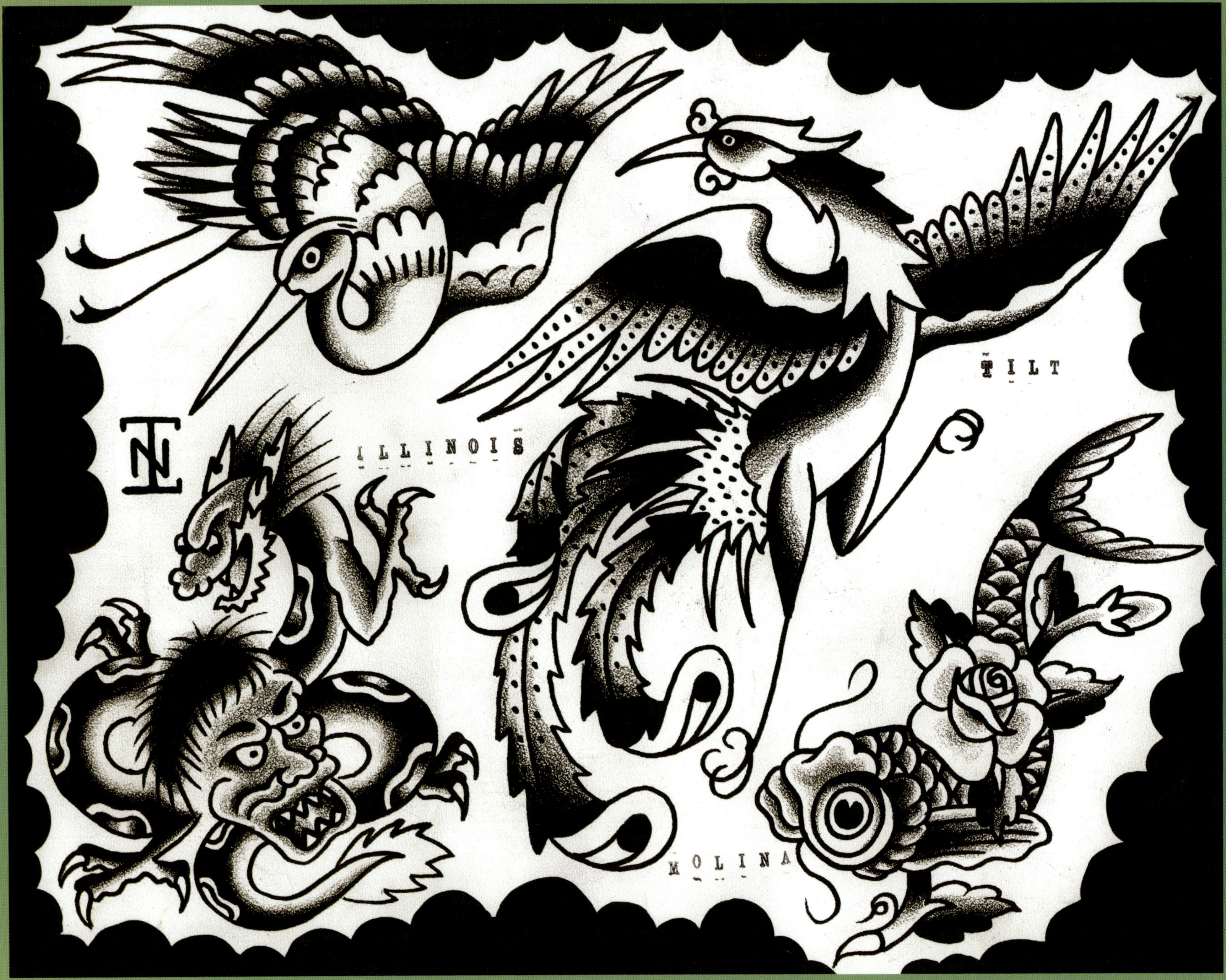

Gentleman Joel and Tilt

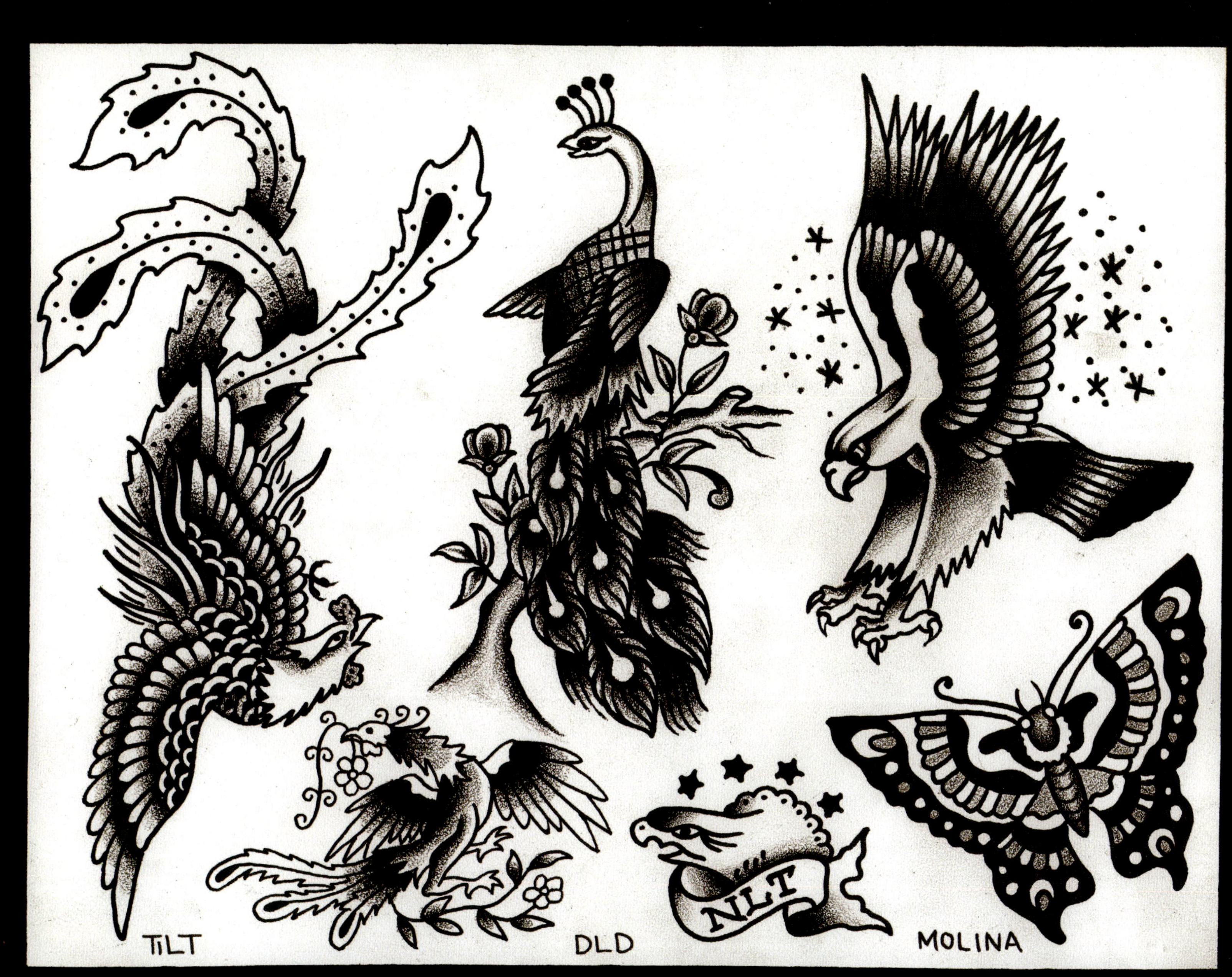

Gentleman Joel and Tilt

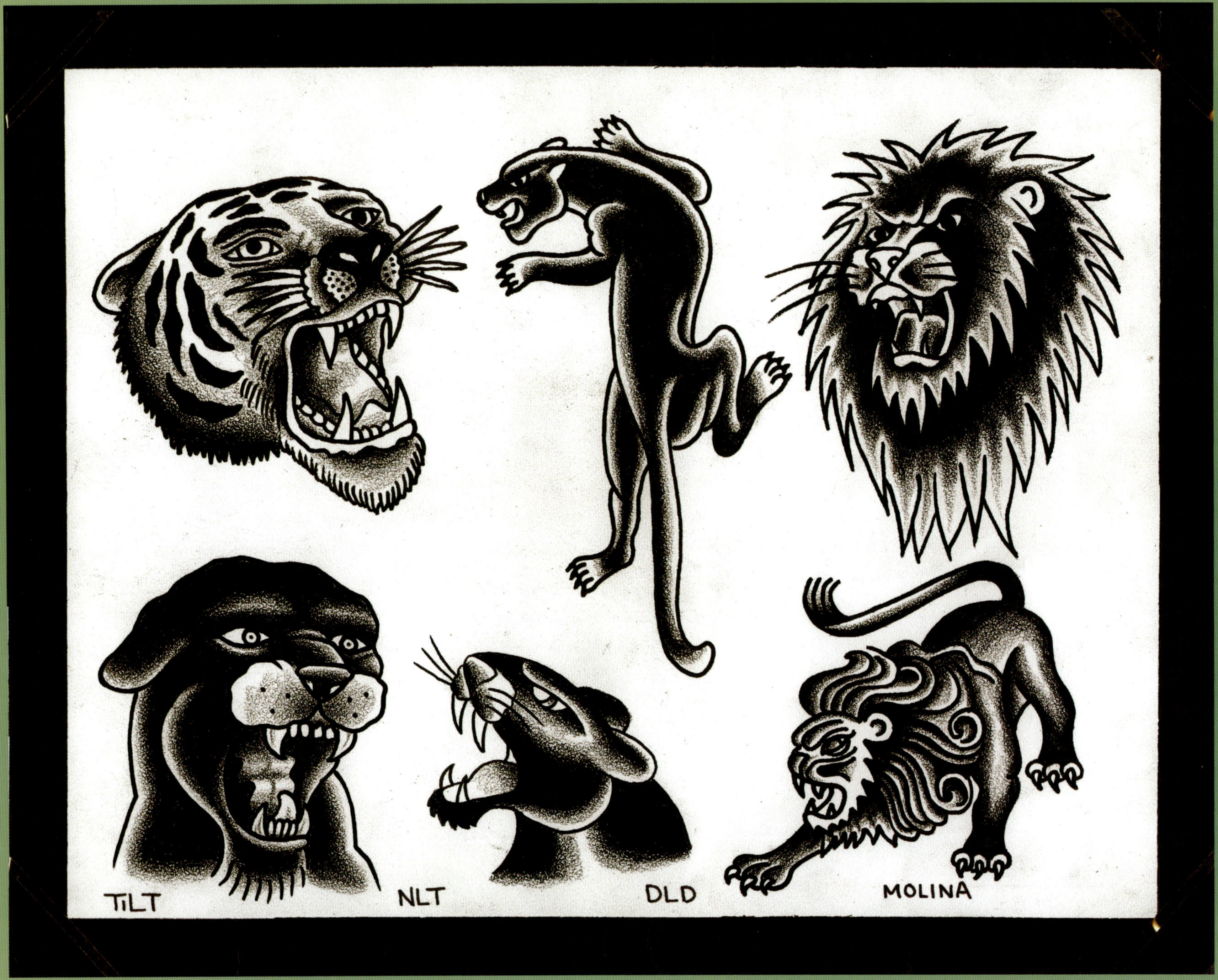

TiLT NLT DLD MOLINA

Gentleman Joel and Tilt

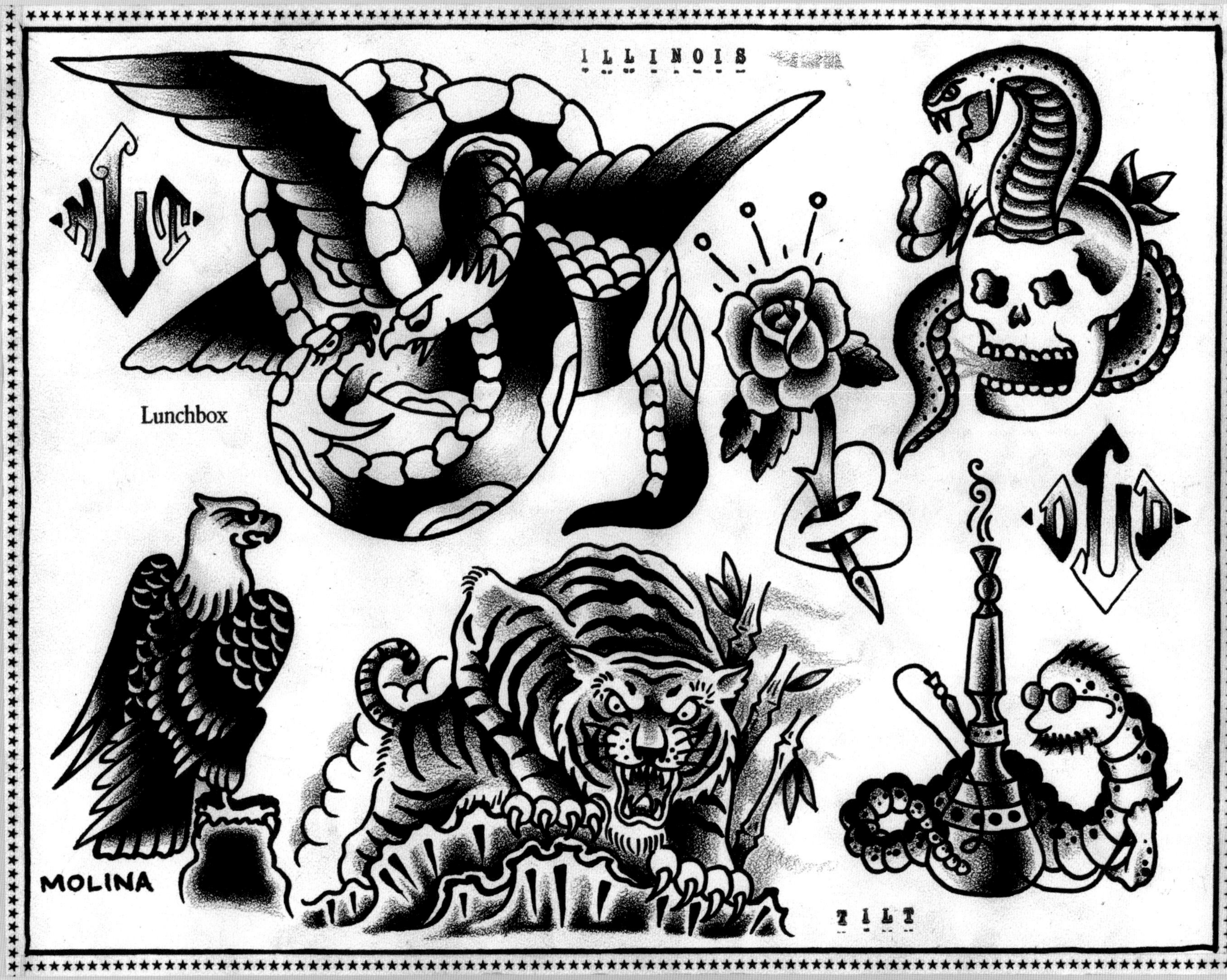

ILLINOIS

Lunchbox

MOLINA

TILT

Ben Cheese and Tilt

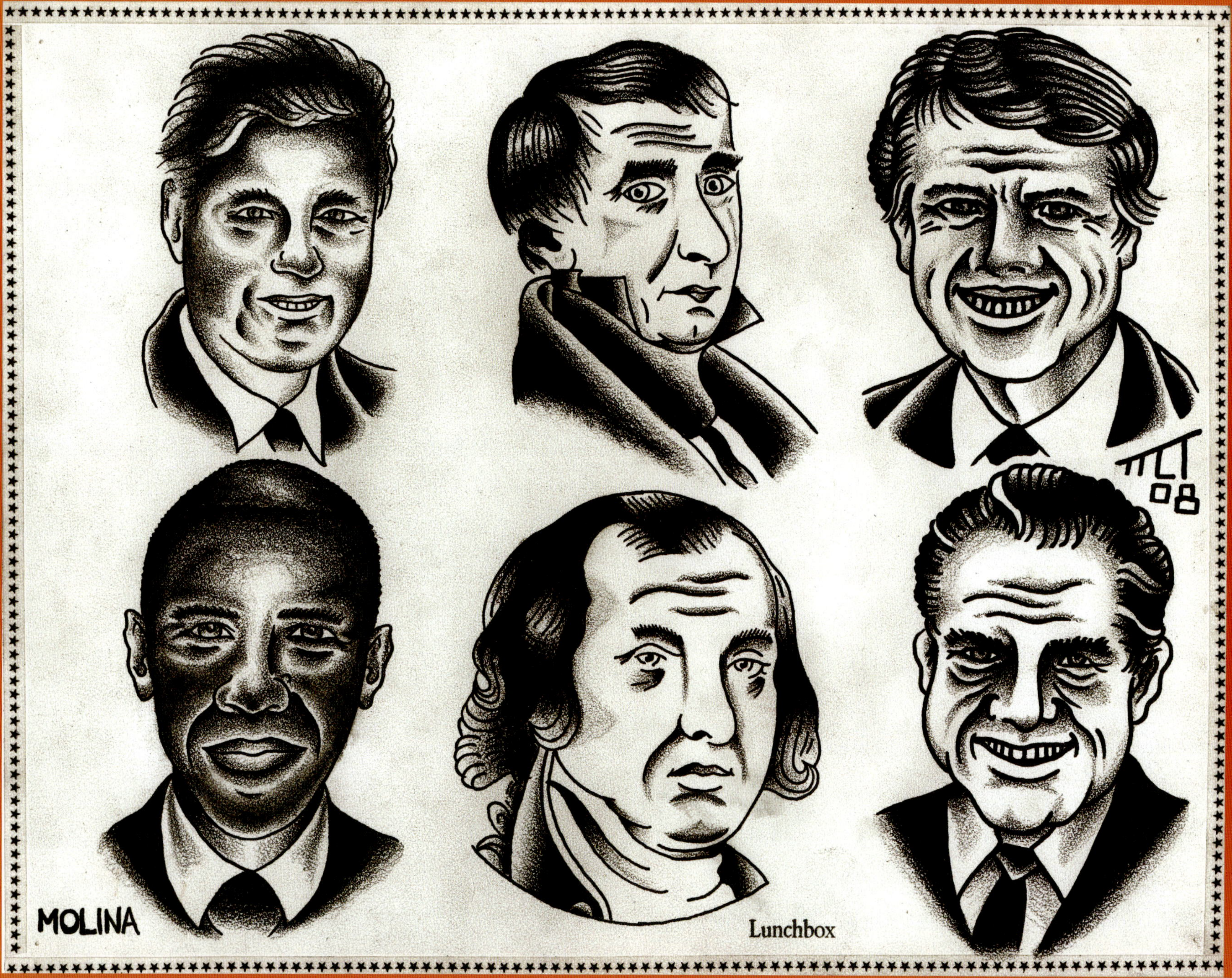

Gentleman Joel, Lunchbox and Tilt

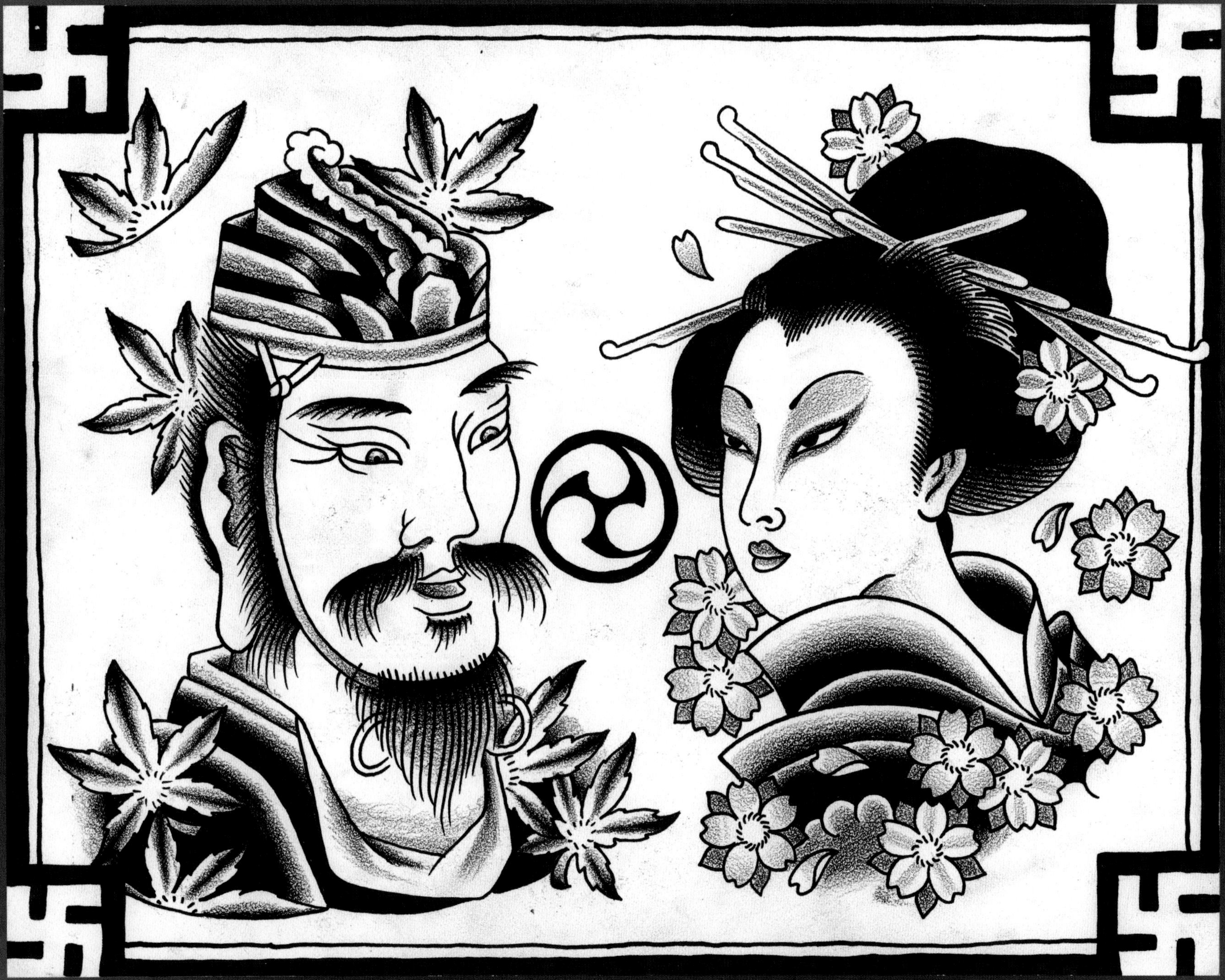

Ben Cheese and Tilt

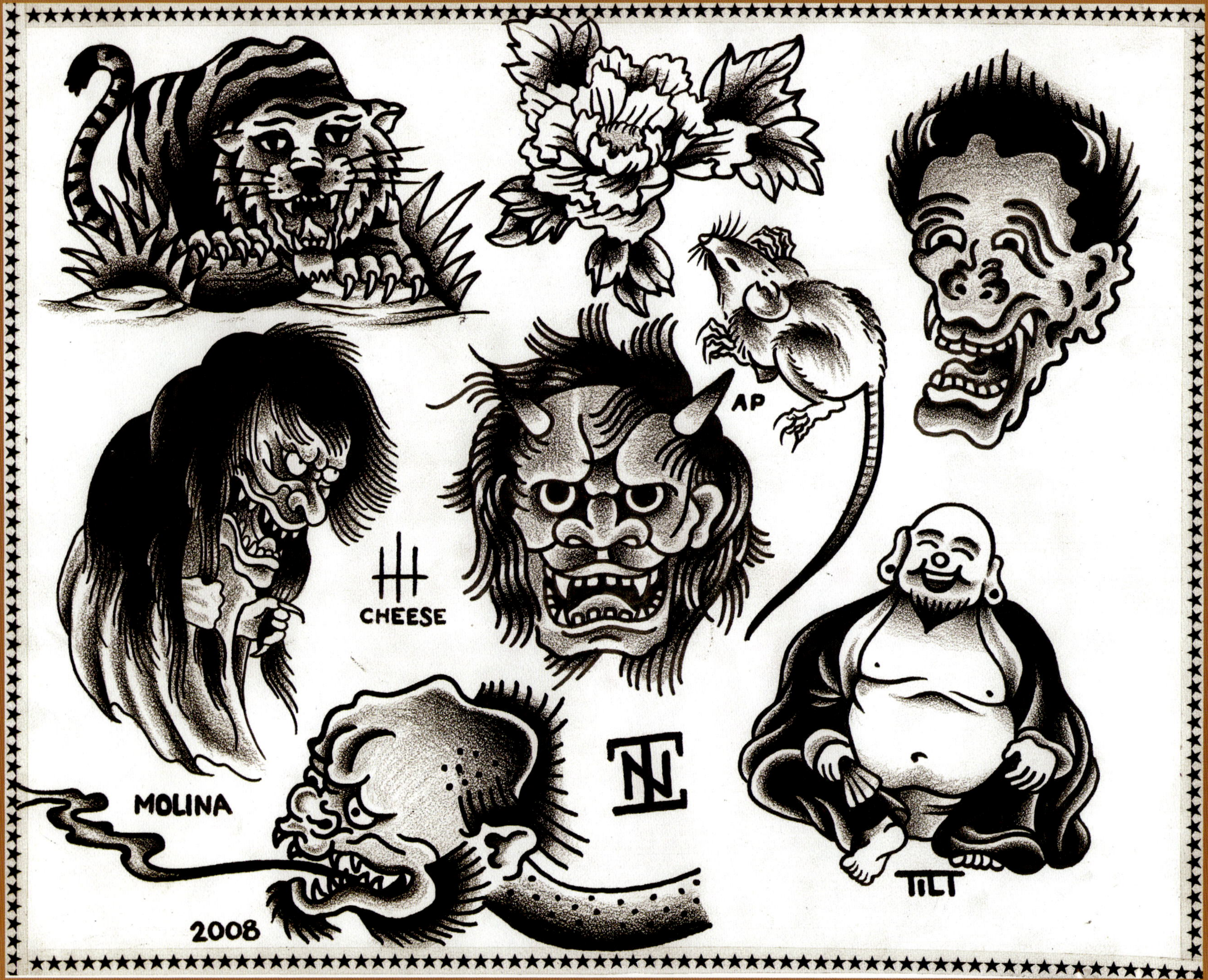

Gentleman Joel, Ben Cheese, A.P. Shrewsbury and Tilt

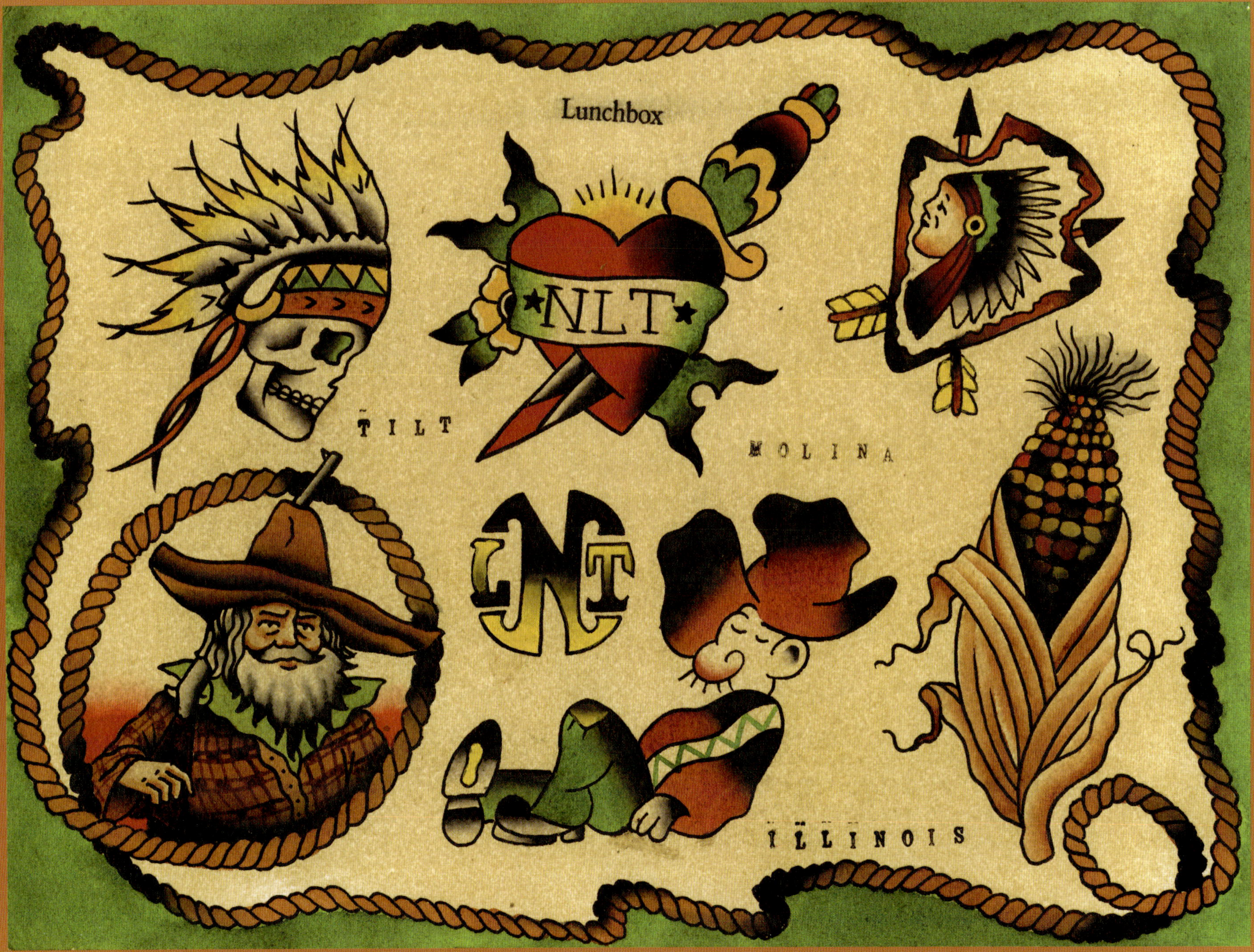

Gentleman Joel, Lunchbox and Tilt

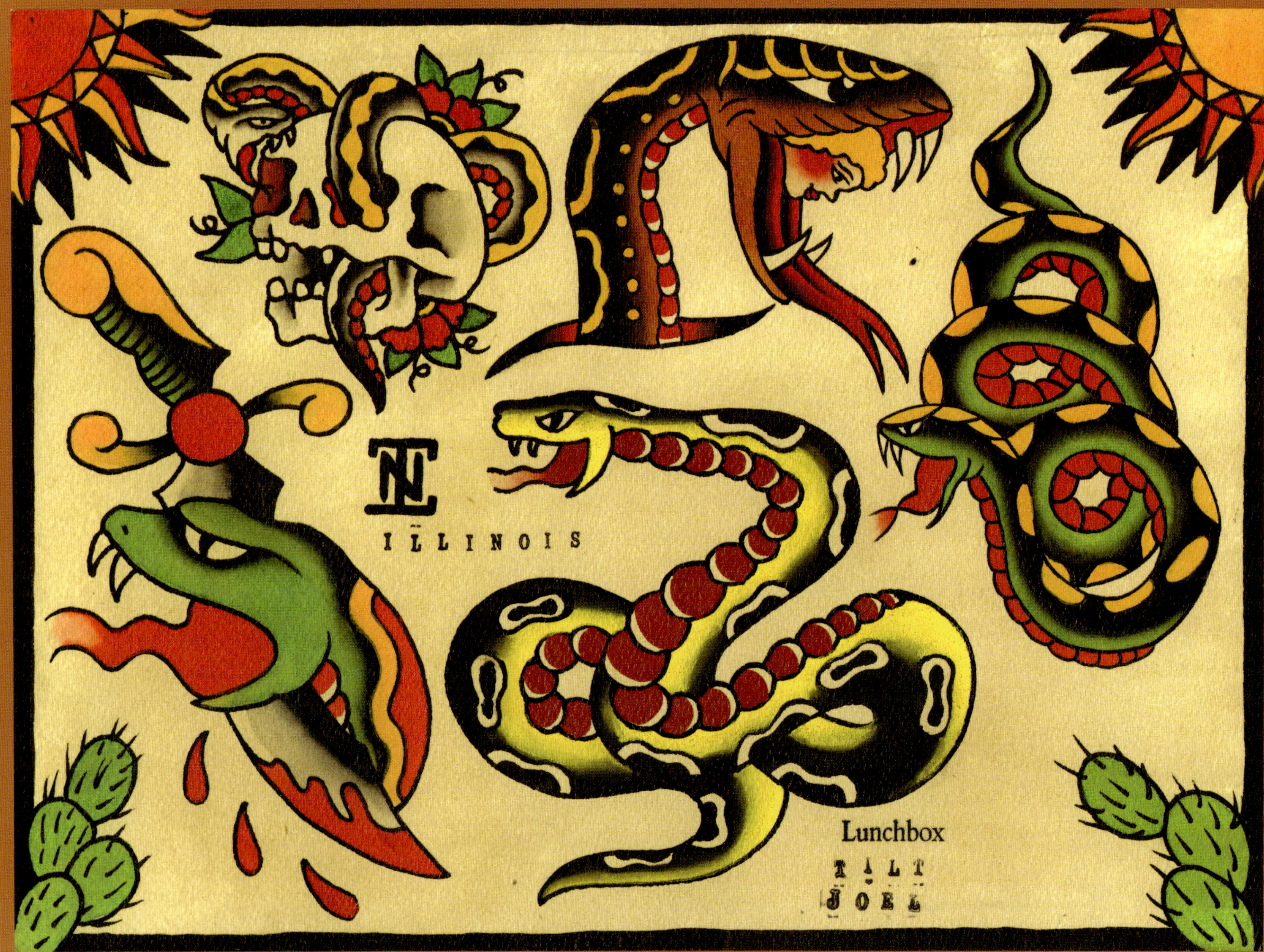

Gentleman Joel, Lunchbox and Tilt

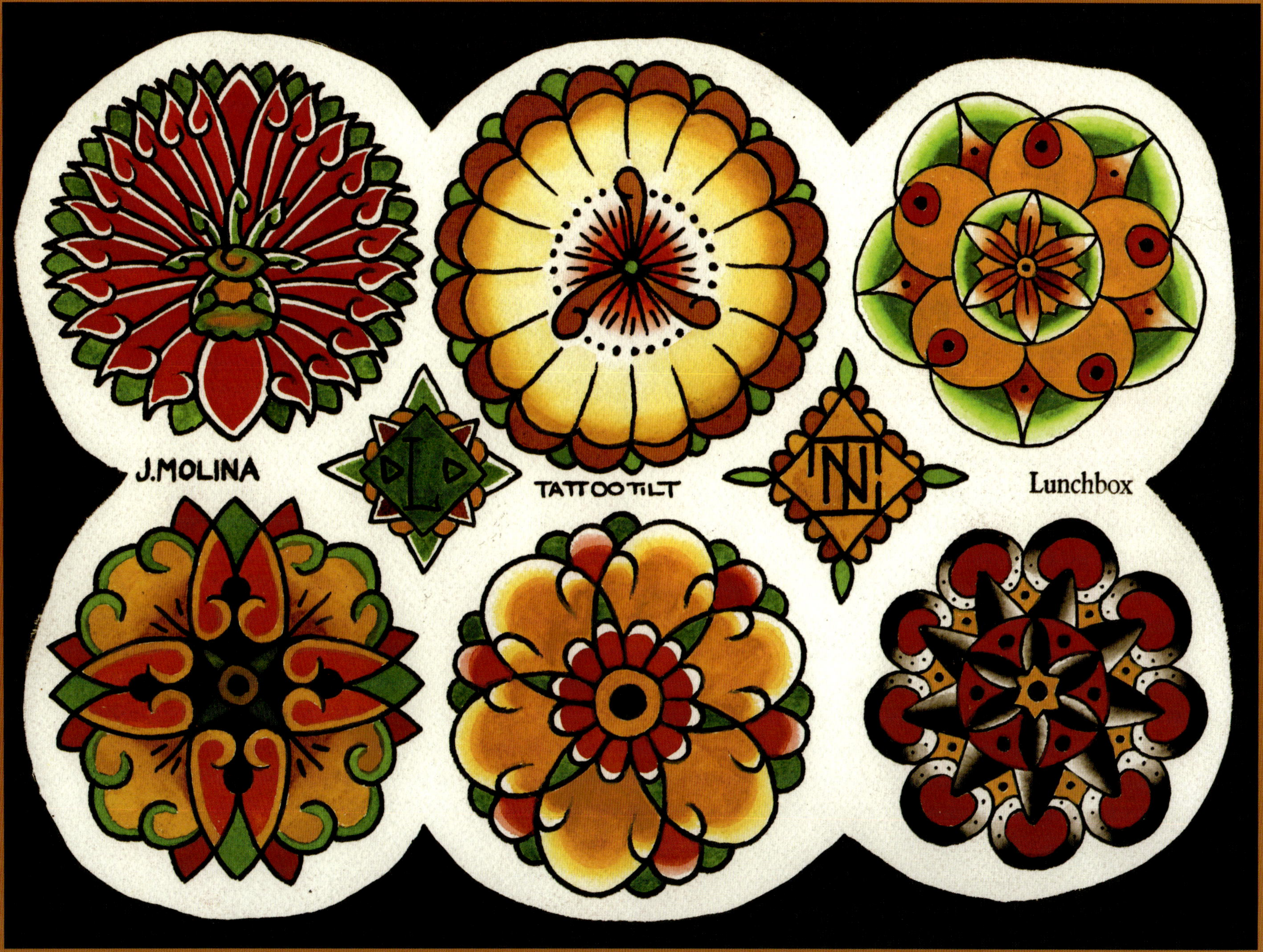

Gentleman Joel, Lunchbox and Tilt

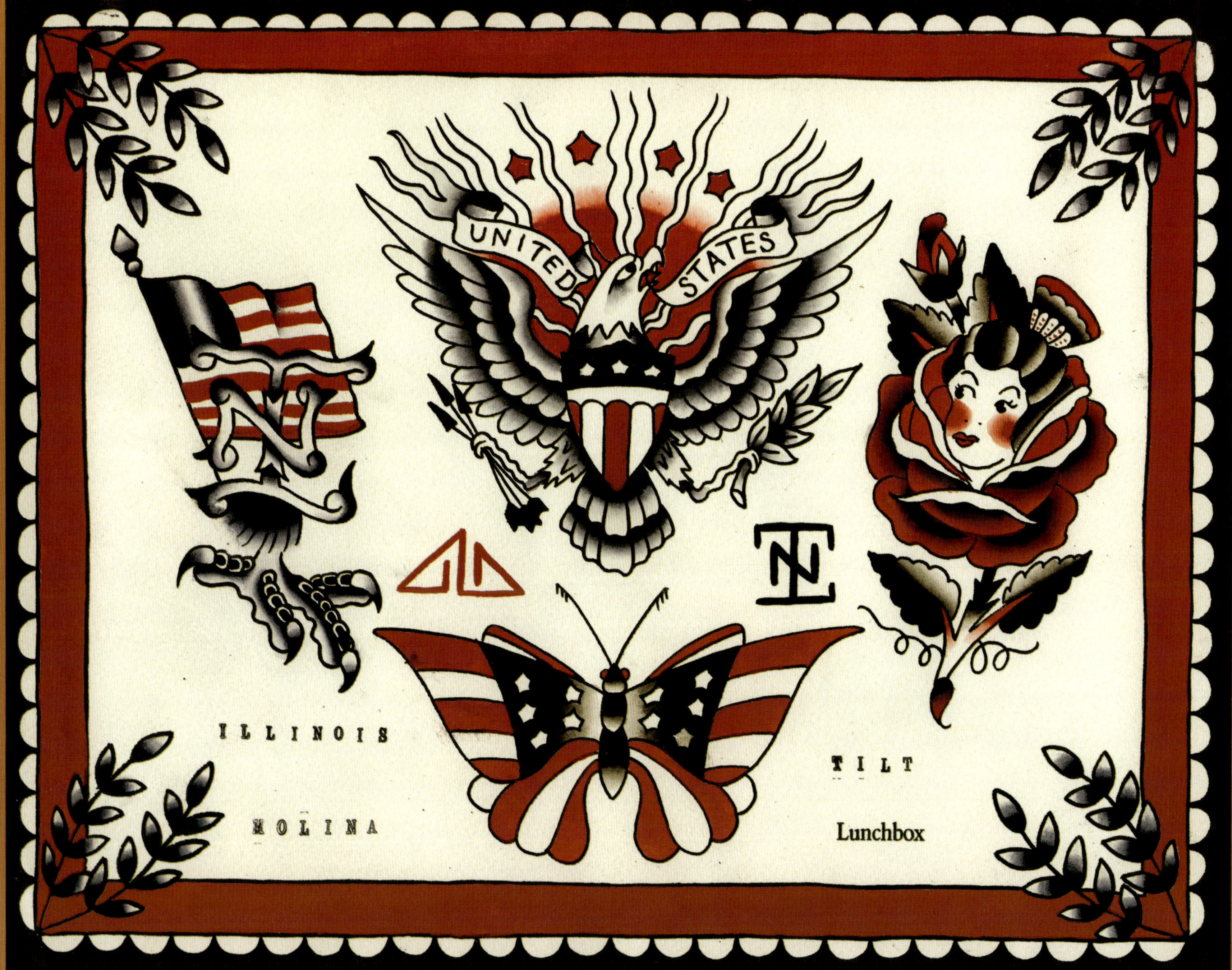

Gentleman Joel, Lunchbox and Tilt

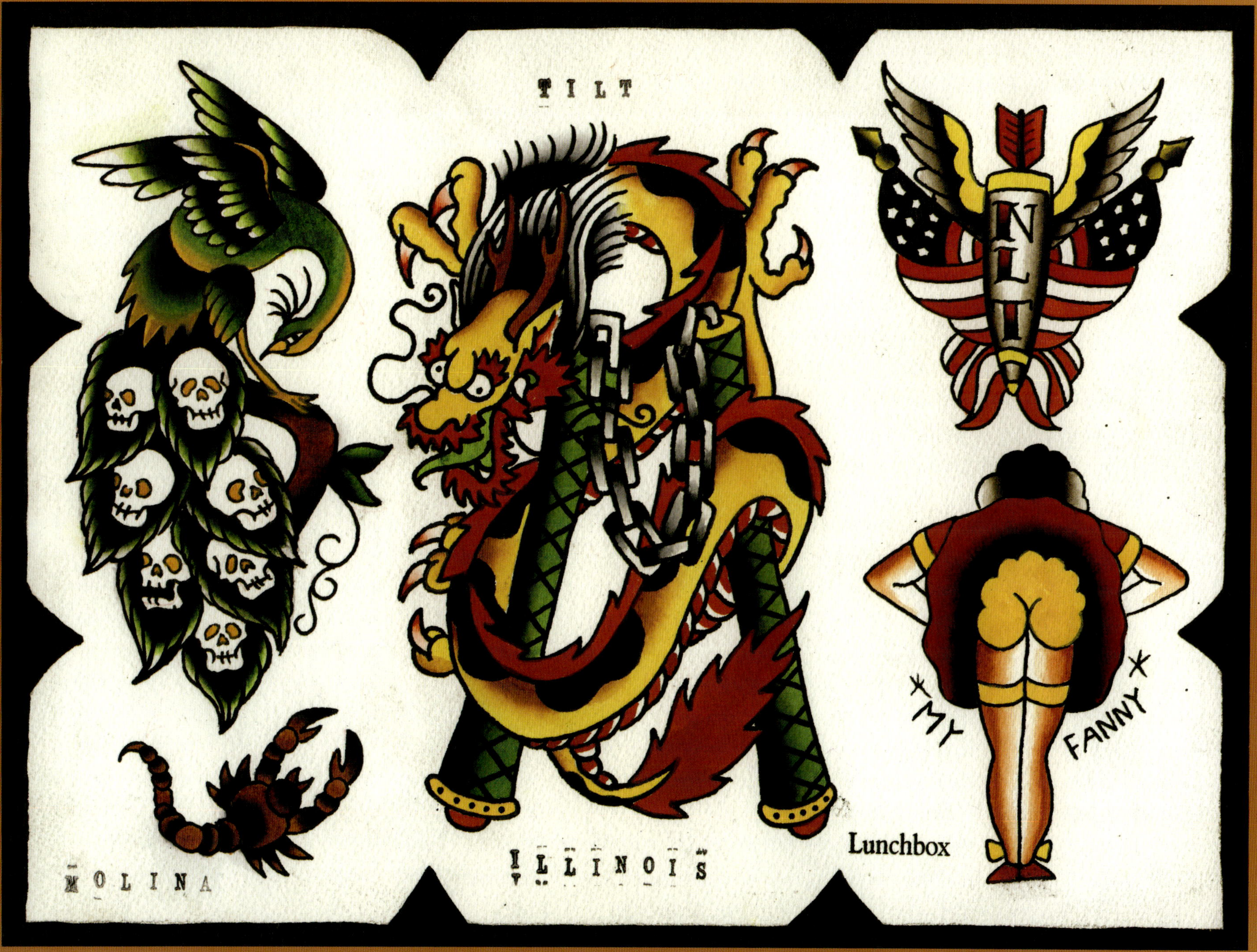

TILT

NLT

MOLINA

ILLINOIS

Lunchbox

MY FANNY

Gentleman Joel, Lunchbox and Tilt

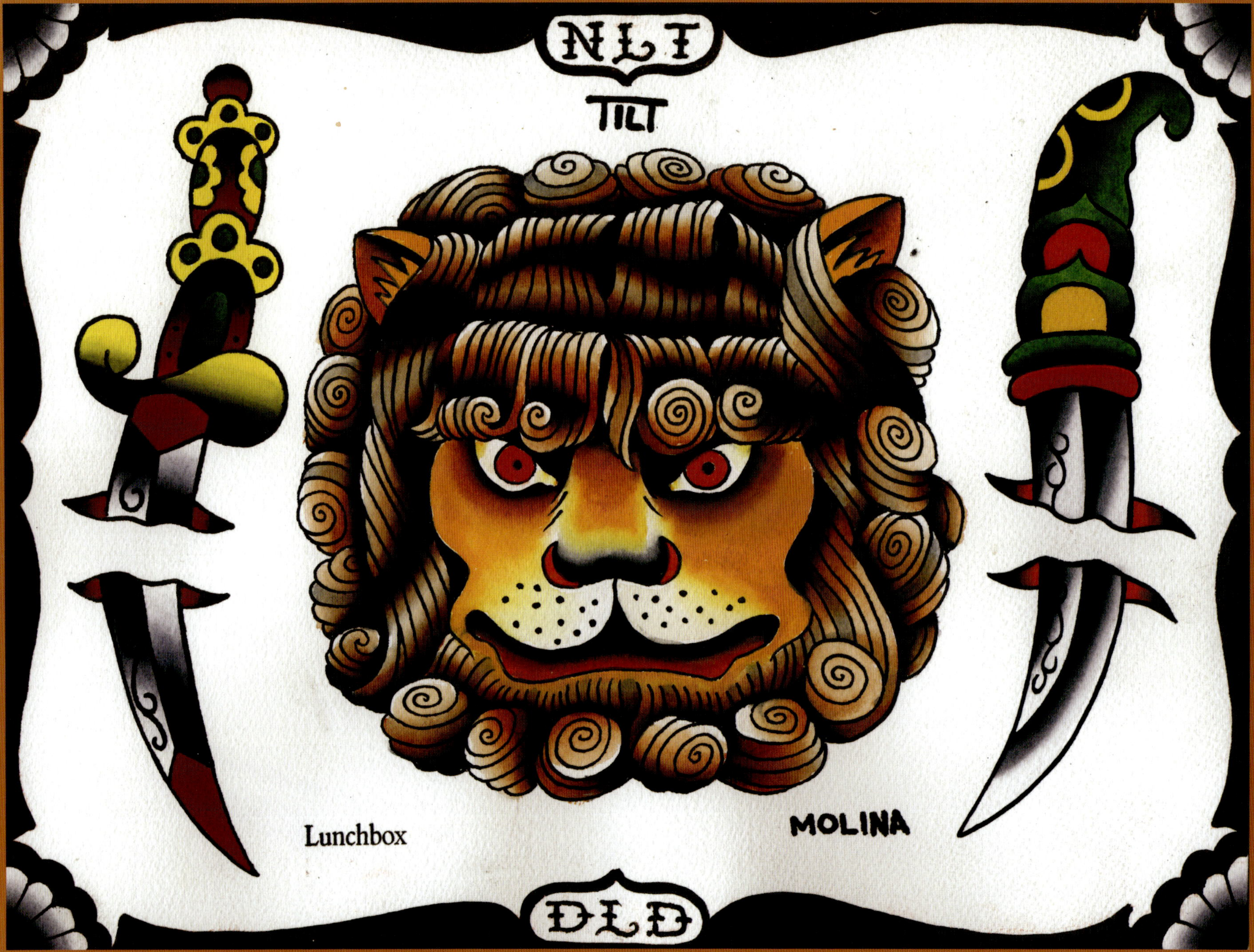

Gentleman Joel, Lunchbox and Tilt

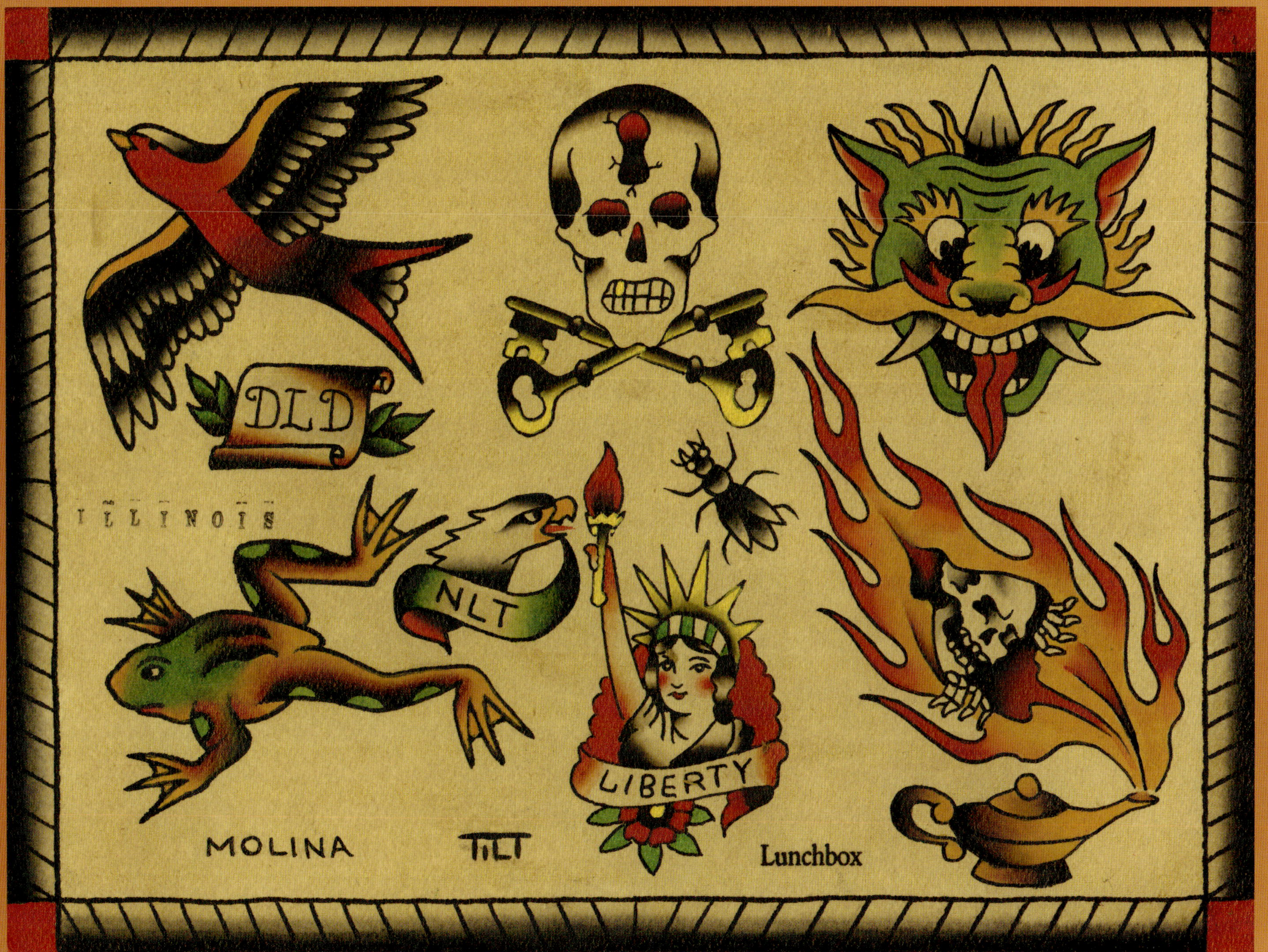

Gentleman Joel, Lunchbox and Tilt

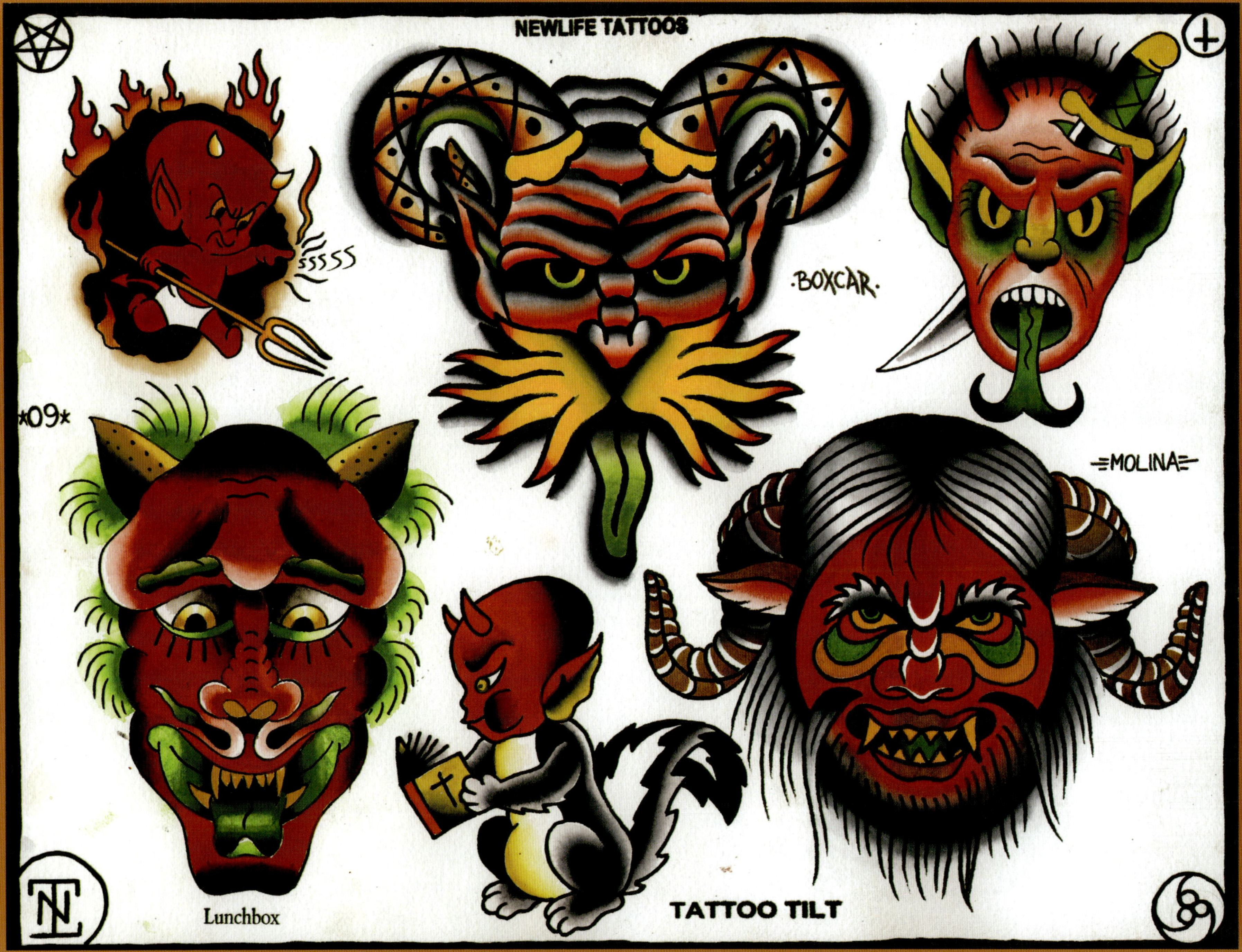

NEWLIFE TATTOOS

SSSSS

BOXCAR.

09

MOLINA

Lunchbox

TATTOO TILT

Gentleman Joel, Lunchbox and Tilt

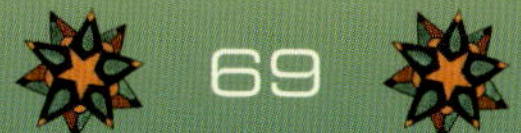

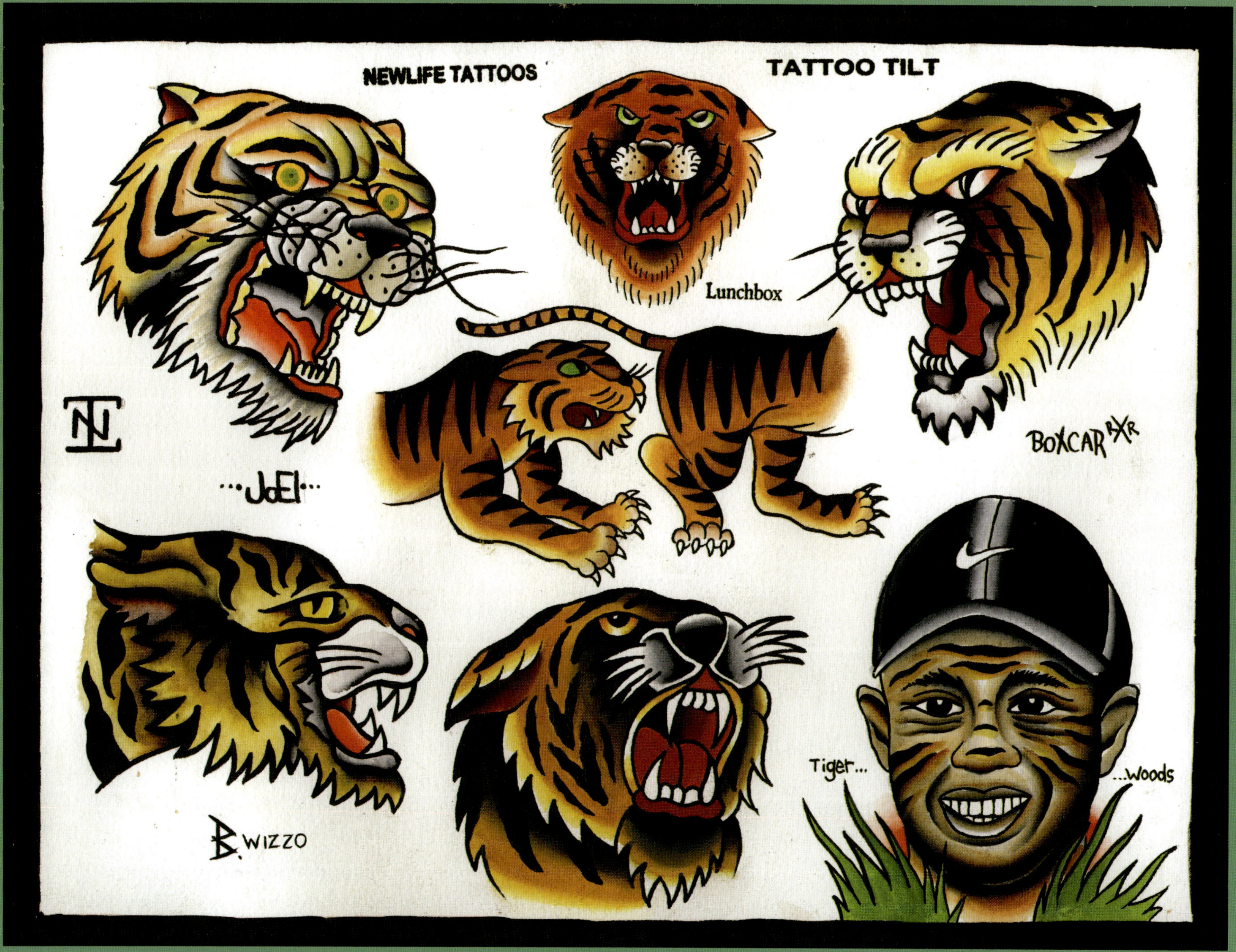

NEWLIFE TATTOOS

TATTOO TILT

Lunchbox

BOXCAR

...JoEl...

B. WIZZO

Tiger...

...Woods

Gentleman Joel, Lunchbox Bud Weeks, Boxcar and Tilt

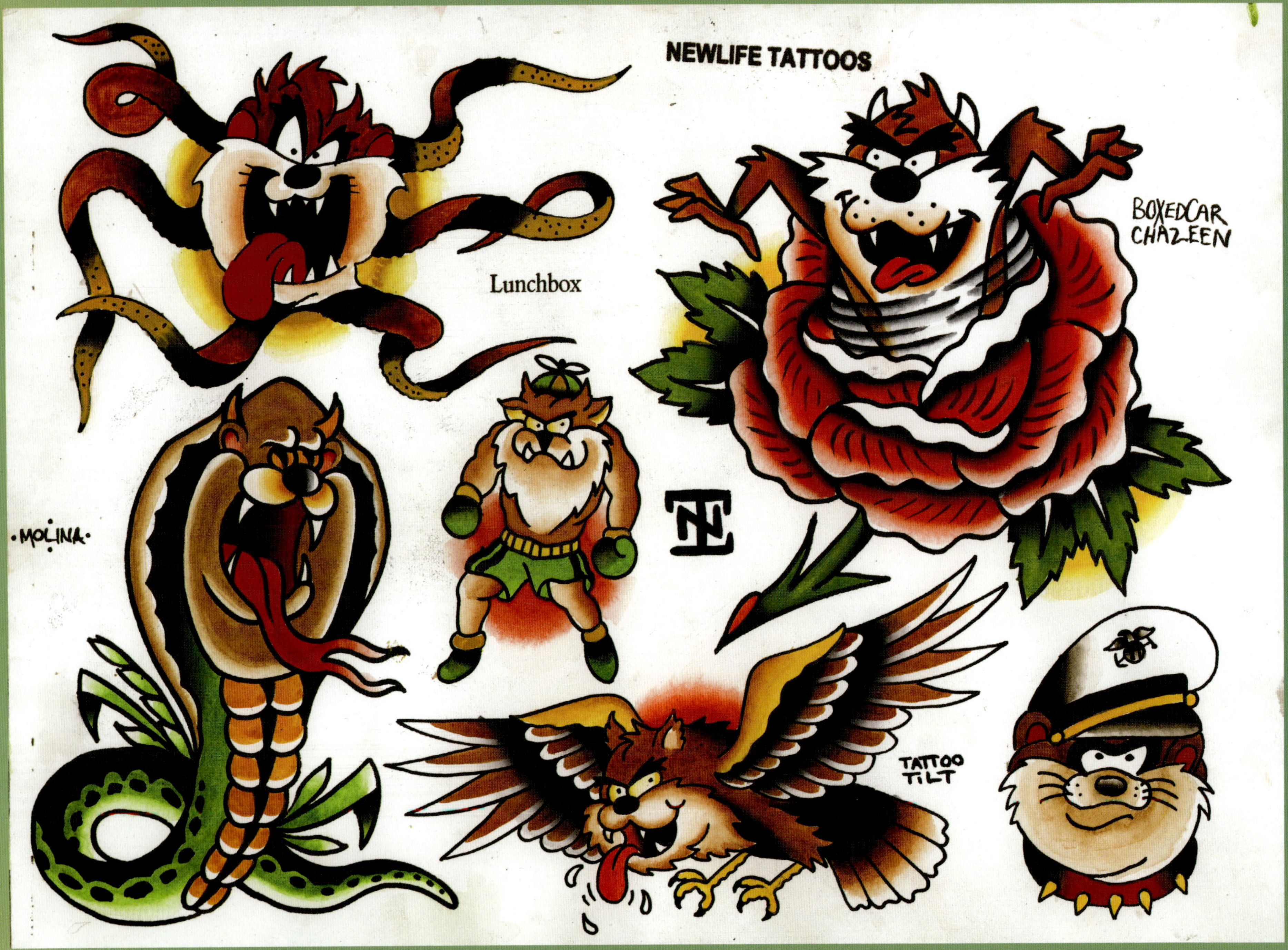

Gentleman Joel, Lunchbox, Boxcar and Tilt

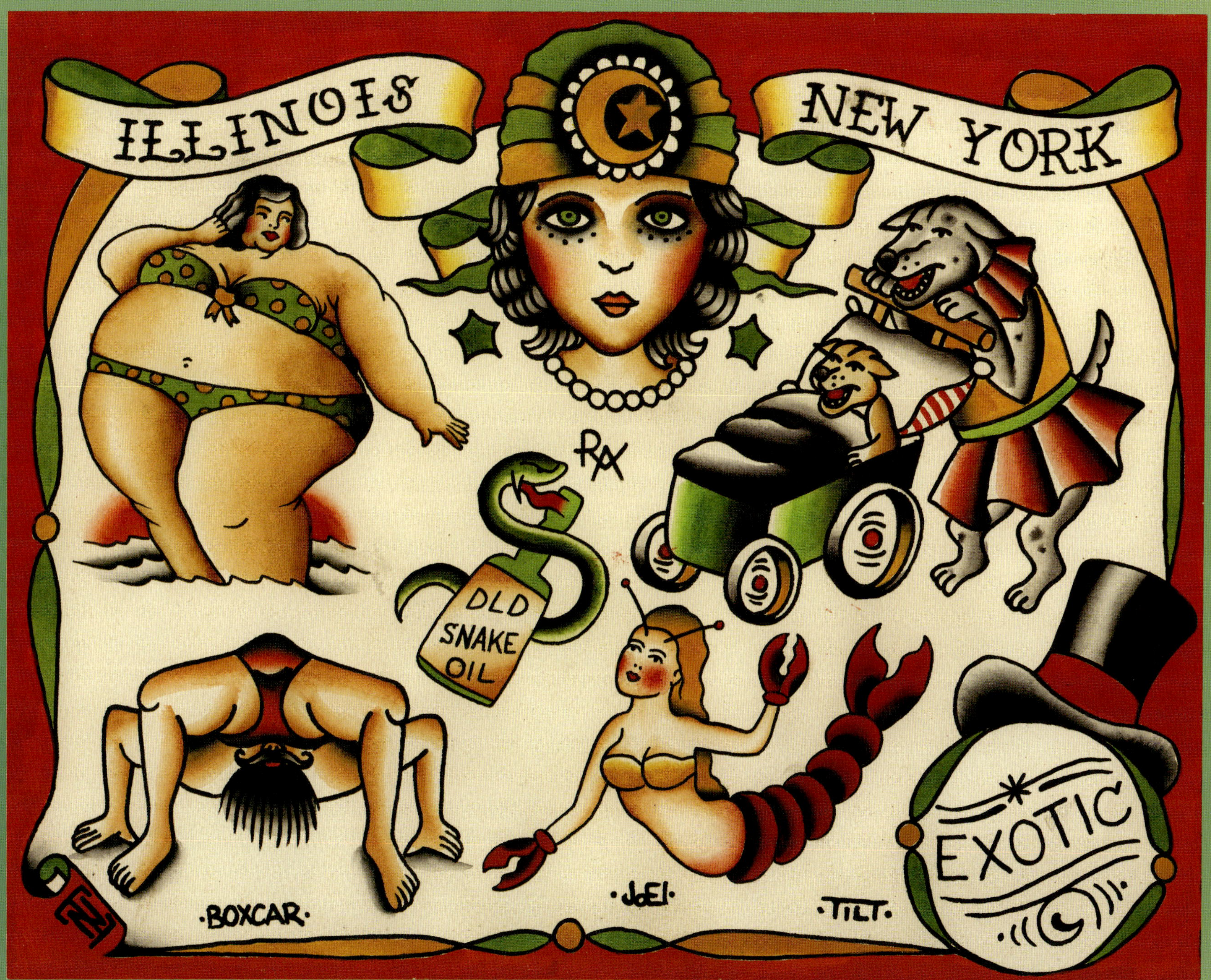

Gentleman Joel, Boxcar and Tilt

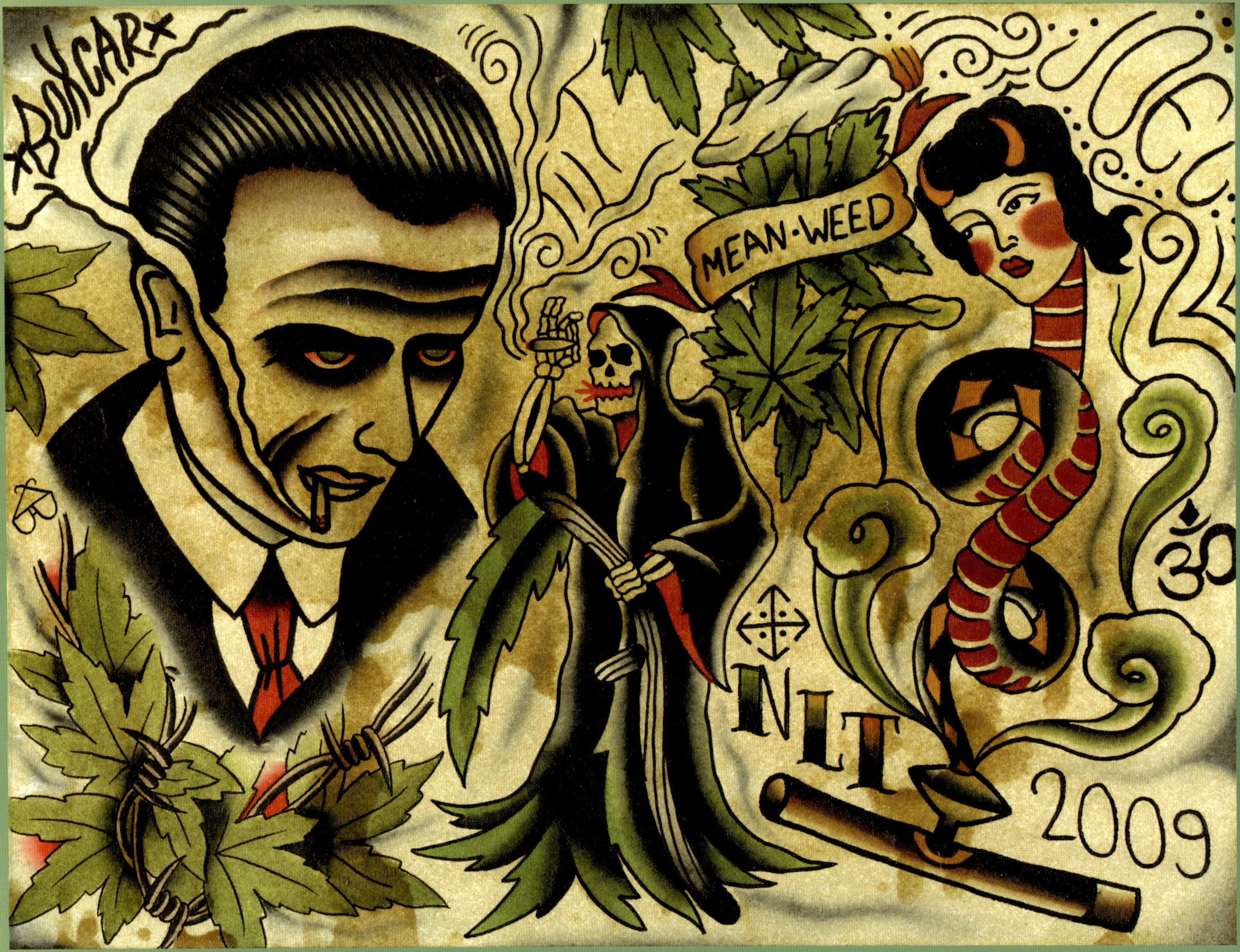

Gentleman Joel, Lunchbox, Boxcar and Tilt

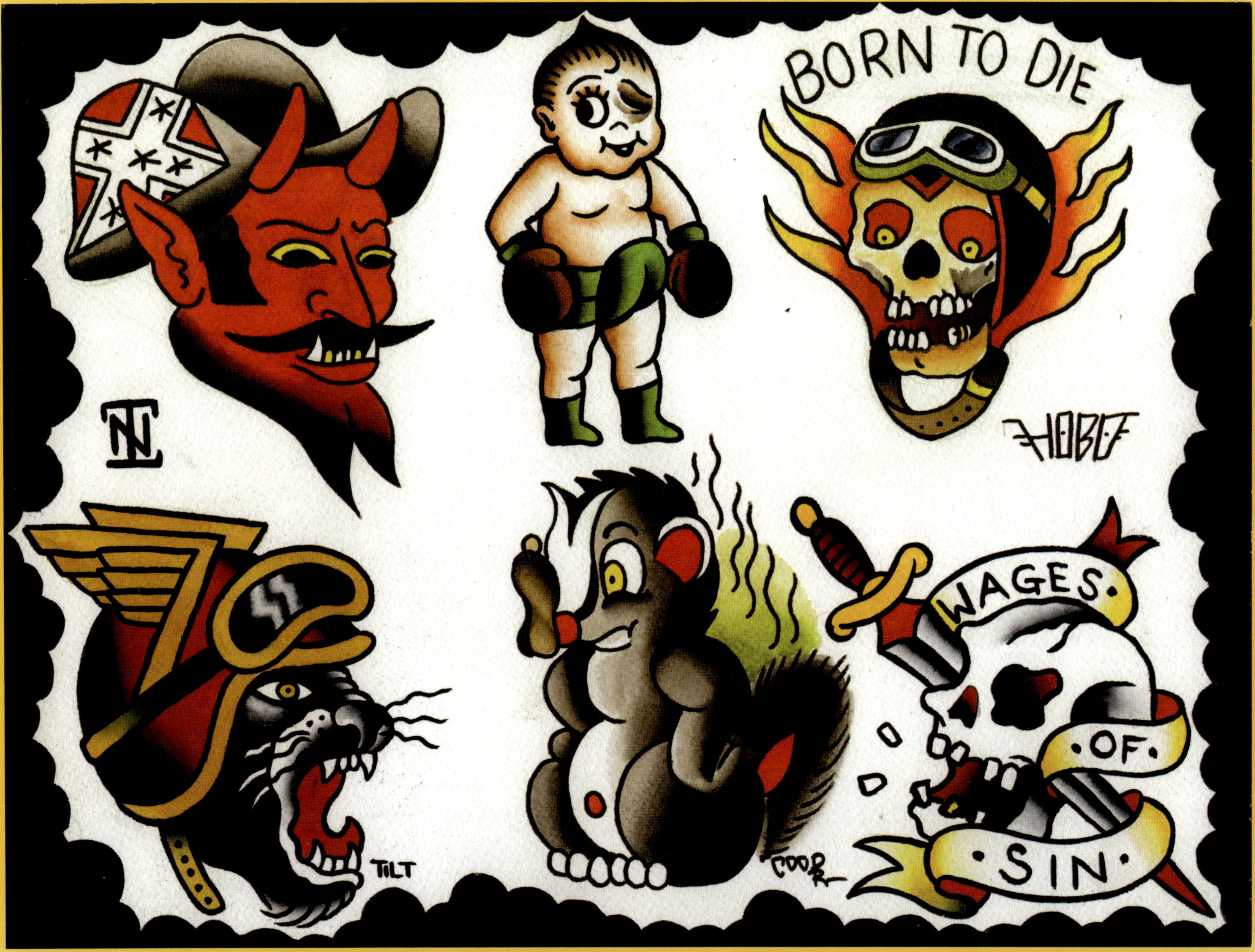

Coopr and Tilt

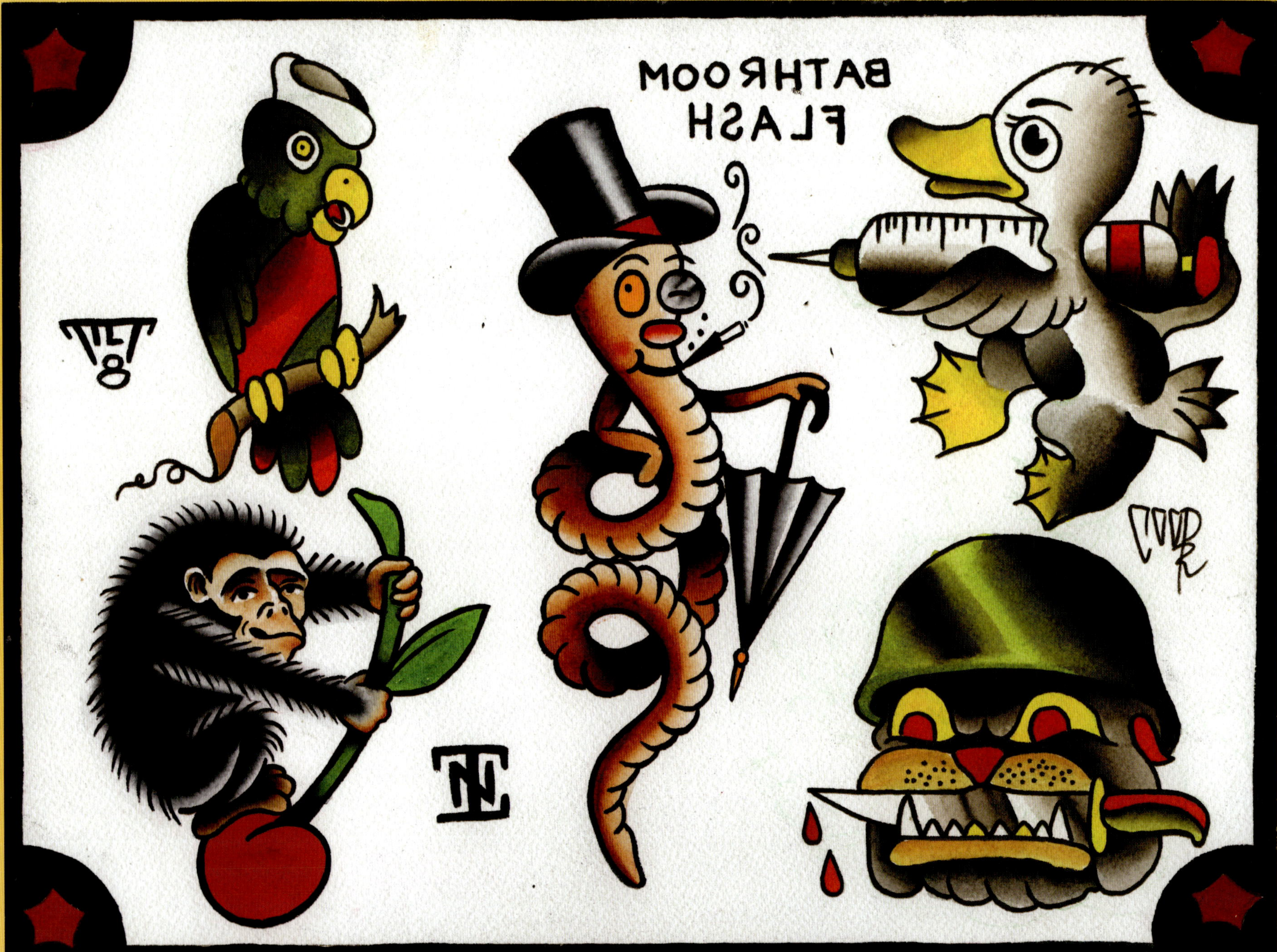

Coopr and Tilt

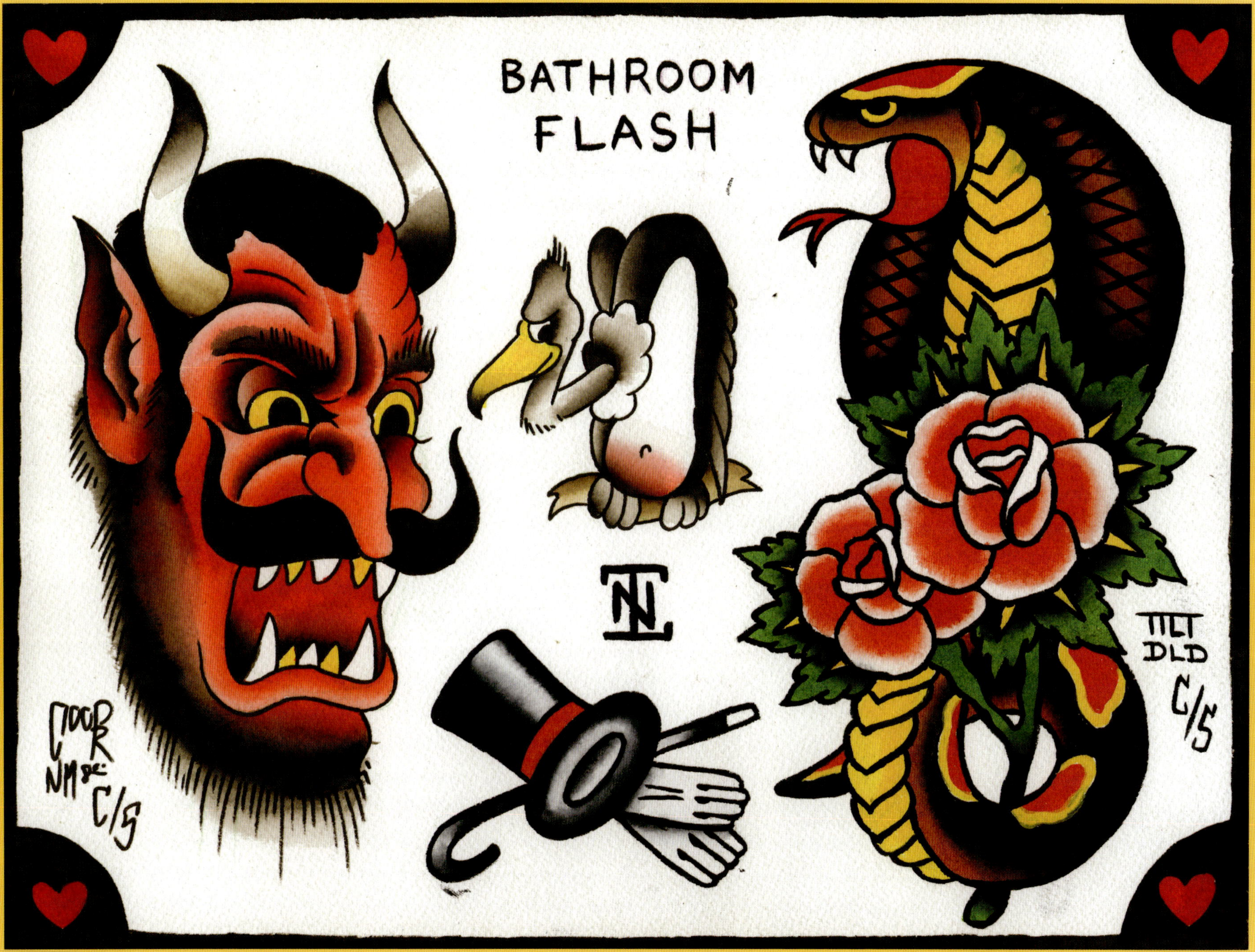

BATHROOM
FLASH

TILT
DLD
C/5

Coopr and Tilt

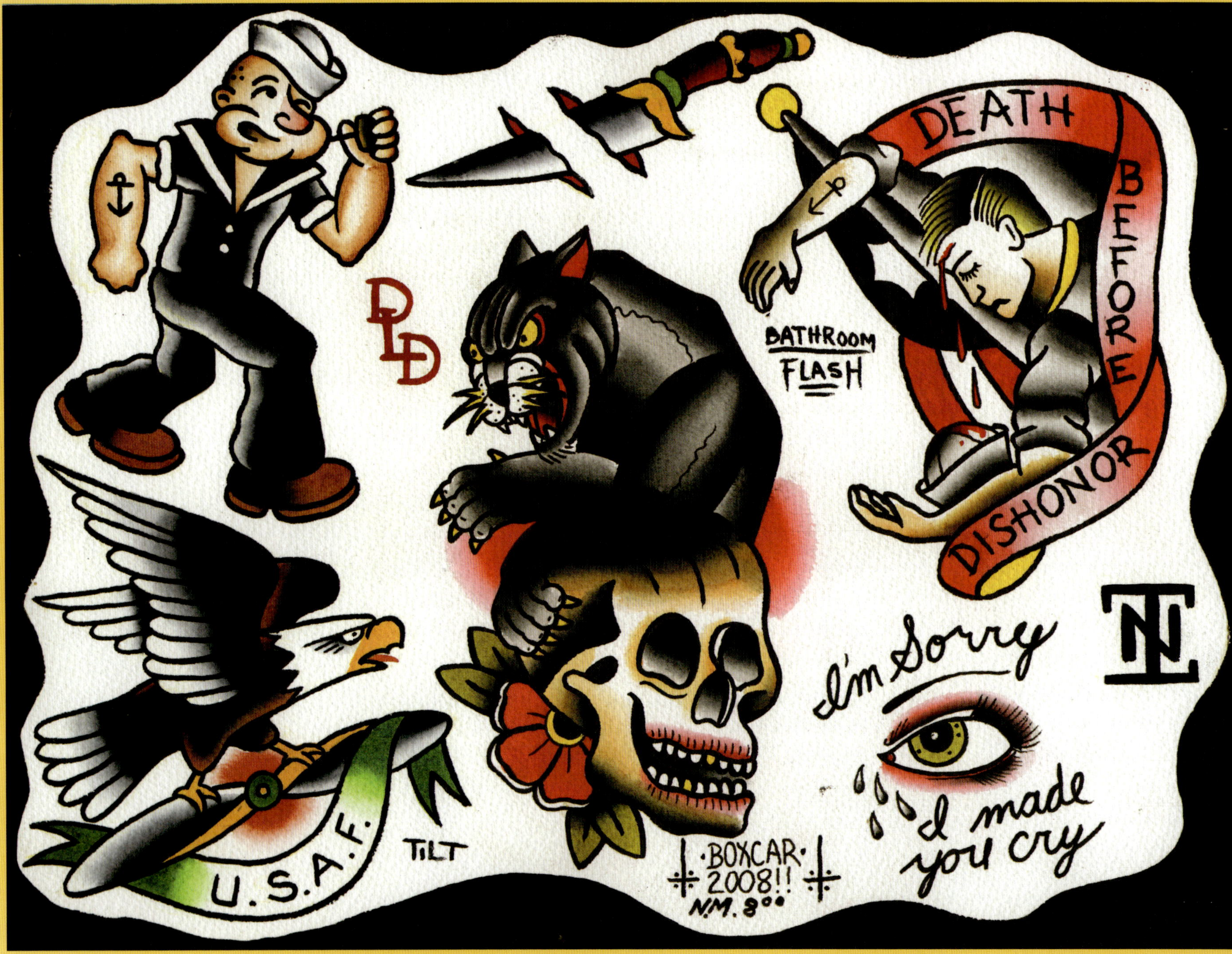

Boxcar and Tilt

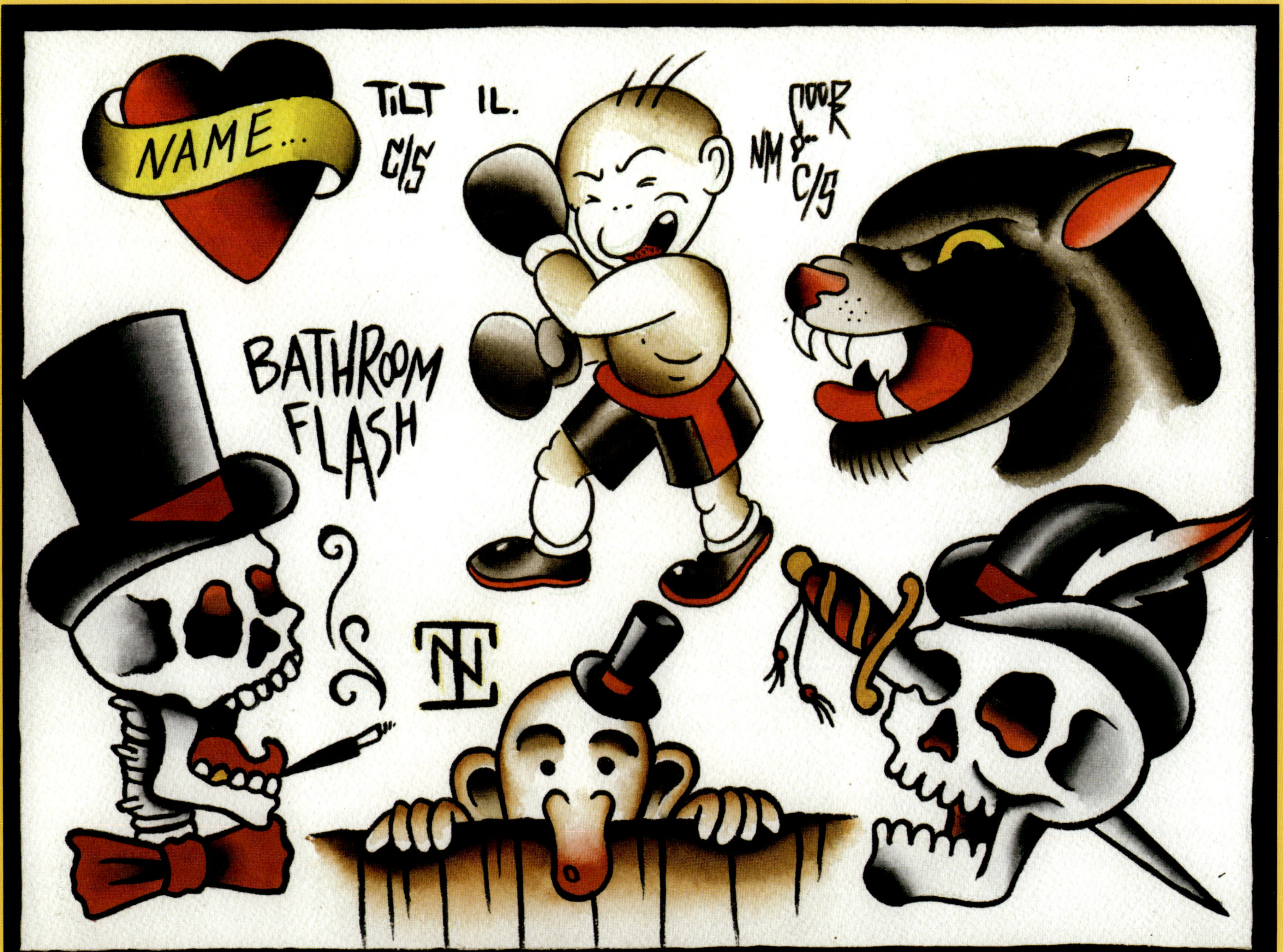

Coopr and Tilt

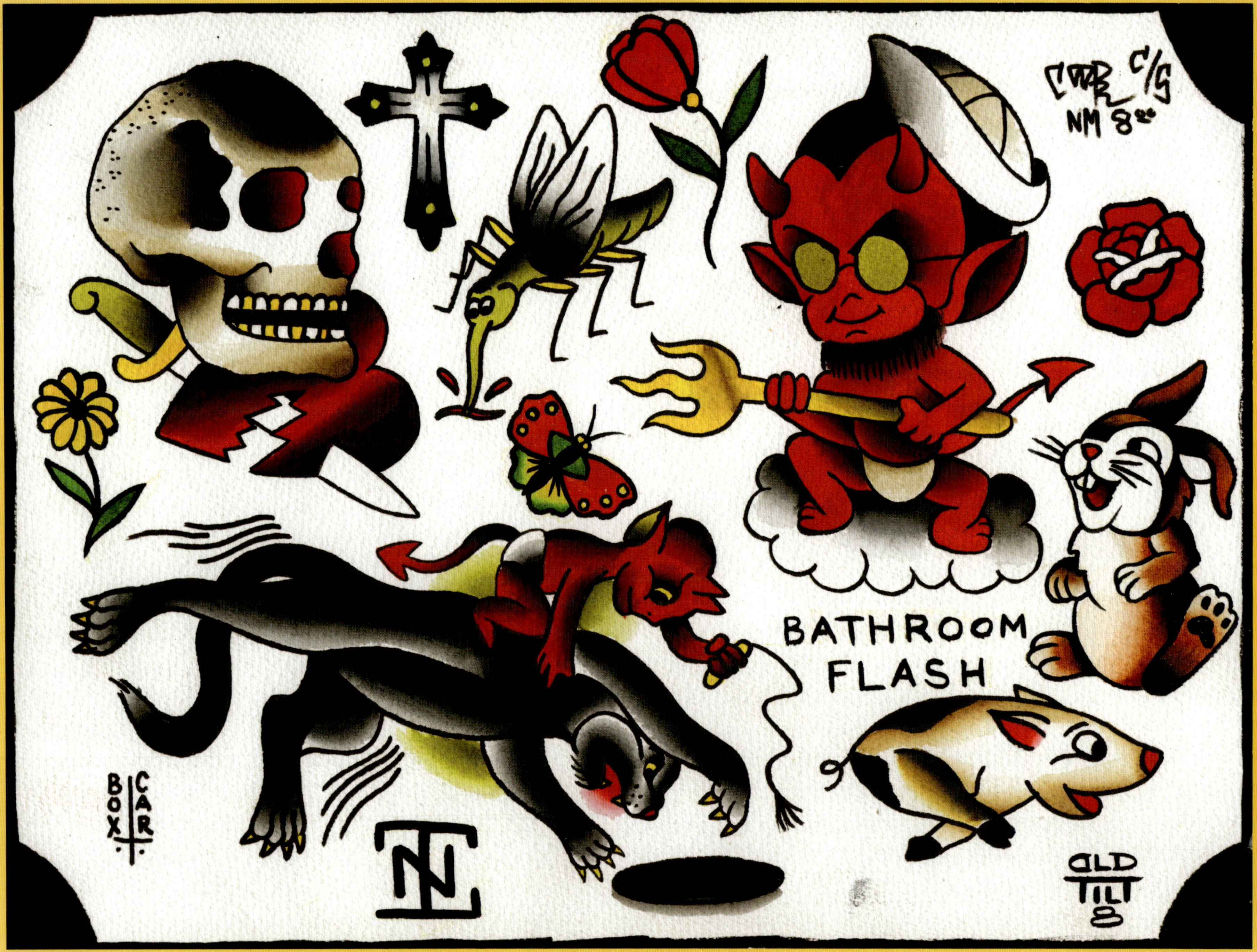

Coopr, Boxcar and Tilt

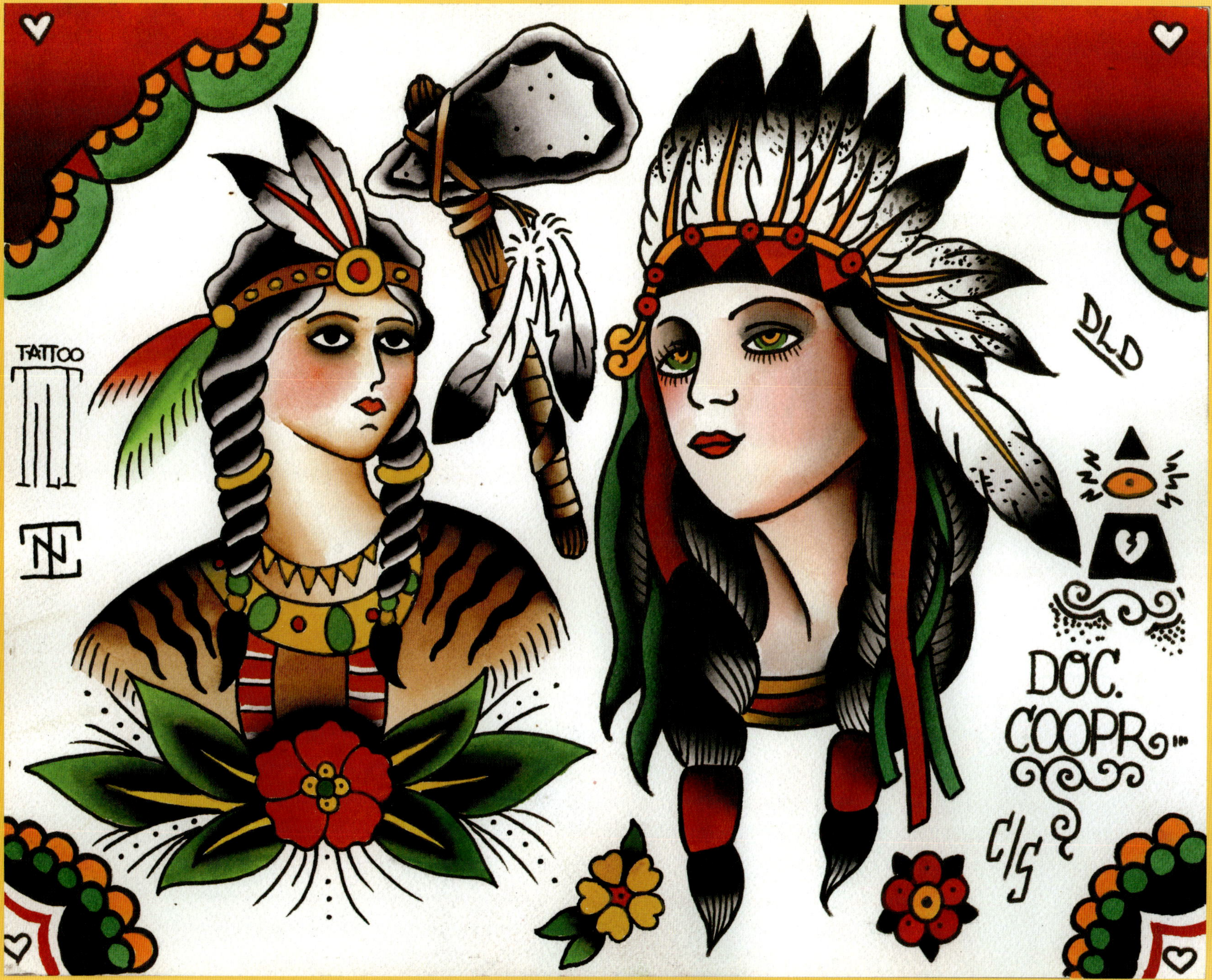

Coopr and Tilt

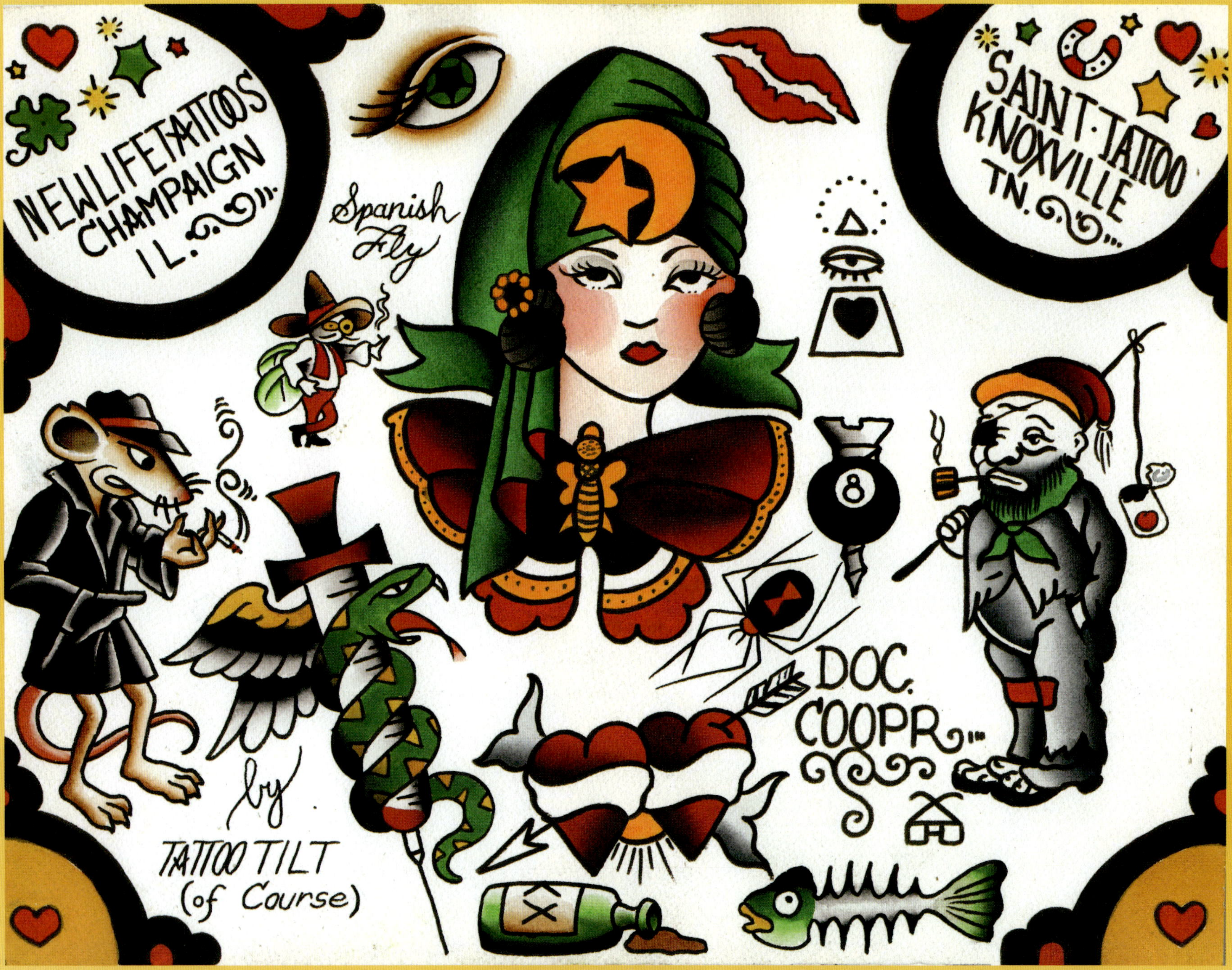

Coopr and Tilt

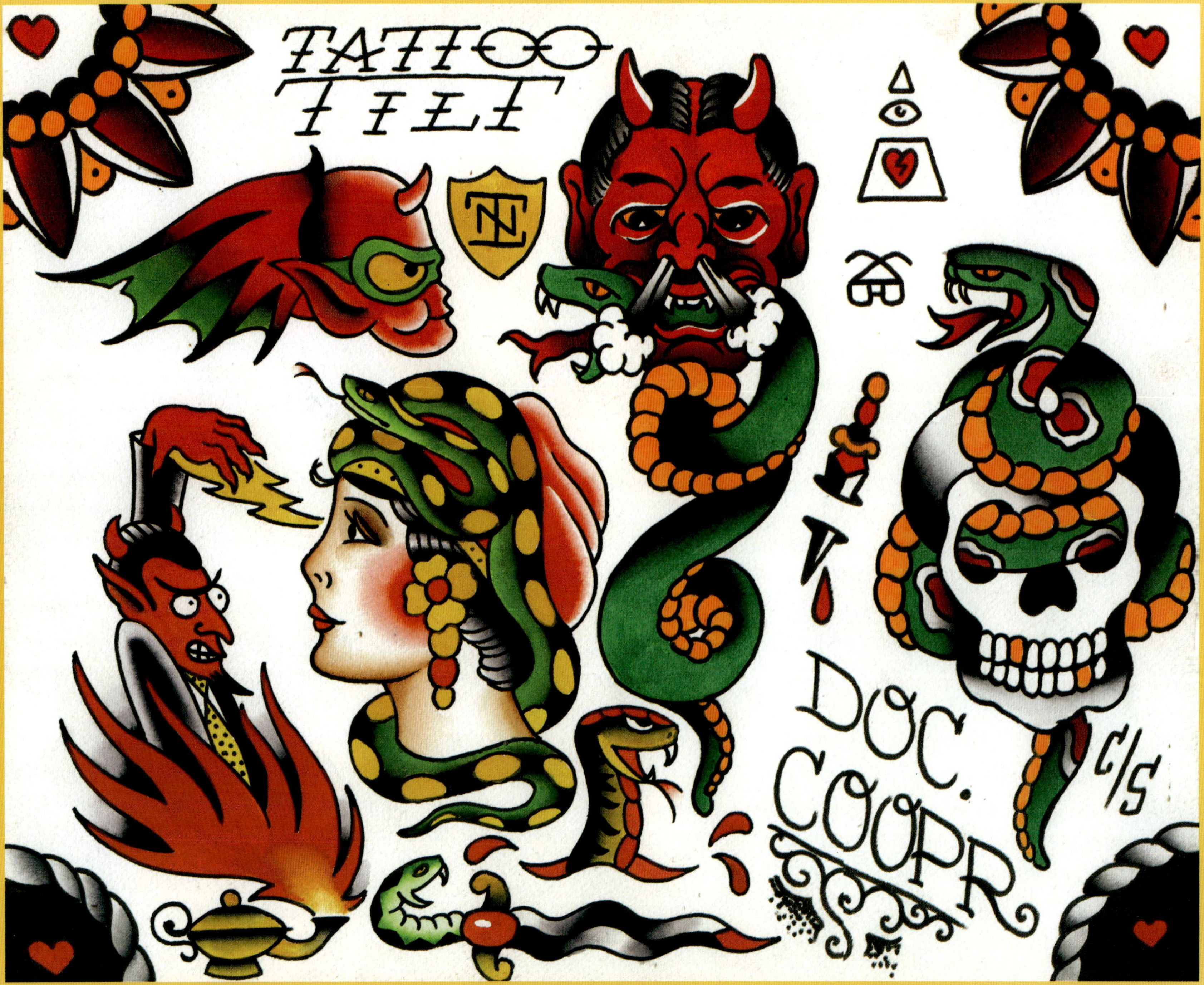

Coopr and Tilt

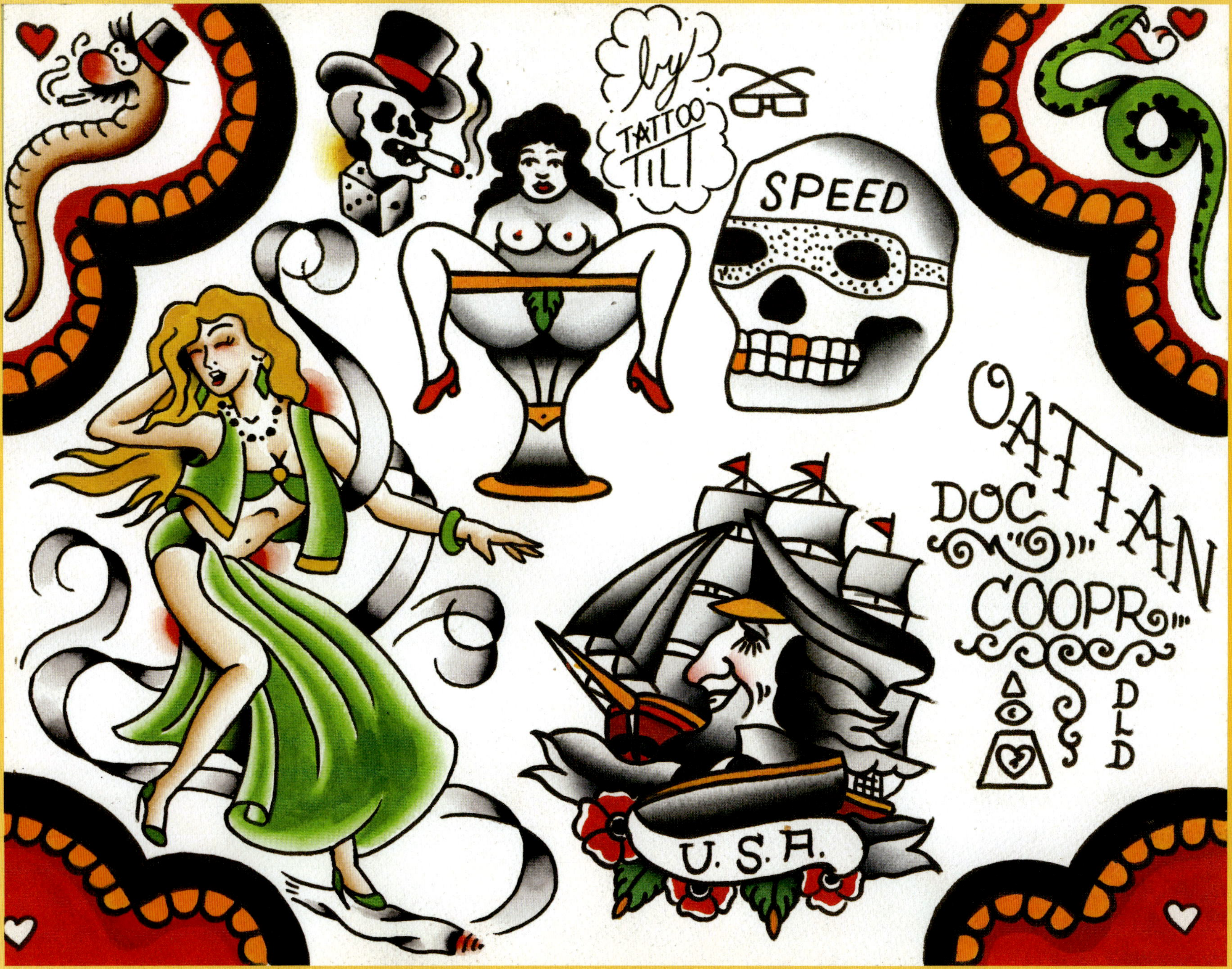

Coopr and Tilt

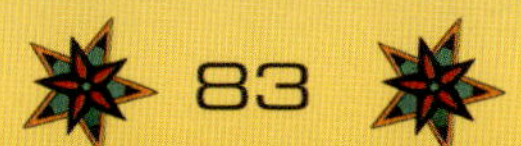

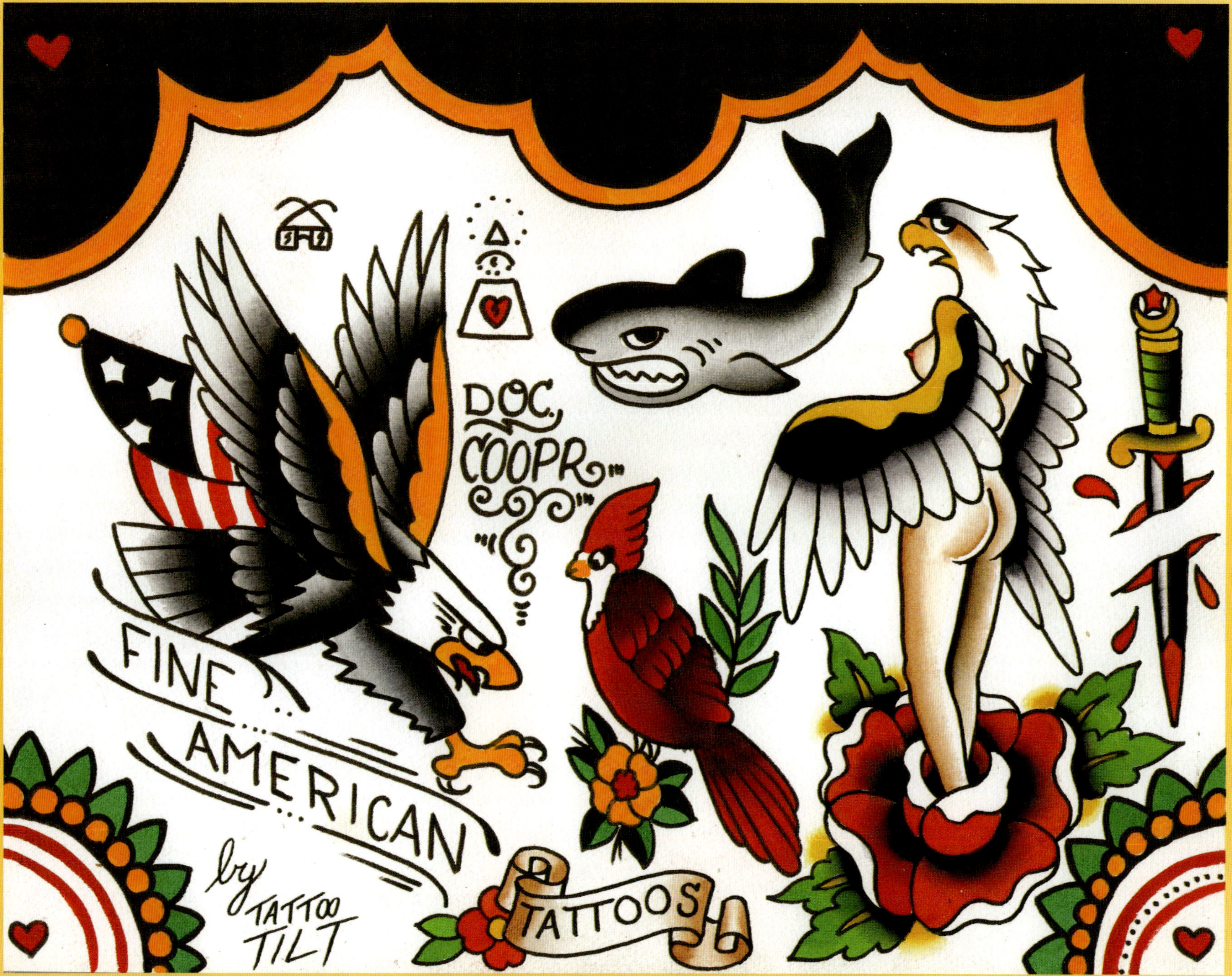

Coopr and Tilt

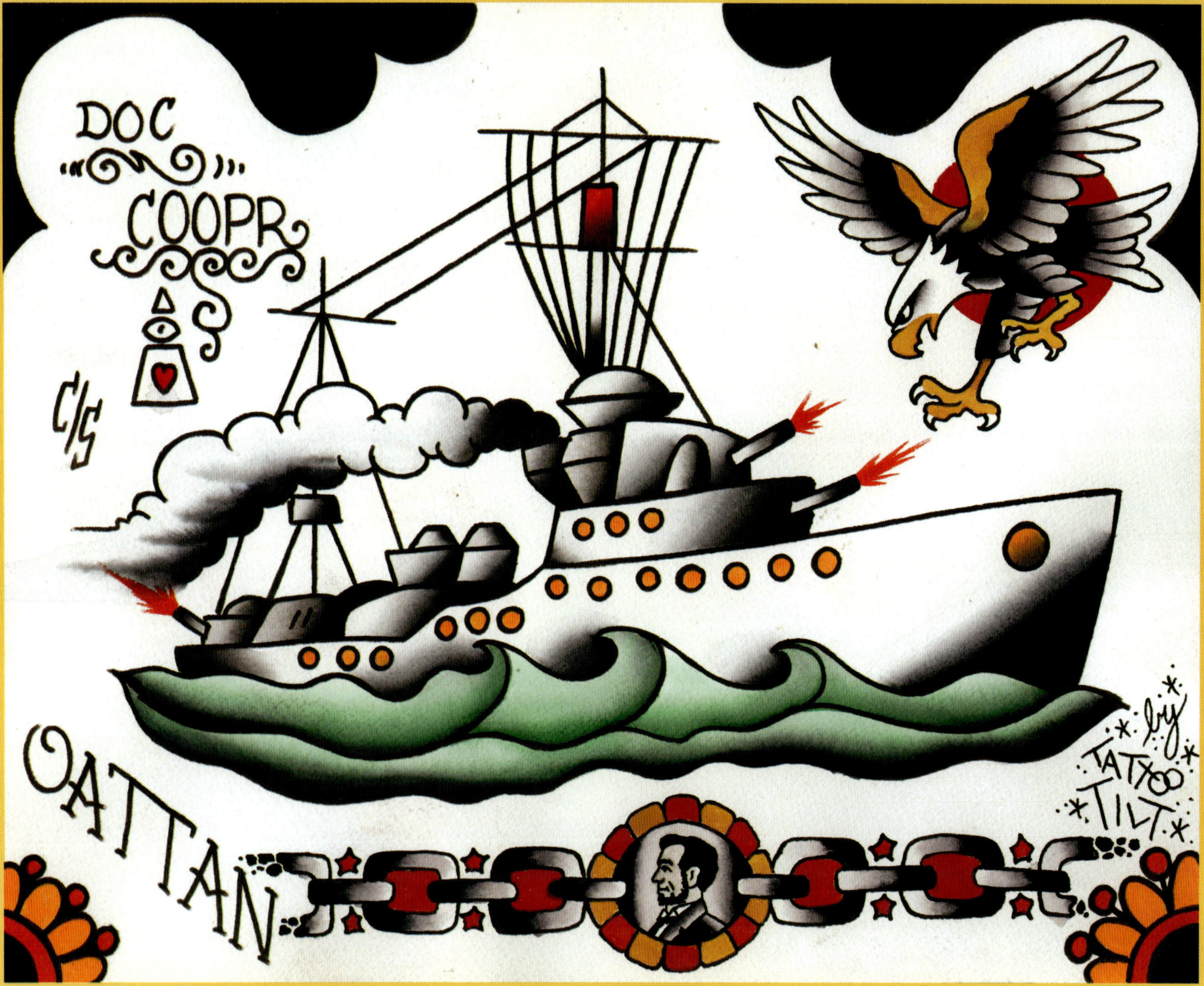

Coopr and Tilt

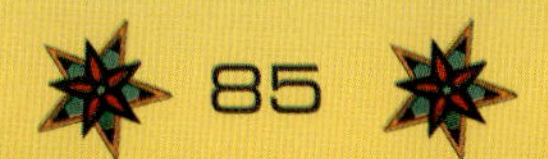

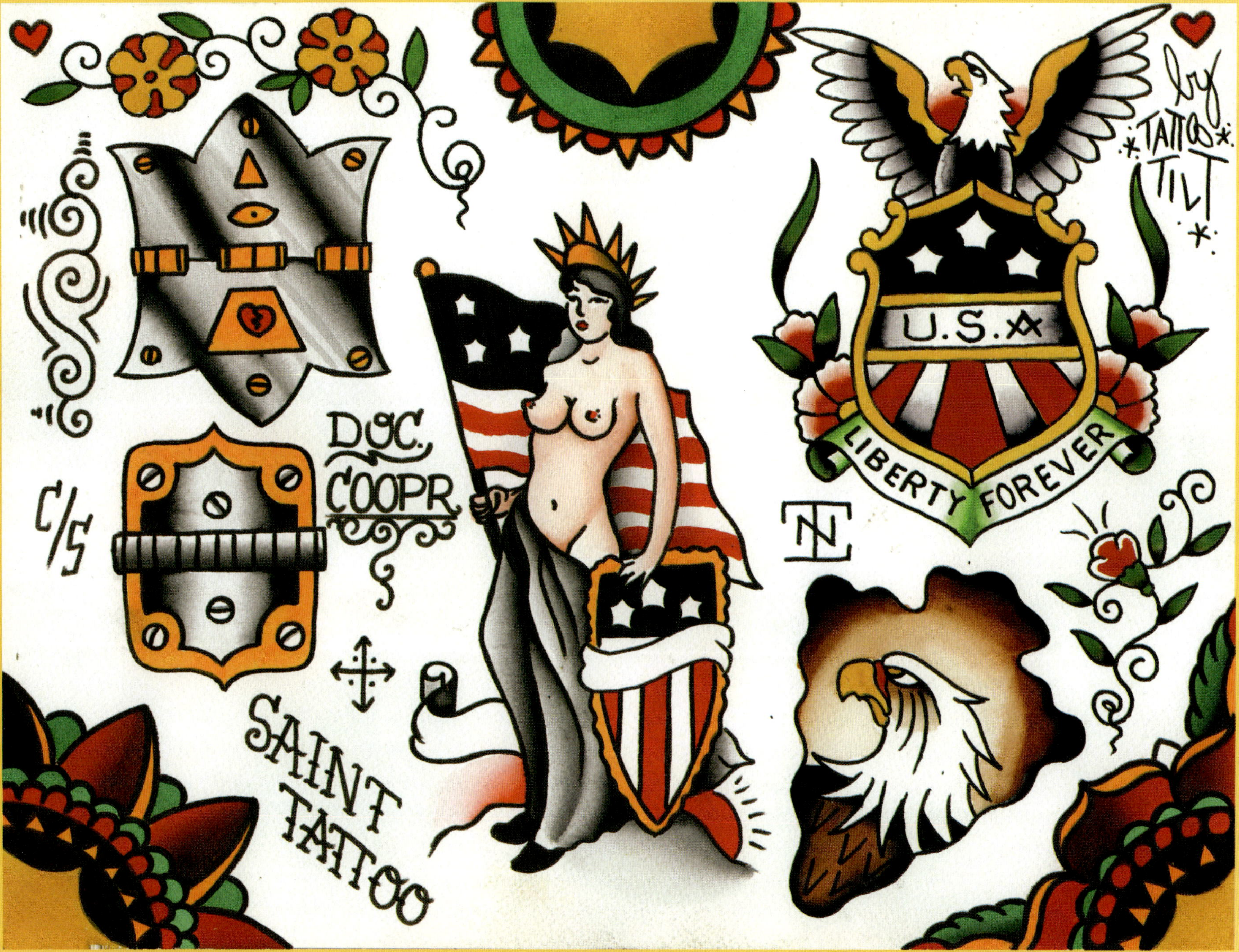

Coopr and Tilt

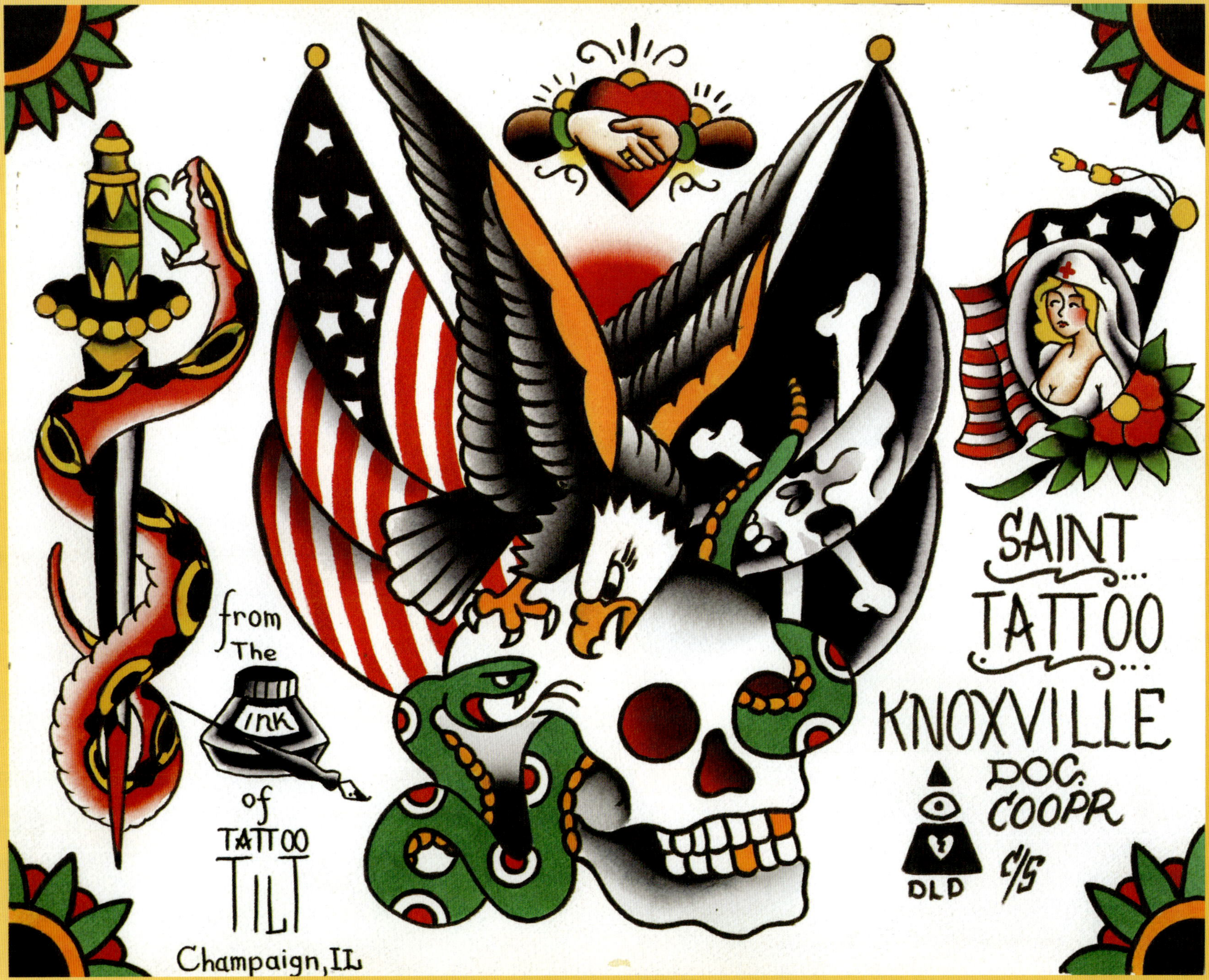

from
The
INK
of
TATTOO
TILT
Champaign, IL

SAINT
TATTOO
KNOXVILLE
DOC.
COOPR
DLD
C/S

Coopr and Tilt

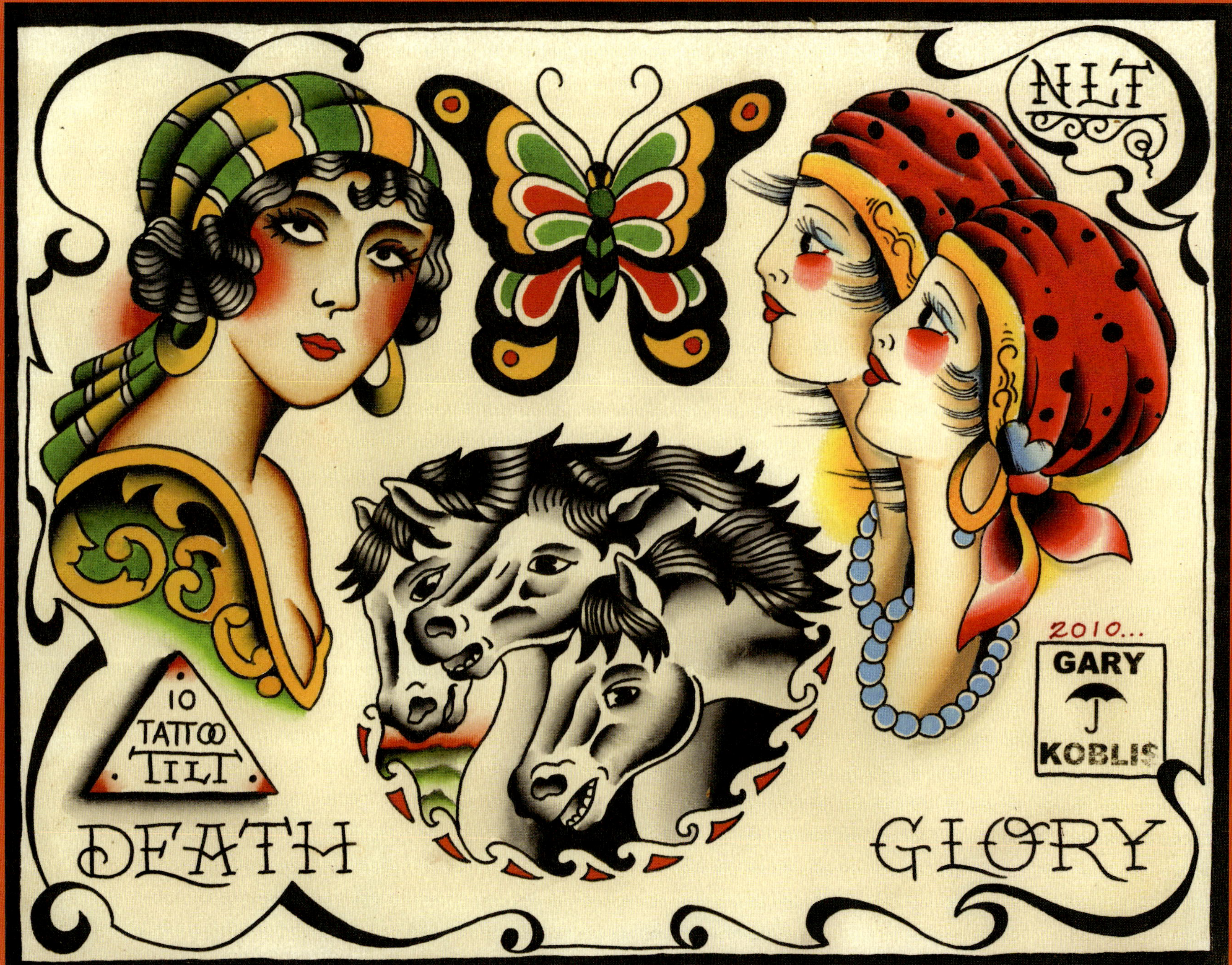

Gary Koblis and Tilt

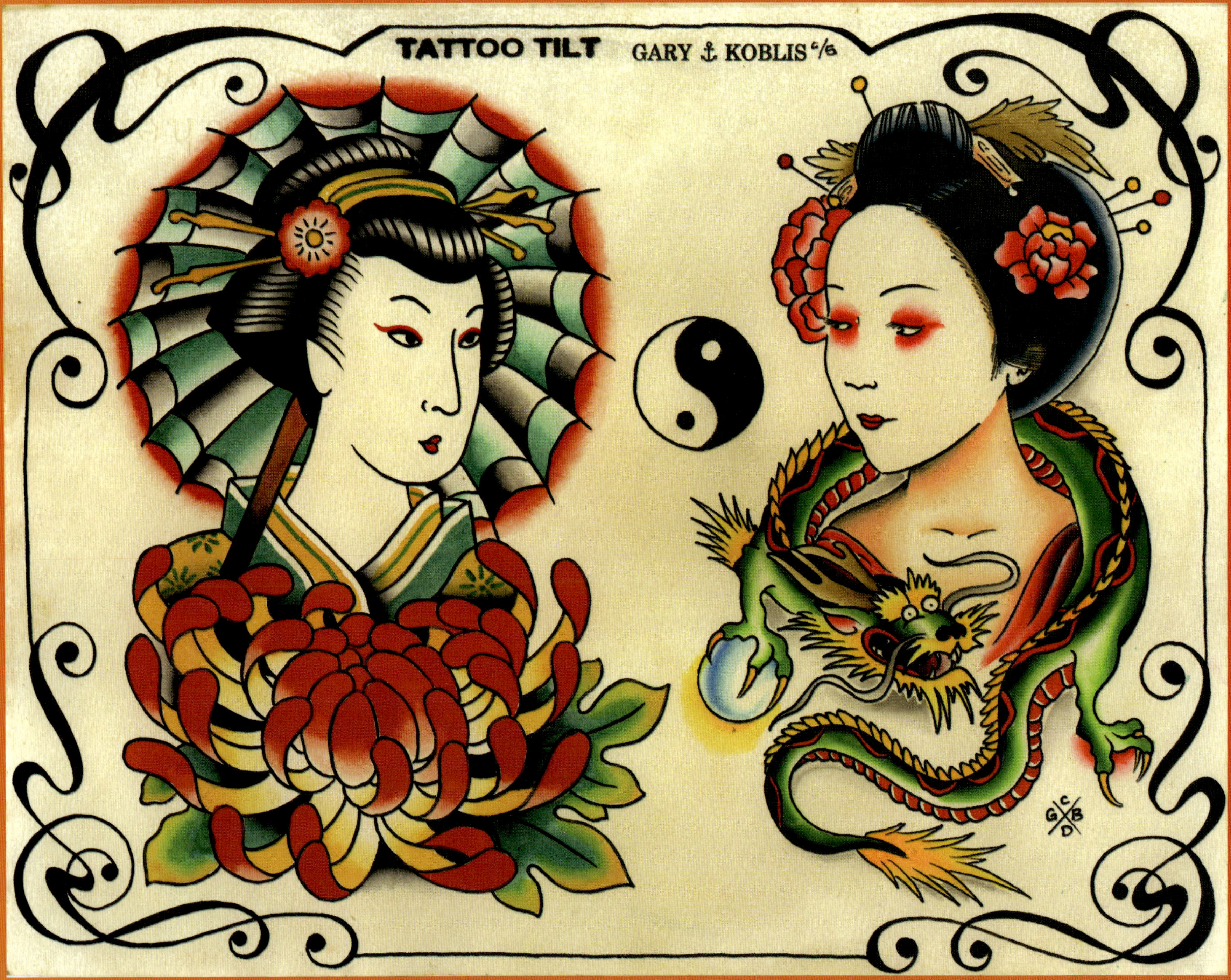

TATTOO TILT

GARY ⚓ KOBLIS c/s

Gary Koblis and Tilt

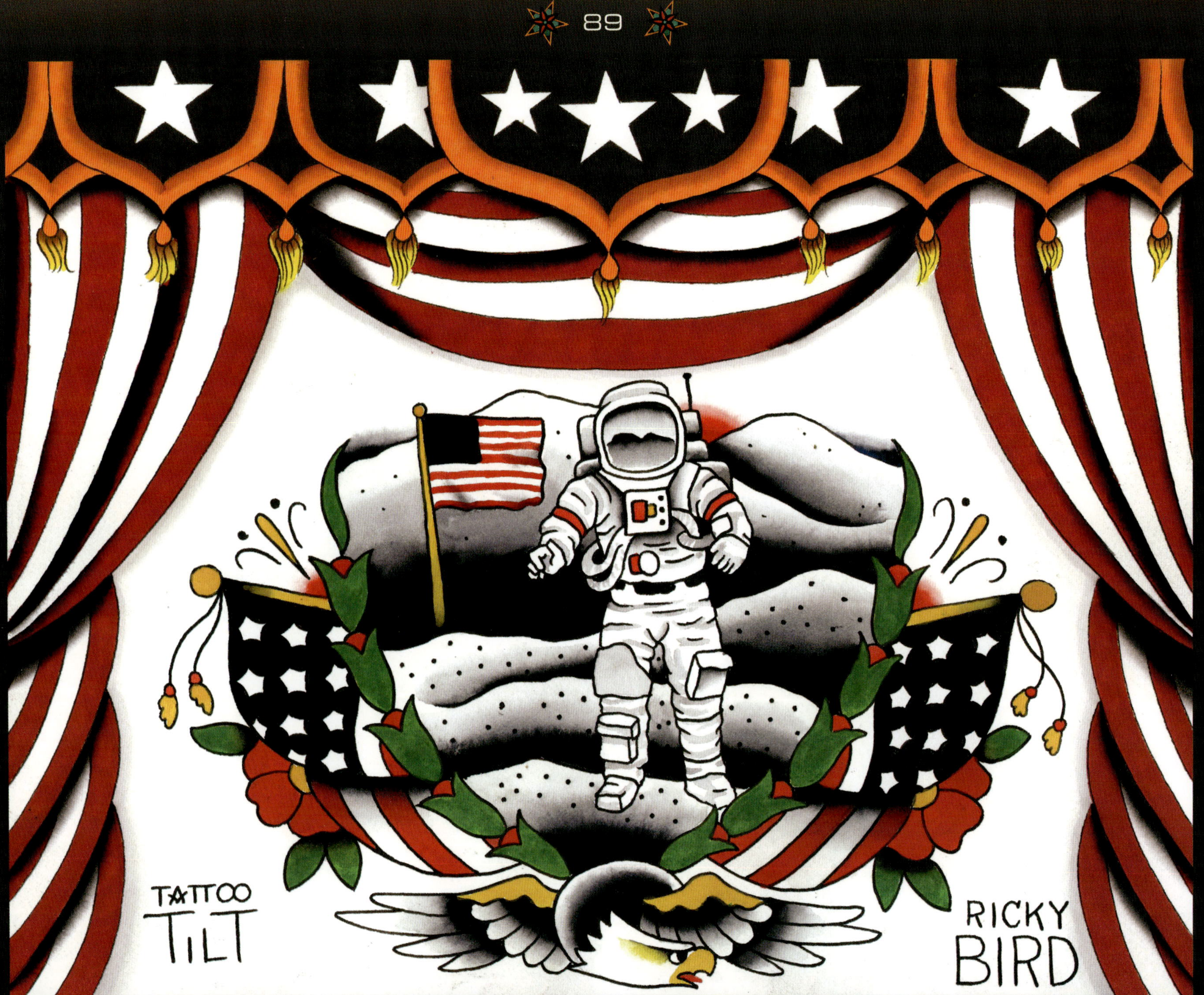

Ricky Bird and Tilt

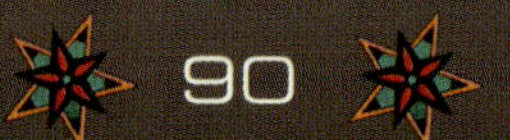

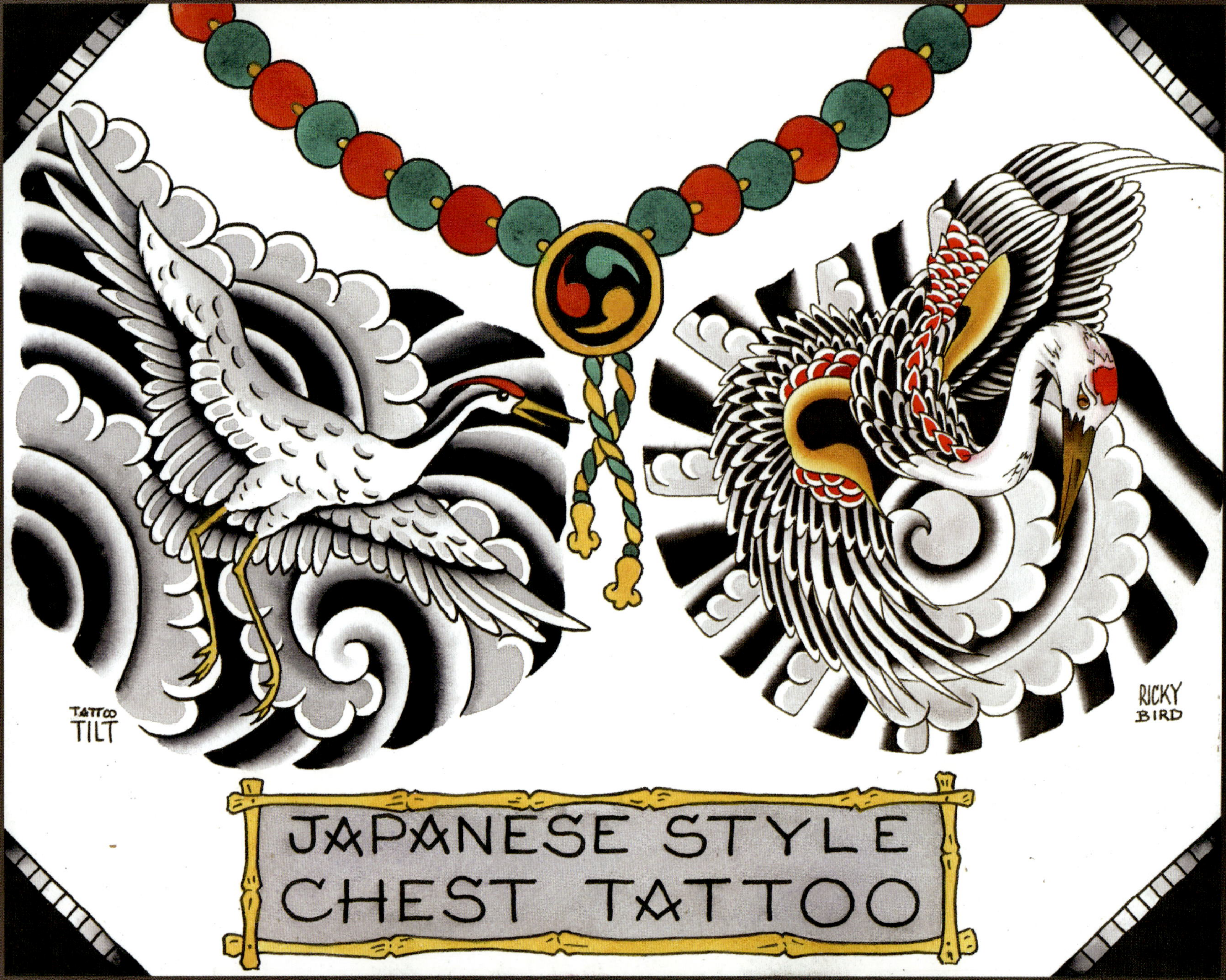

JAPANESE STYLE CHEST TATTOO

TATTOO TILT

RICKY BIRD

Ricky Bird and Tilt

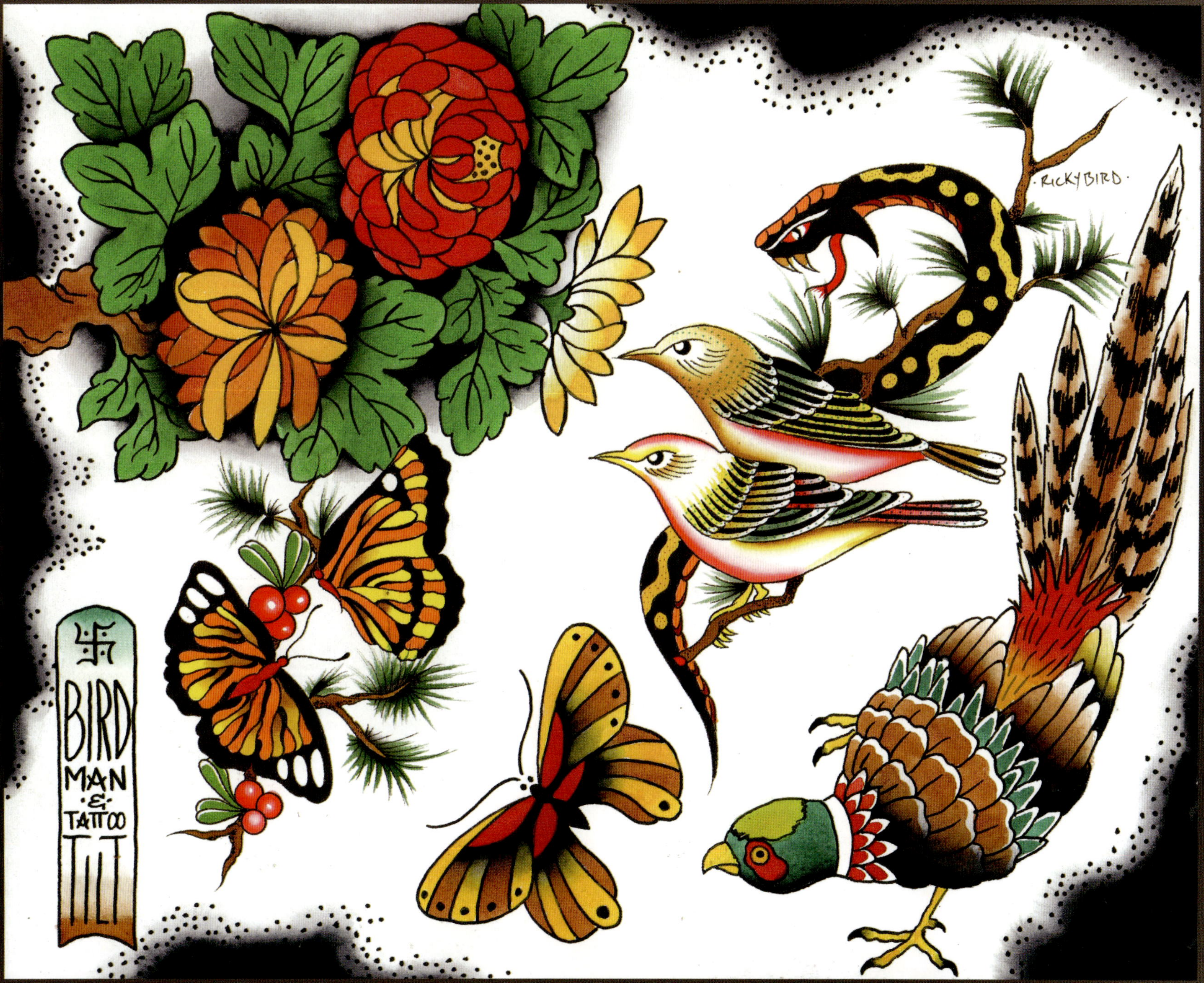

Ricky Bird and Tilt

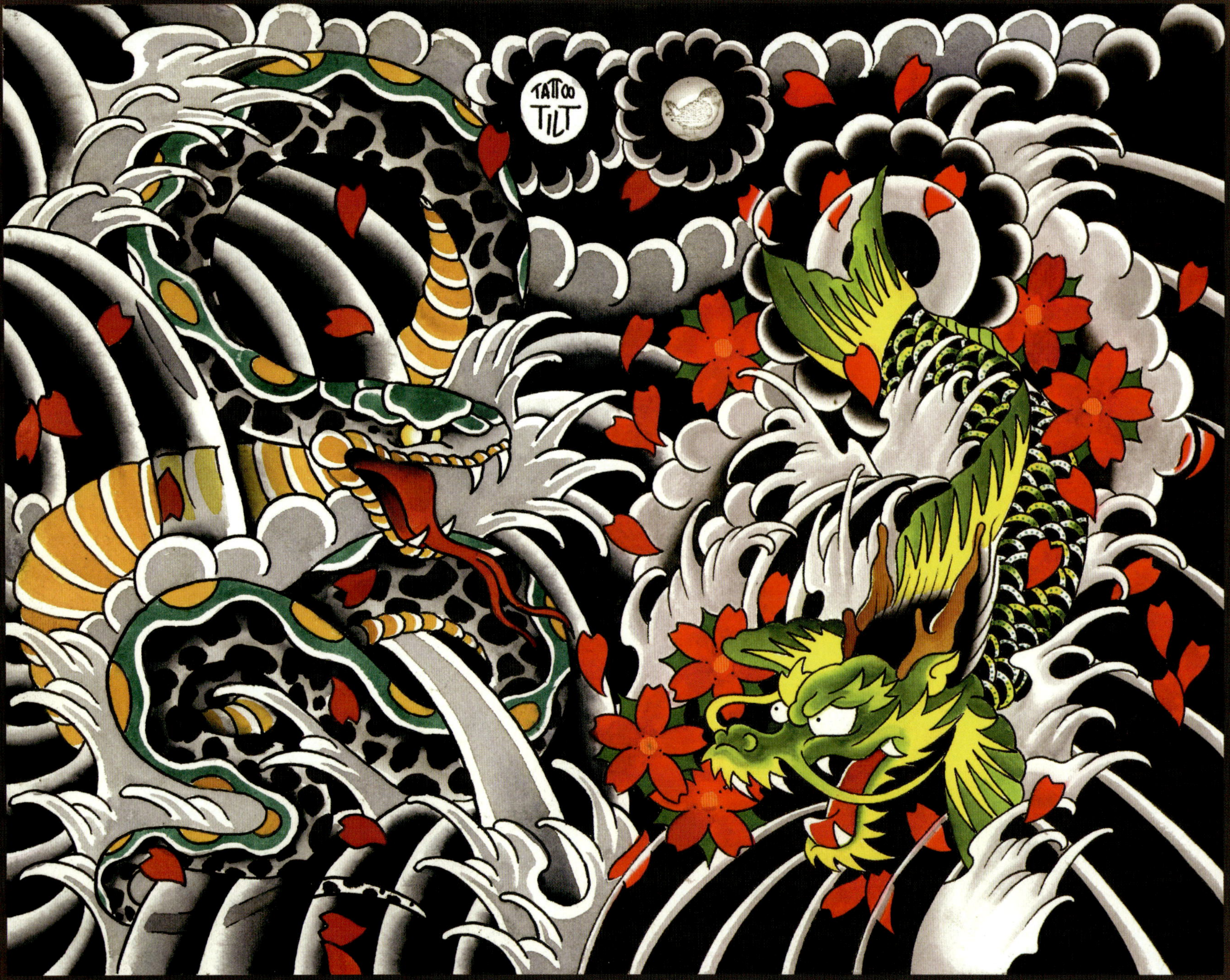

Ricky Bird and Tilt

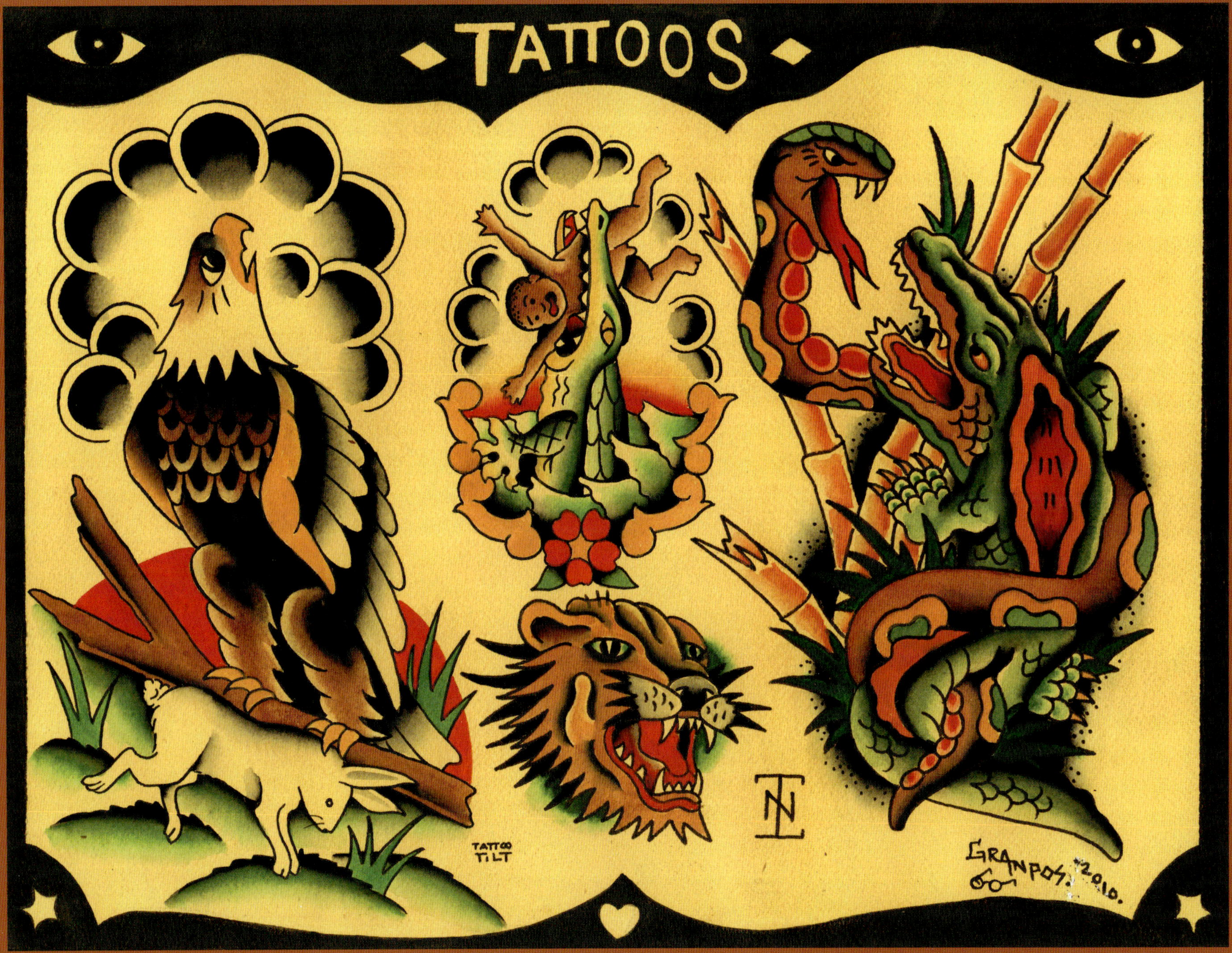

Granpos and Tilt

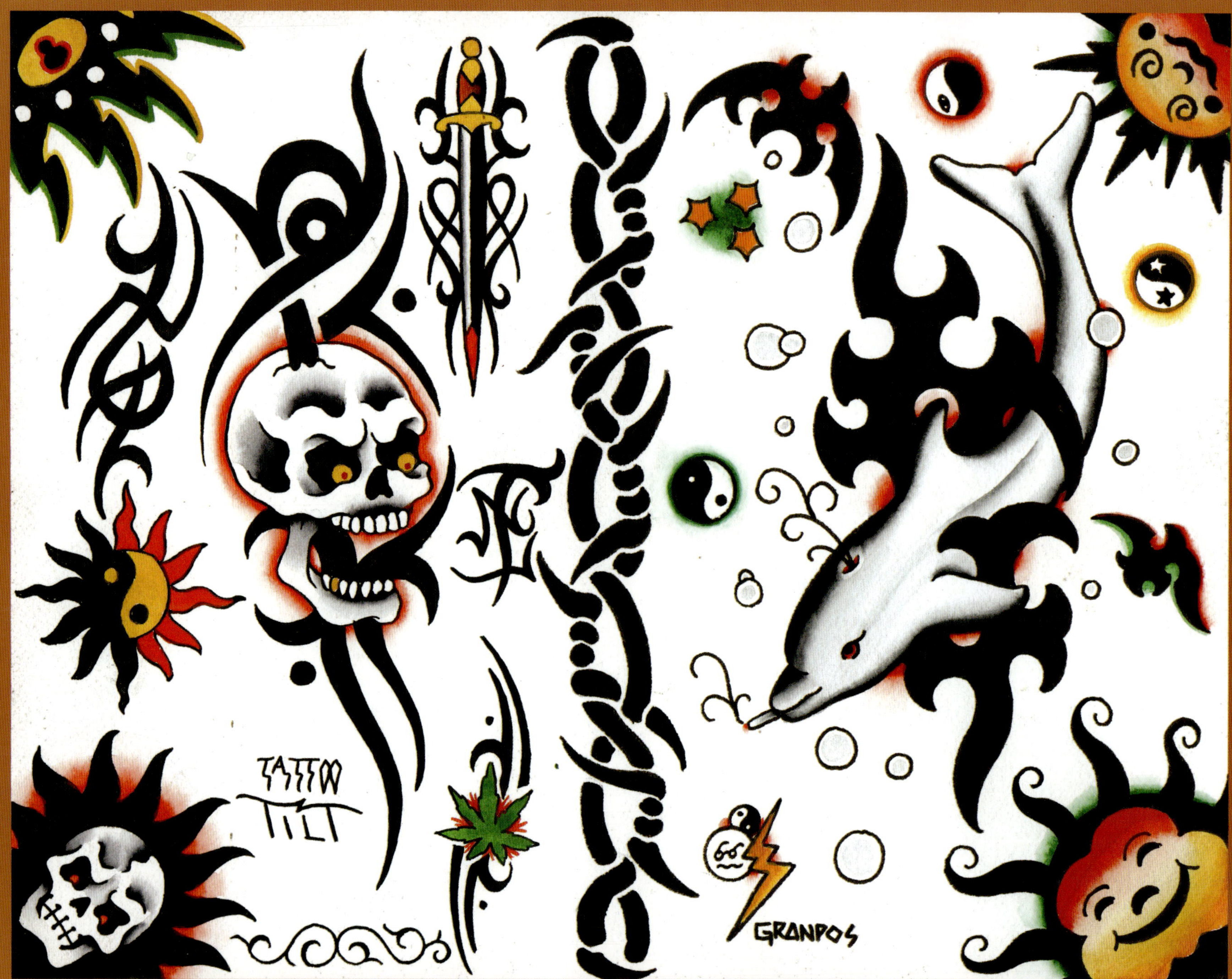

Granpos and Tilt

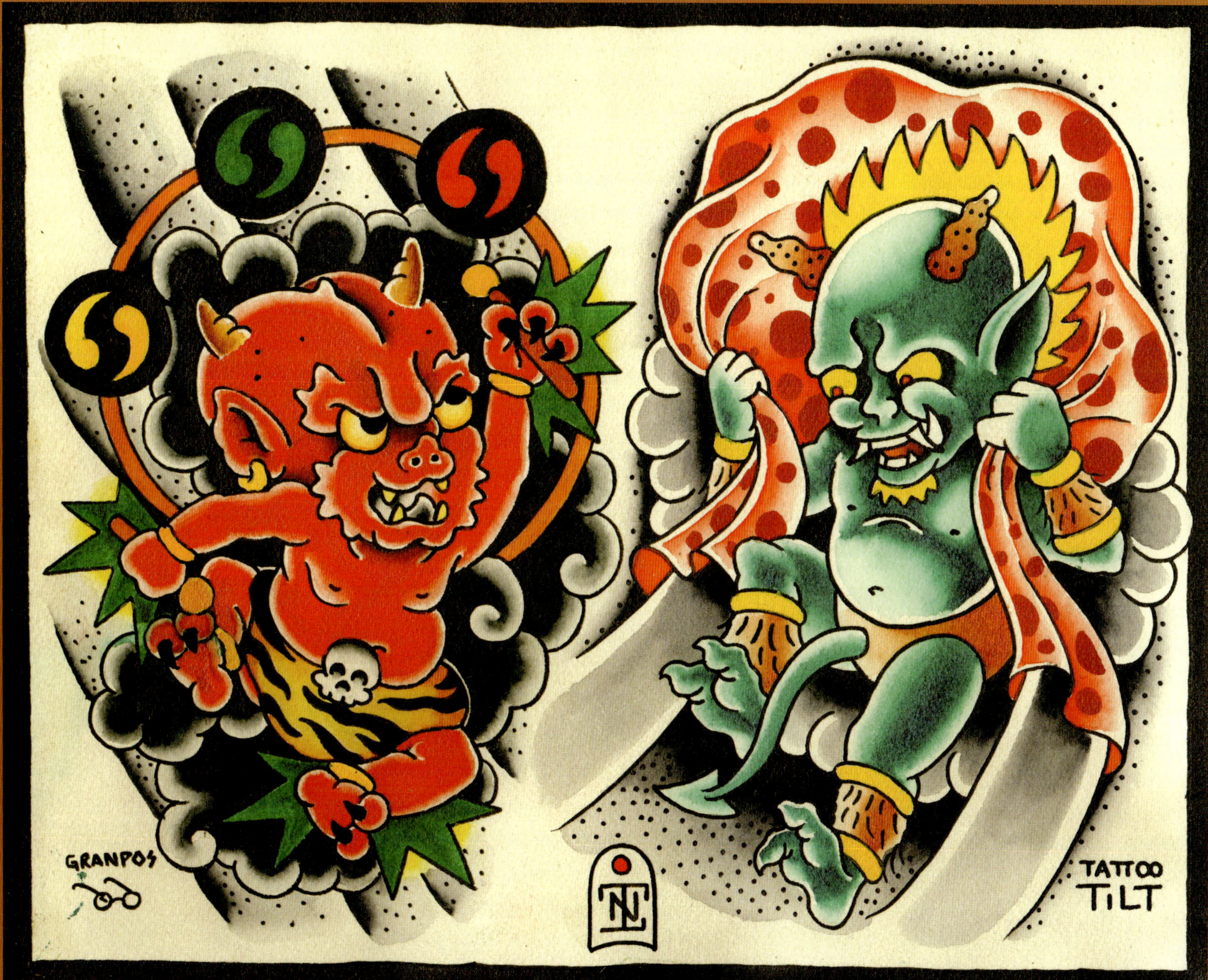

Granpos and Tilt

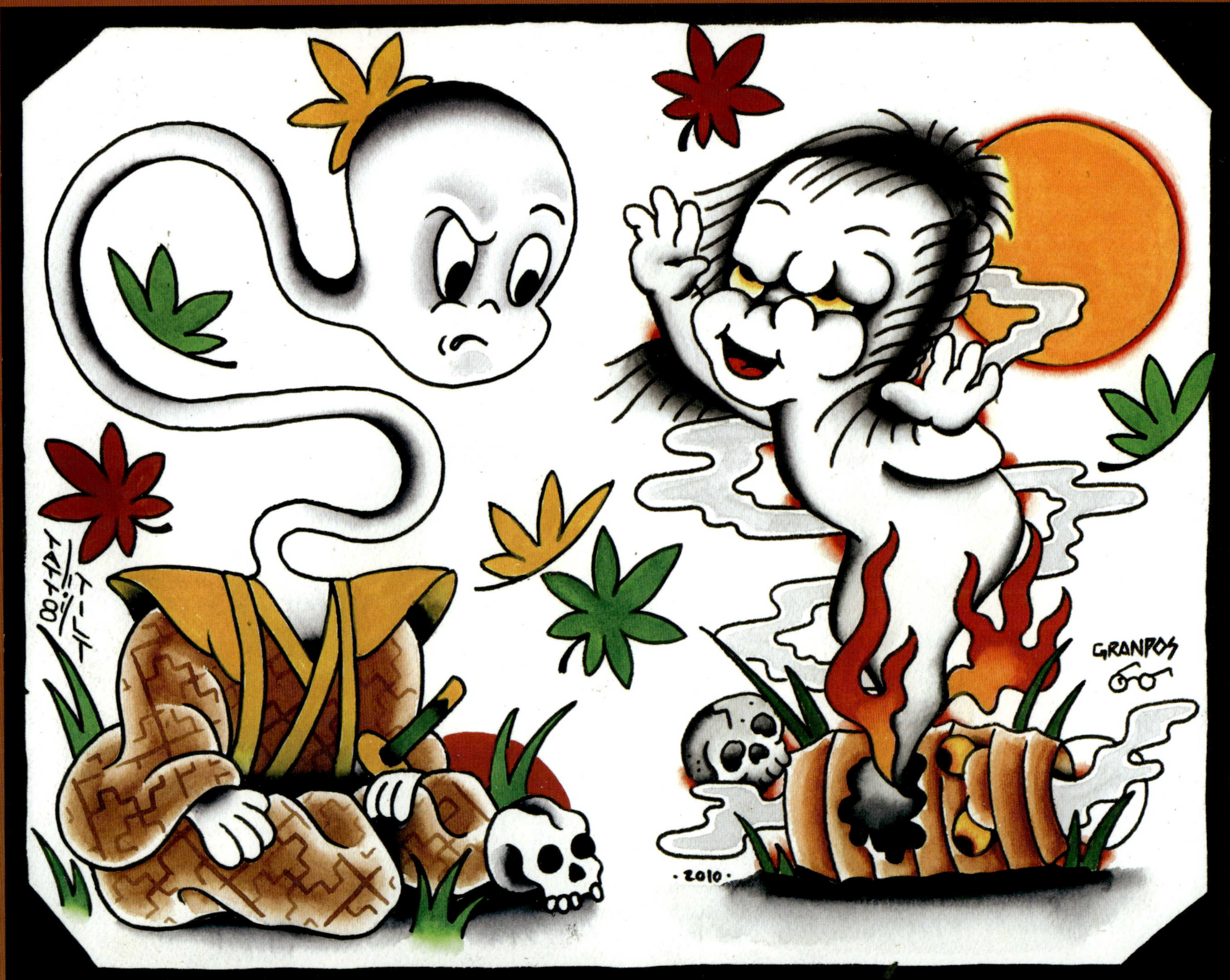

Granpos and Tilt

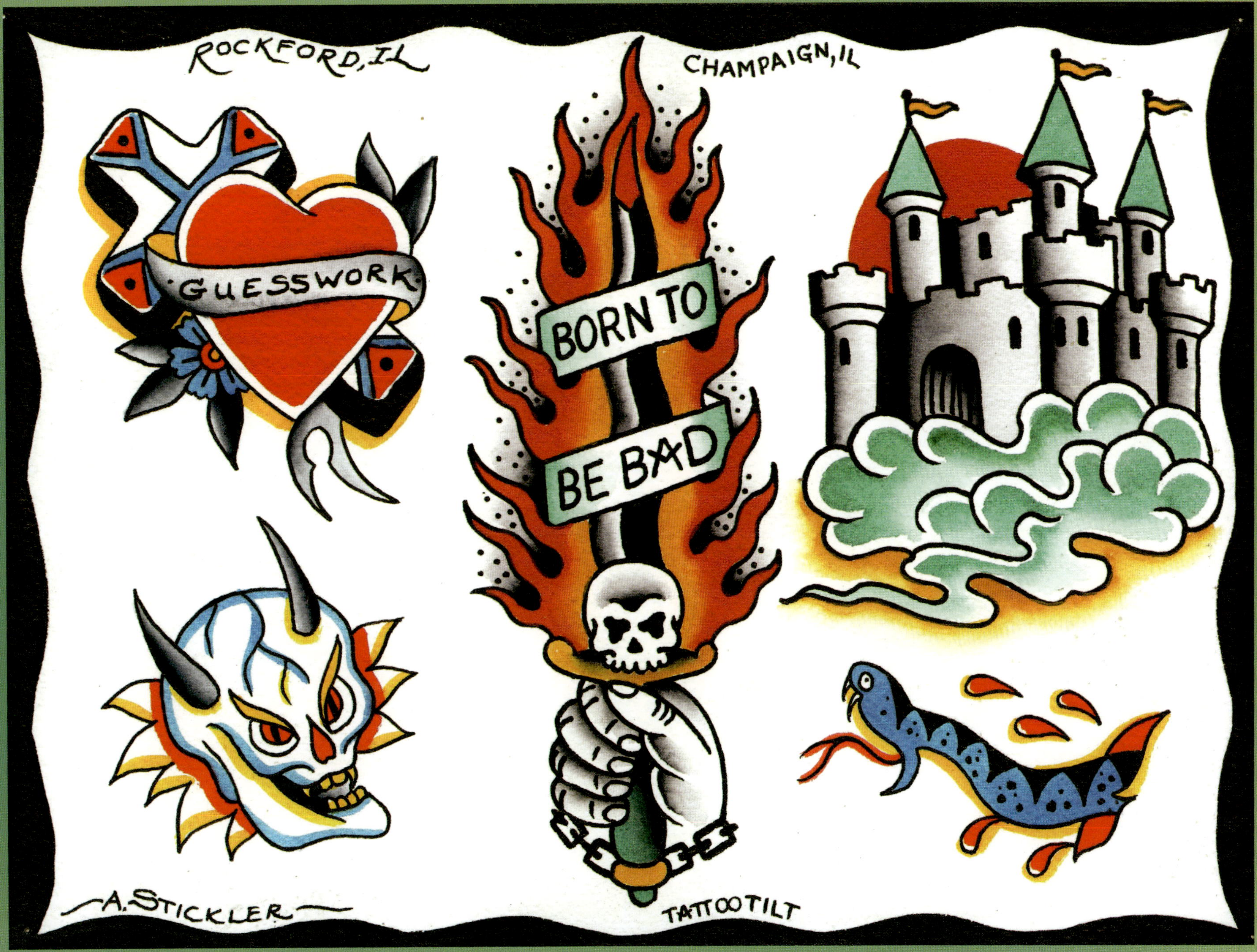

Andrew Stickler and Tilt

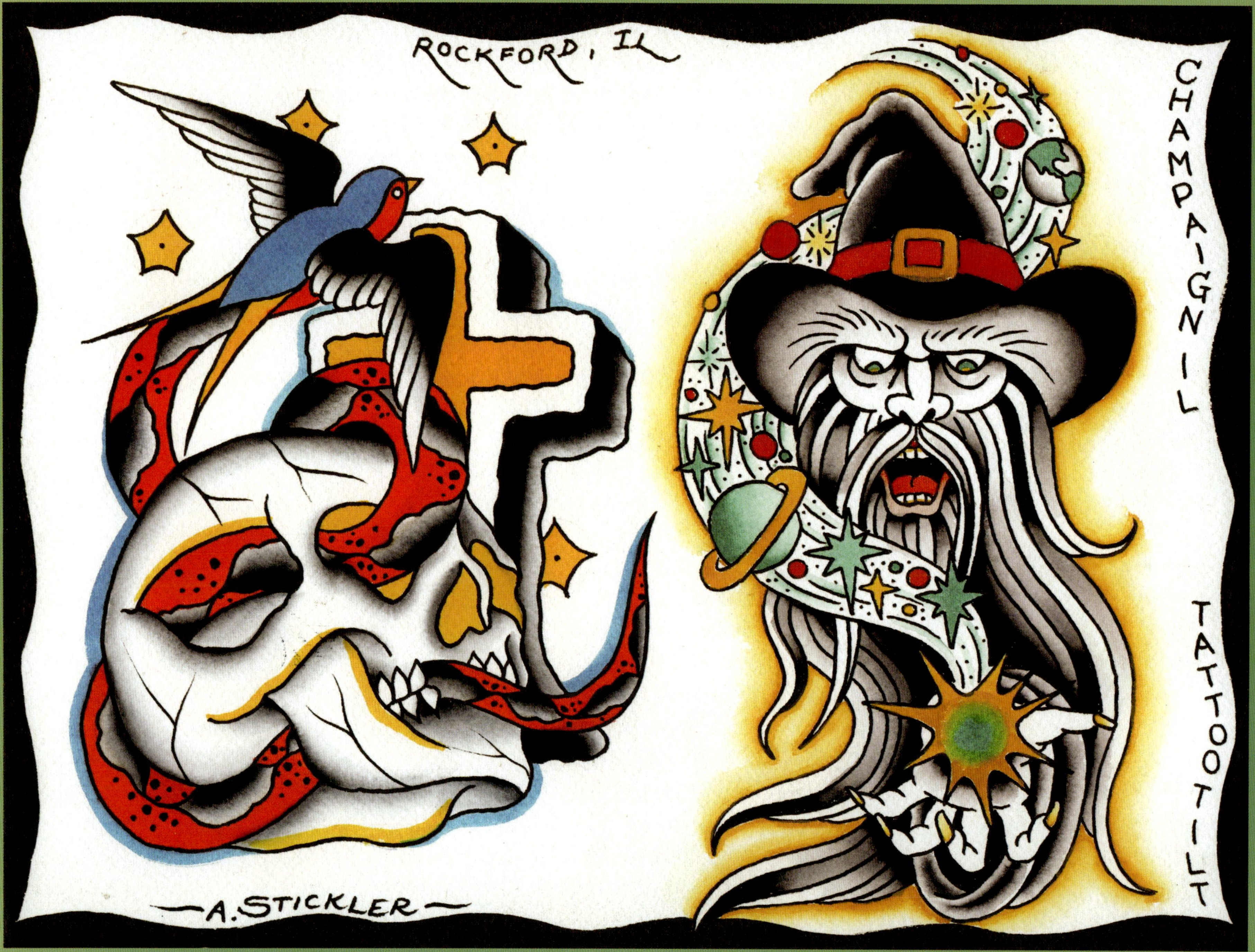

ROCKFORD, IL

A. STICKLER

CHAMPAIGN IL

TATTOO TILT

Andrew Stickler and Tilt

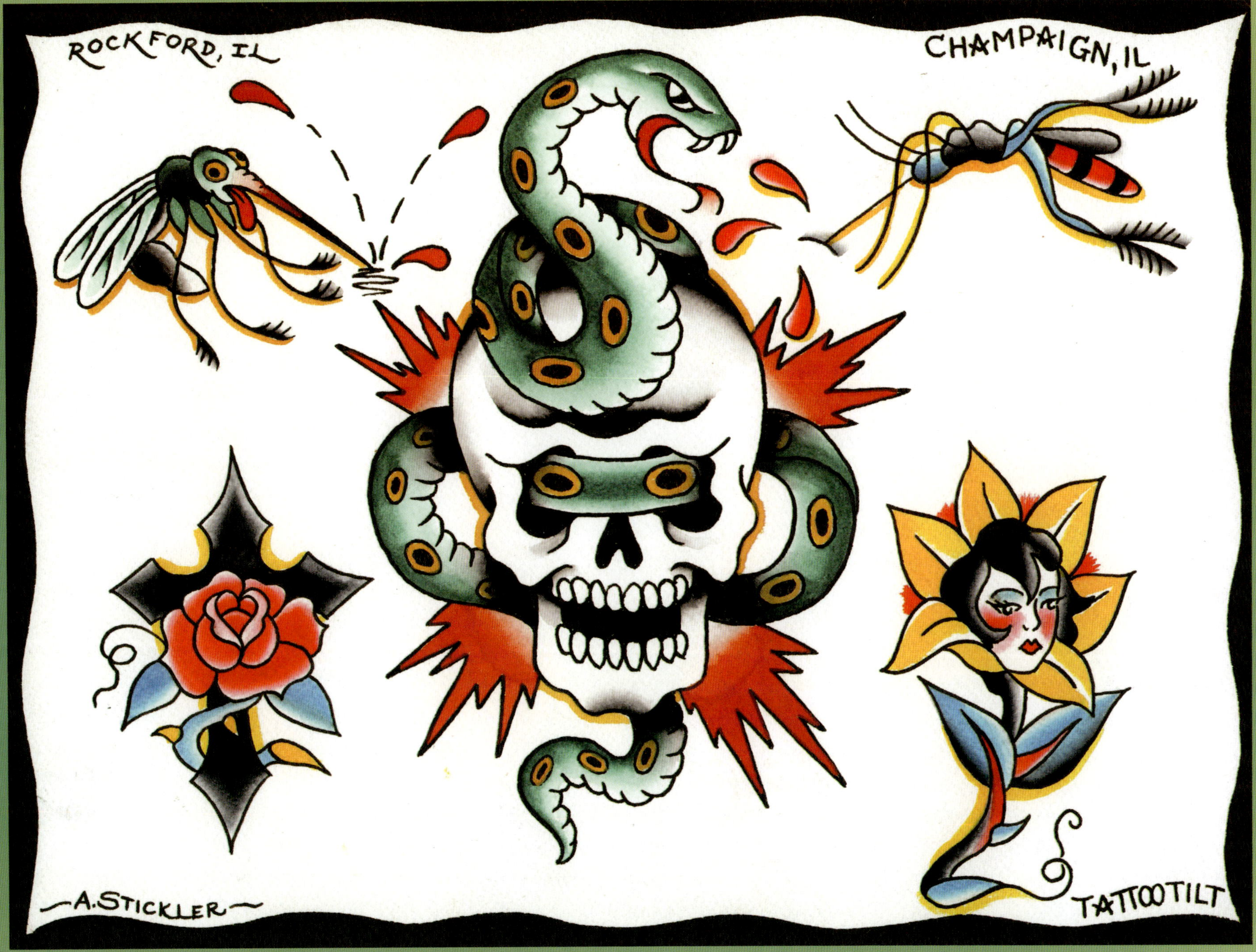

ROCKFORD, IL

CHAMPAIGN, IL

A.STICKLER

TATTOOTILT

Andrew Stickler and Tilt

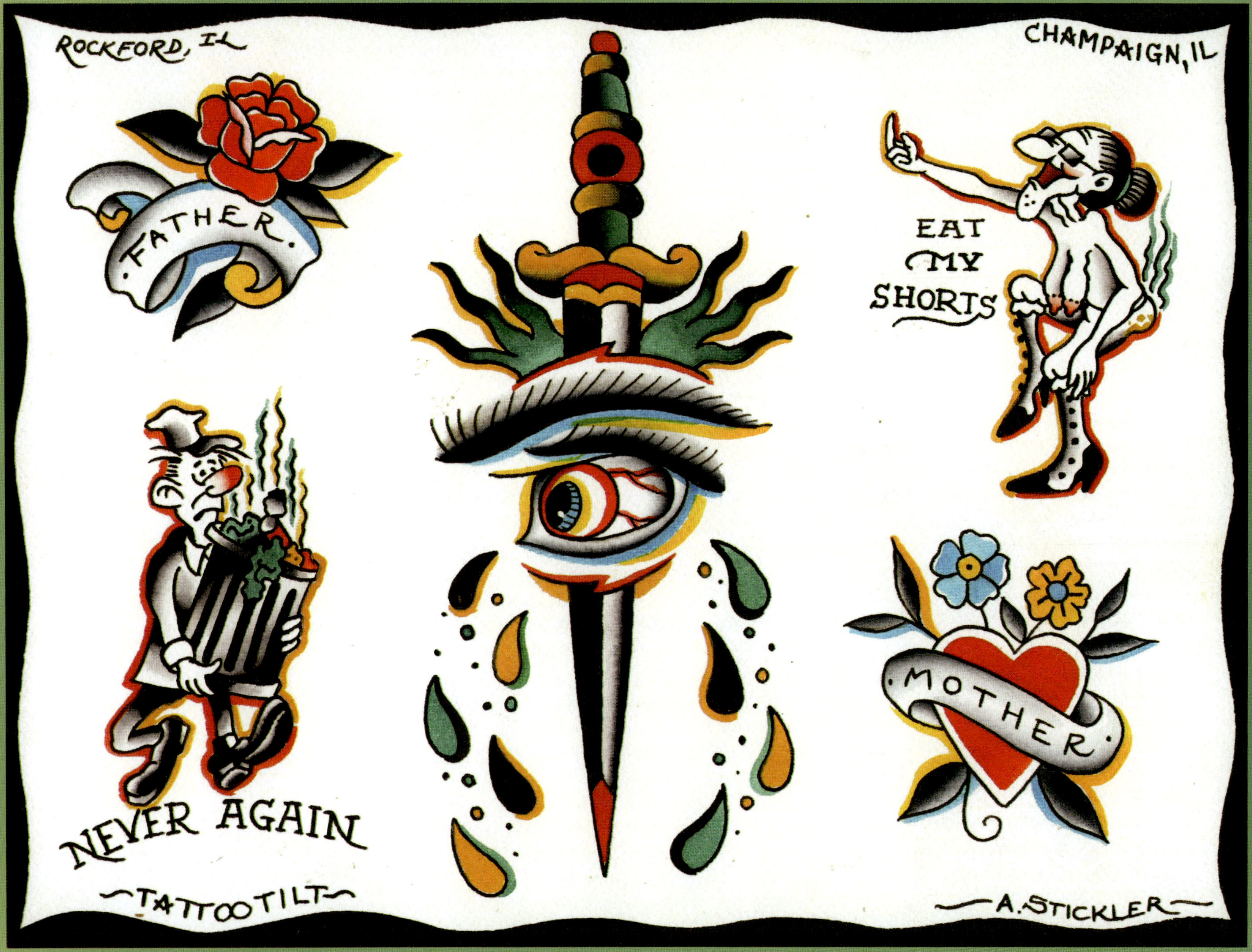

Andrew Stickler and Tilt

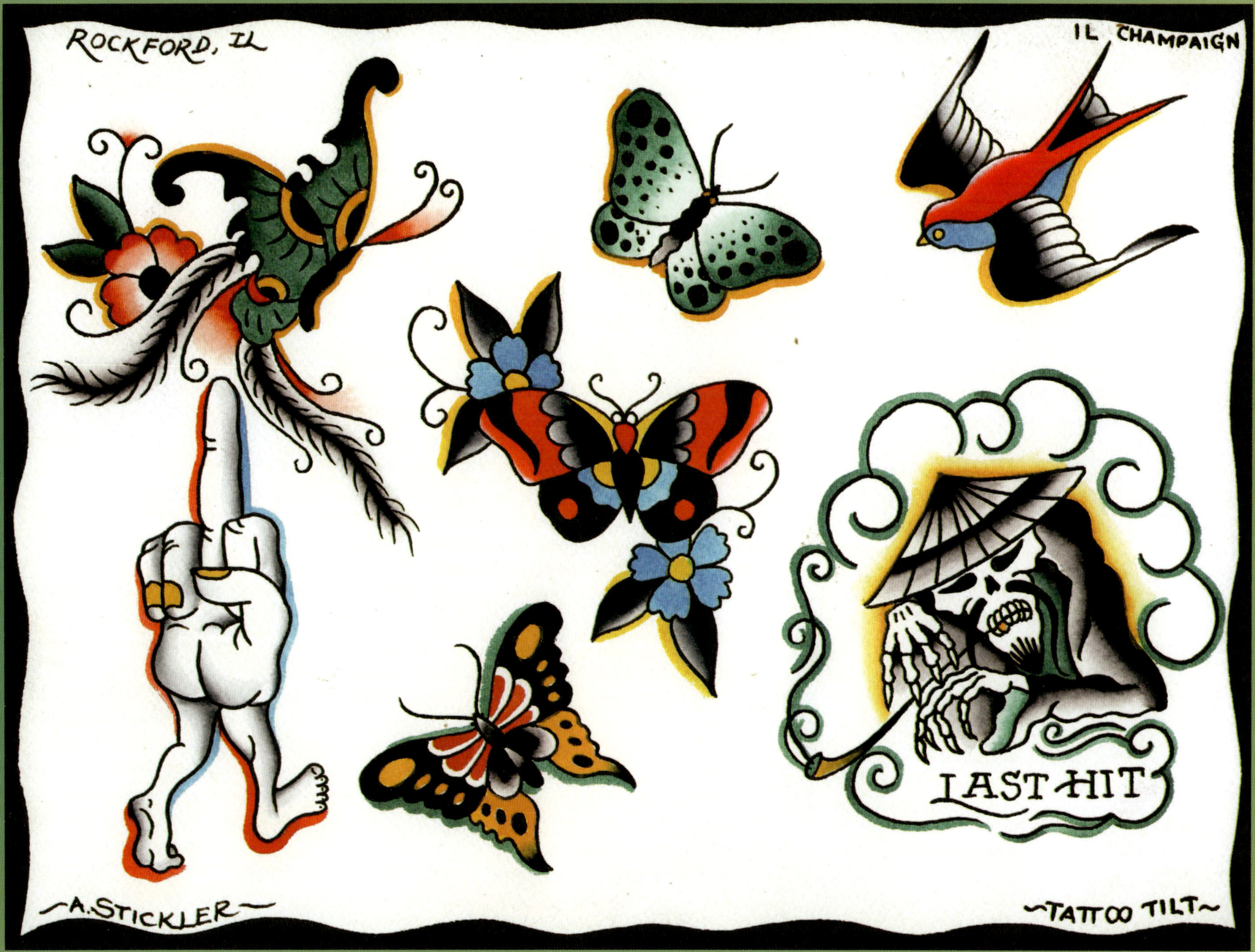

Andrew Stickler and Tilt

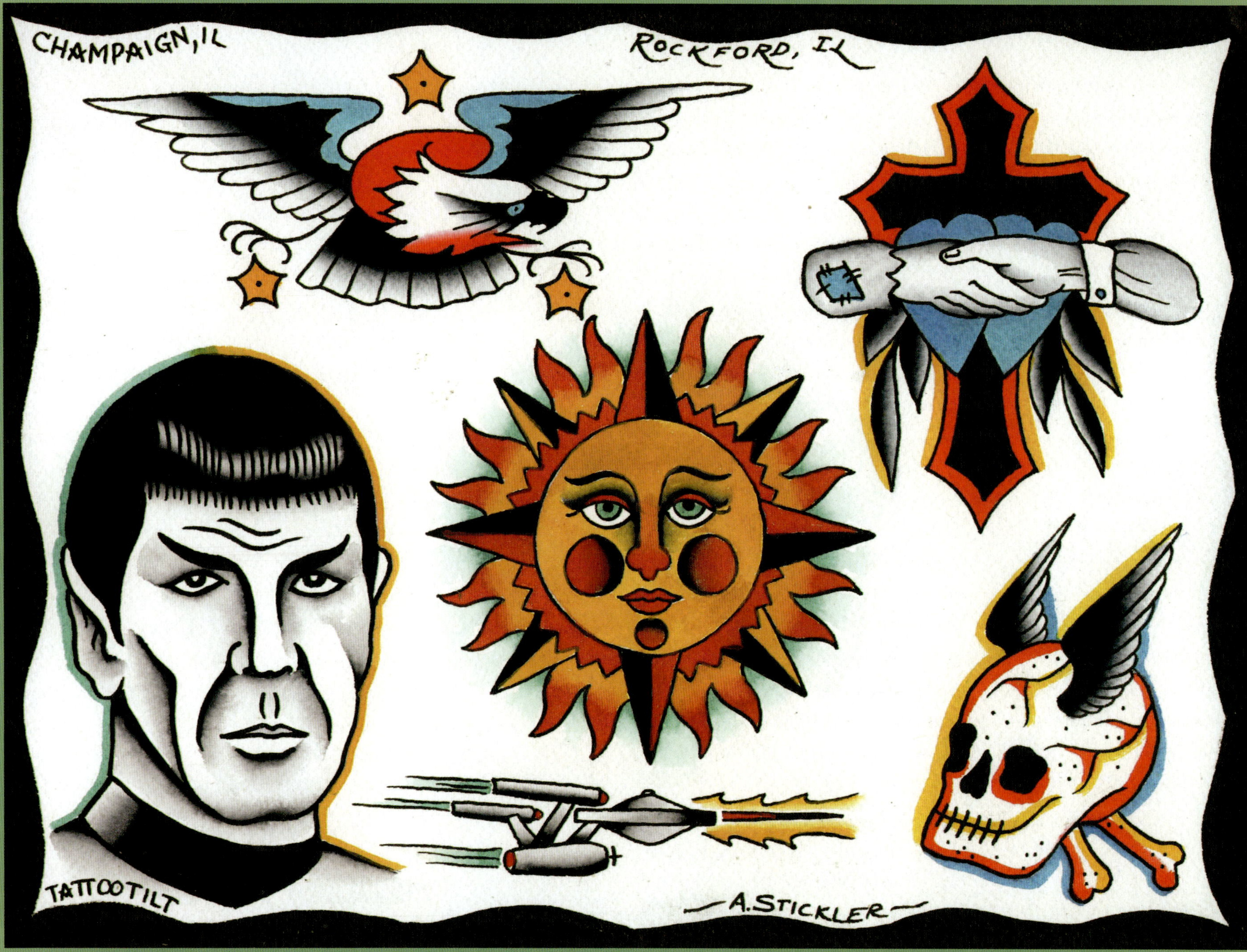

Andrew Stickler and Tilt

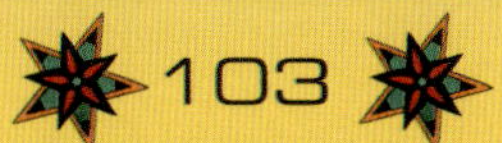

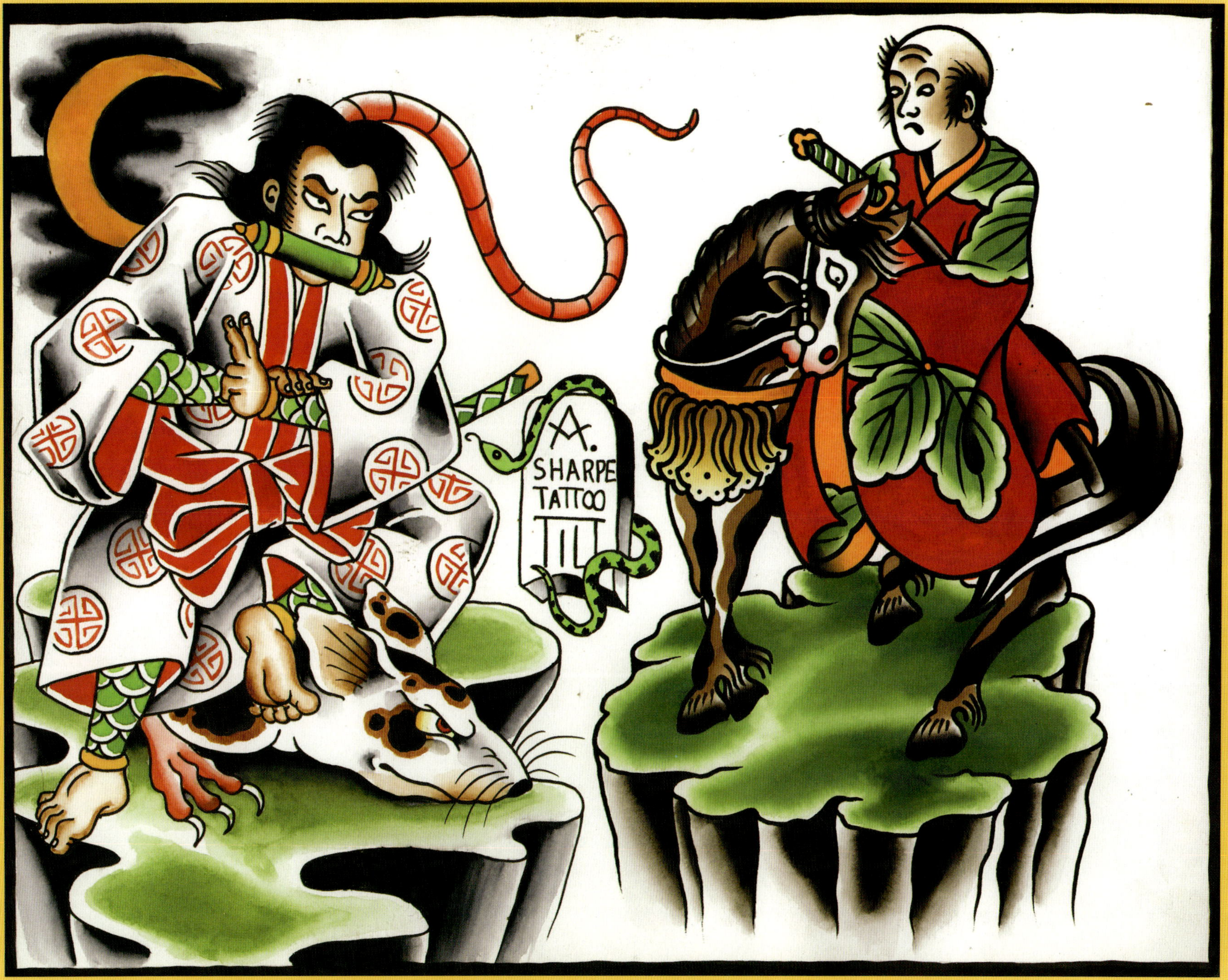

Andy Sharpe and Tilt

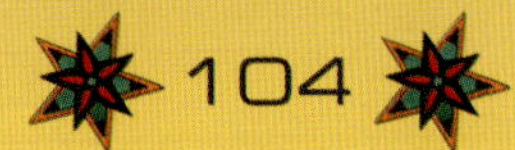

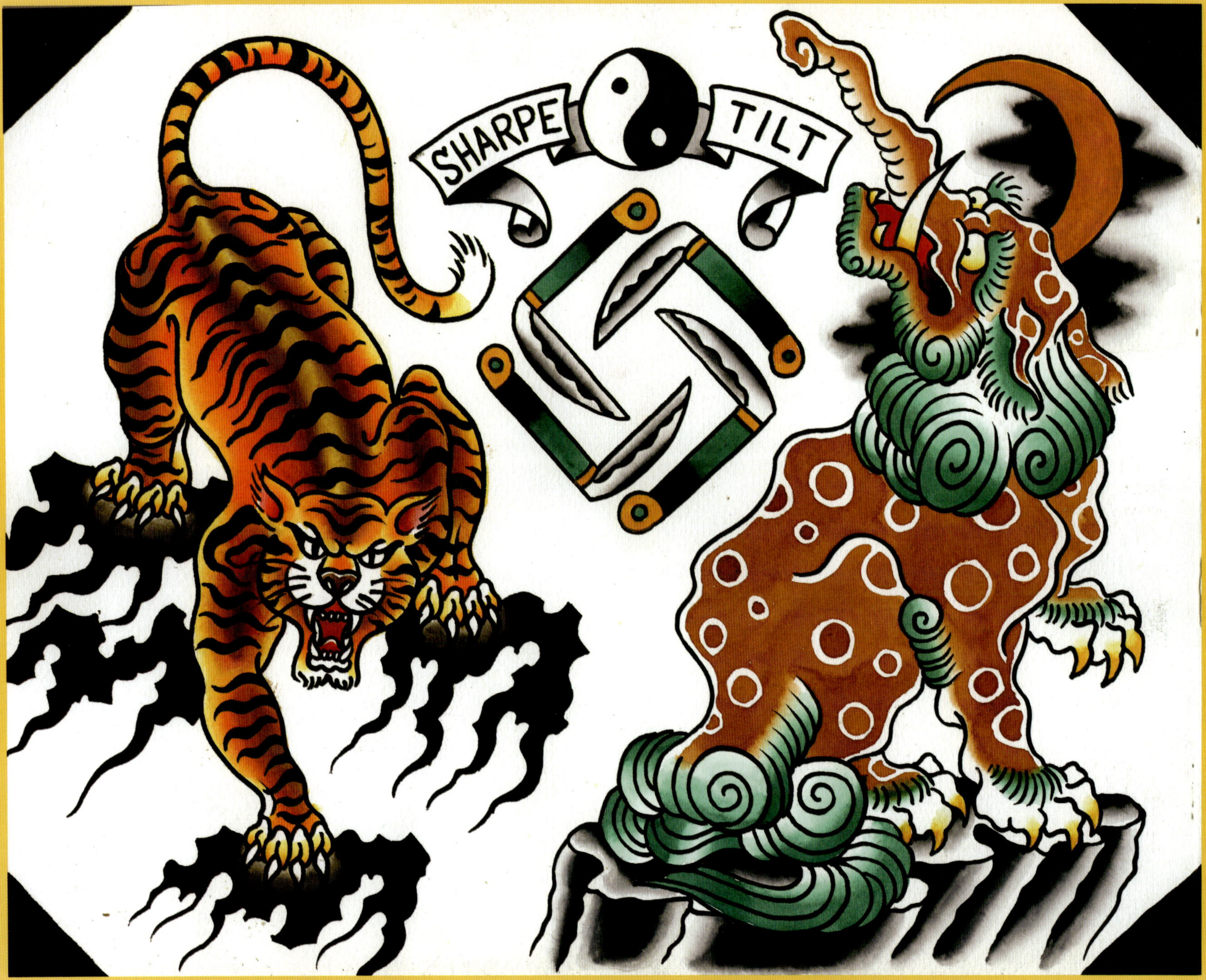

Andy Sharpe and Tilt

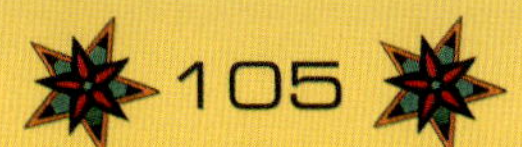

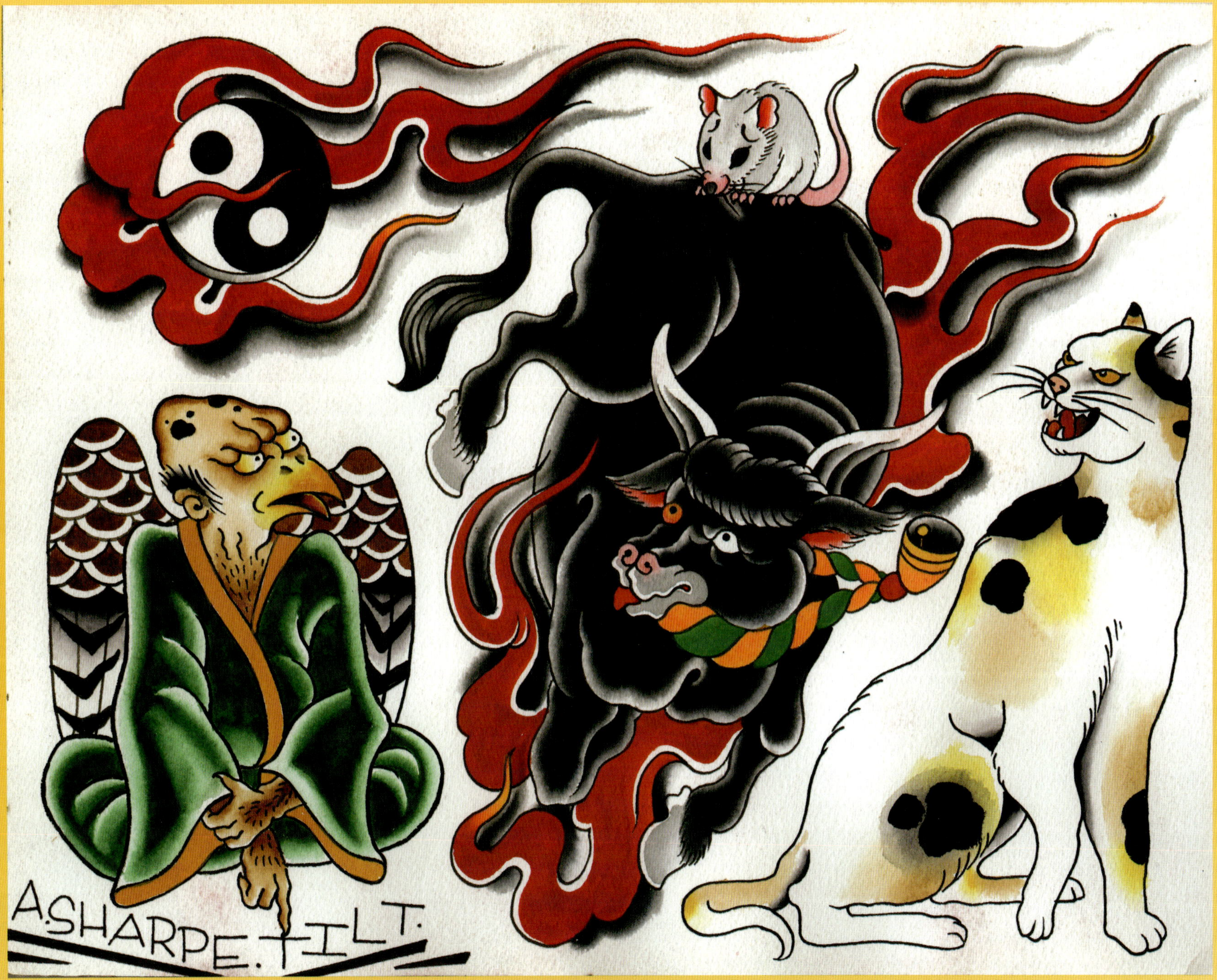

Andy Sharpe and Tilt

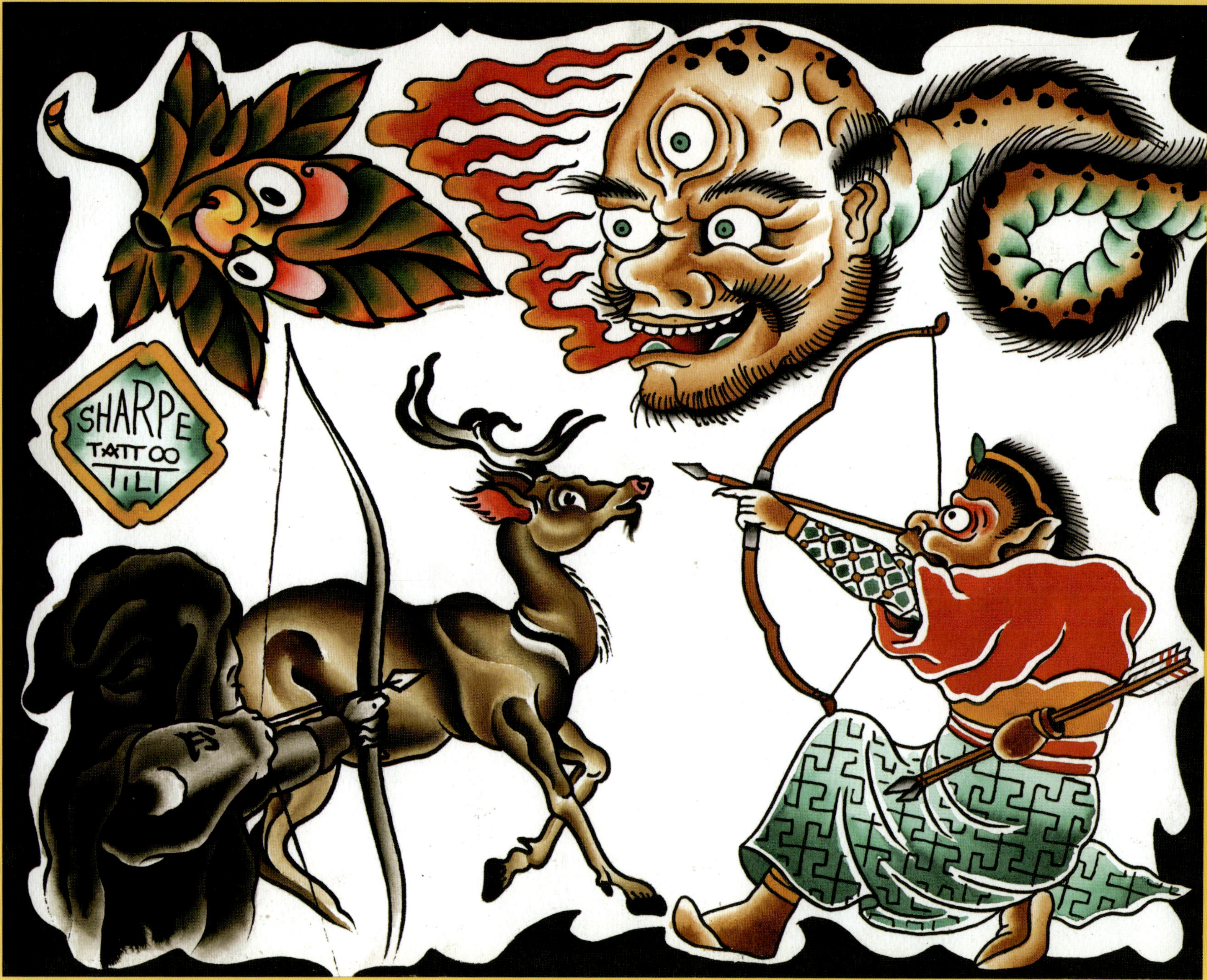

Andy Sharpe and Tilt

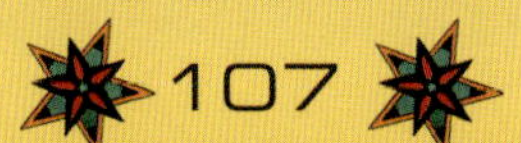

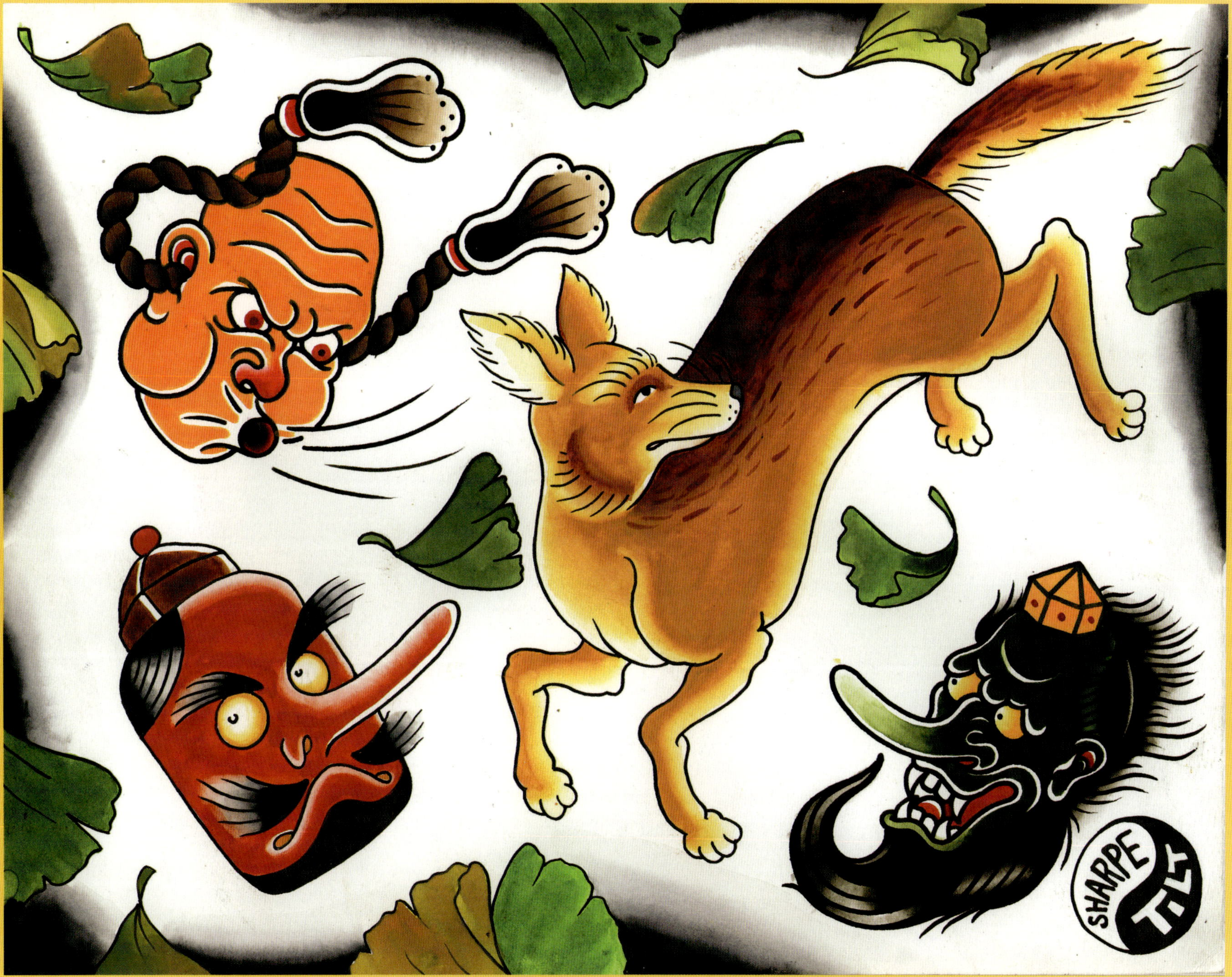

Andy Sharpe and Tilt

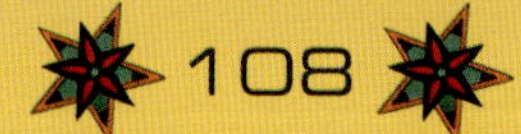

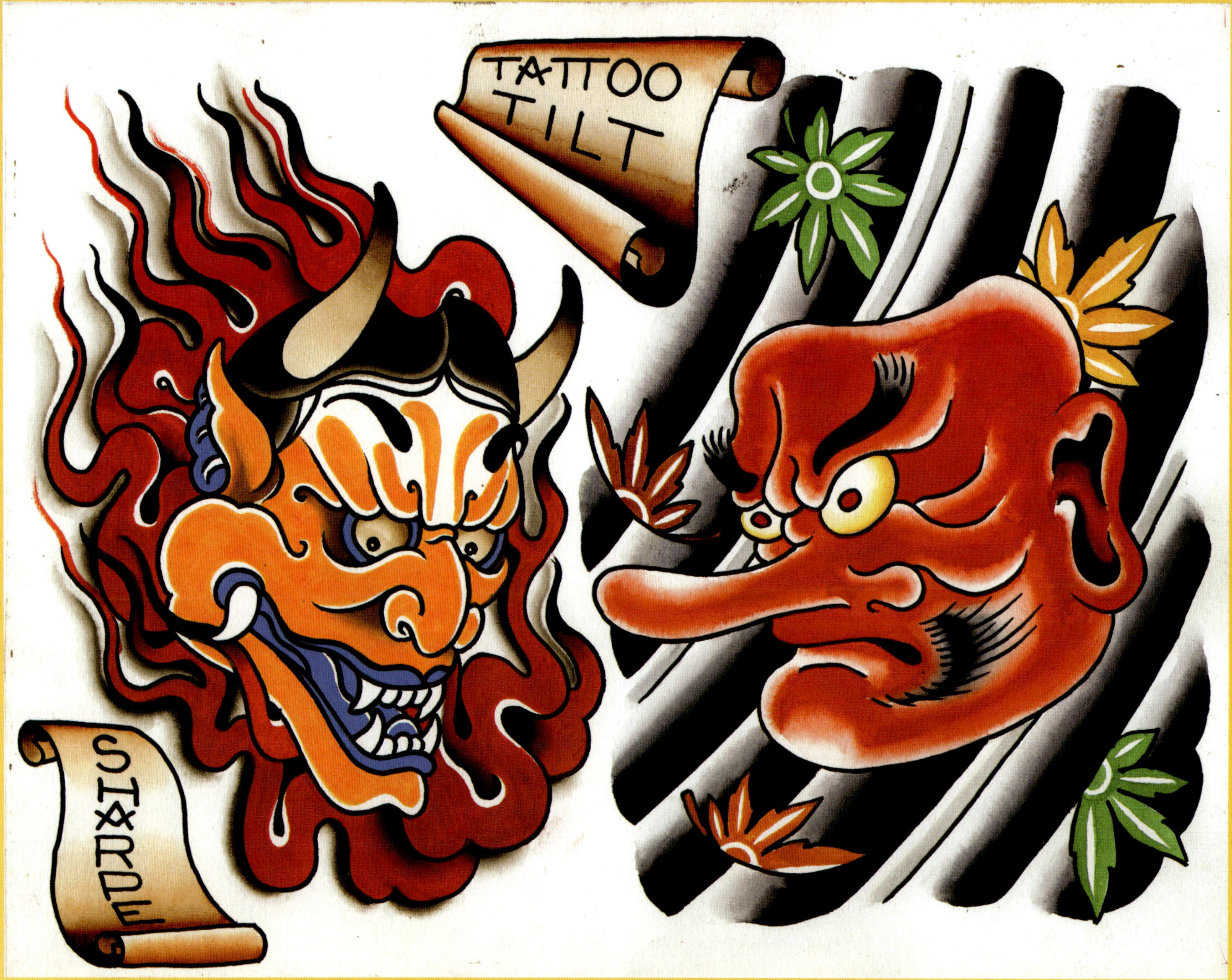

Andy Sharpe and Tilt

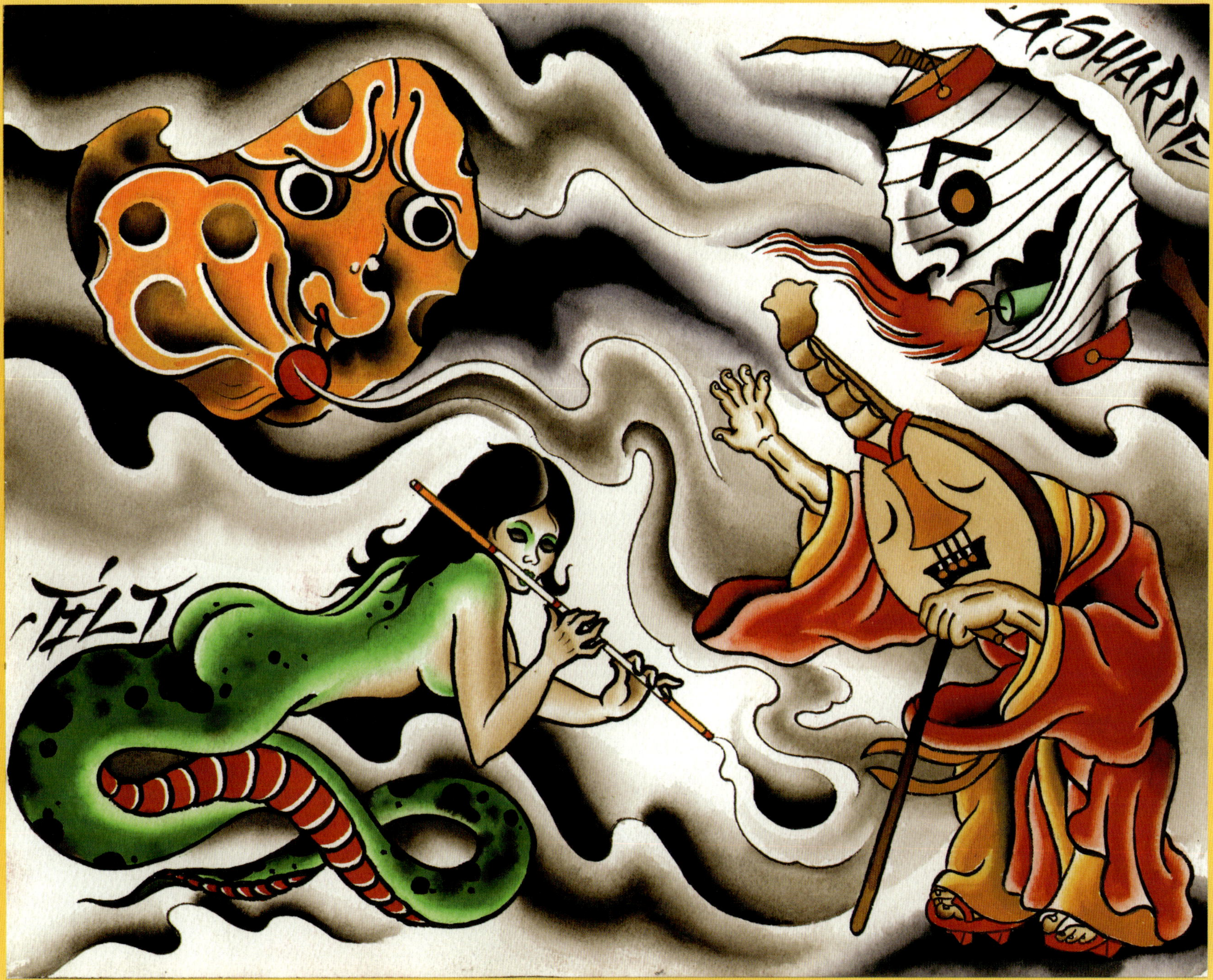

Andy Sharpe and Tilt

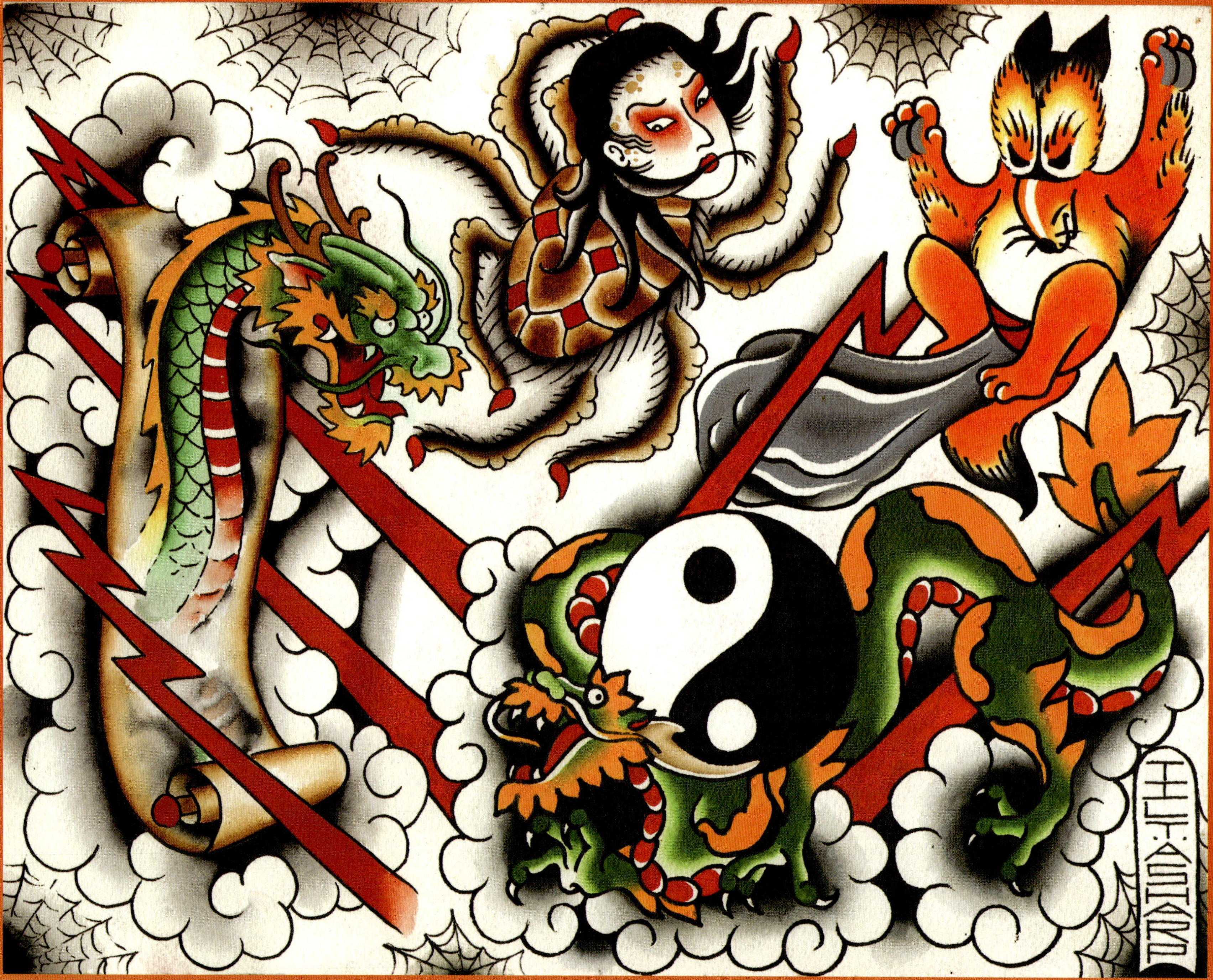

Andy Sharpe and Tilt

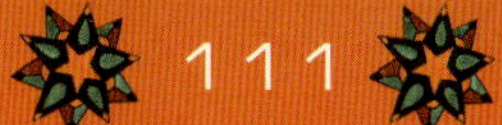

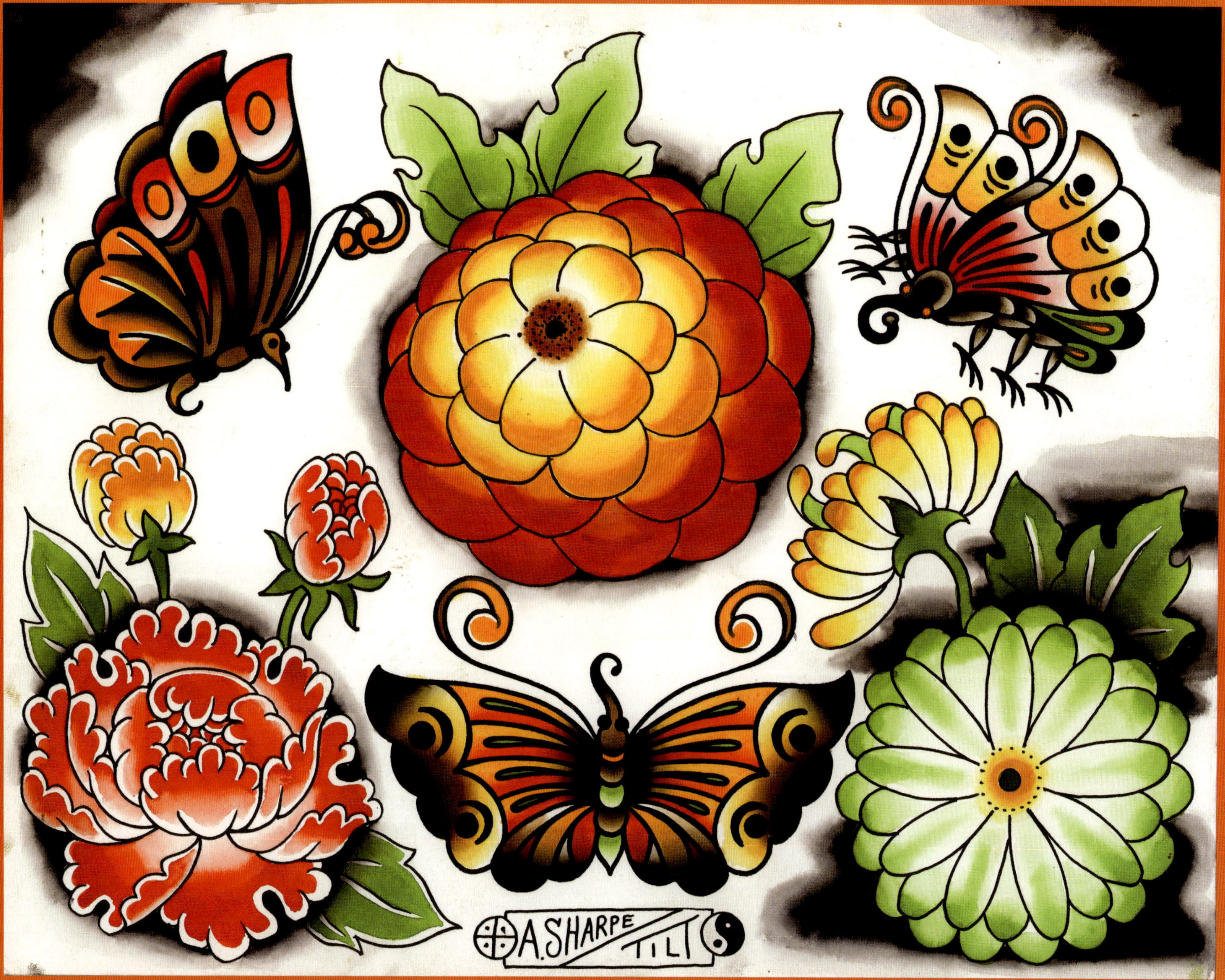

Andy Sharpe and Tilt

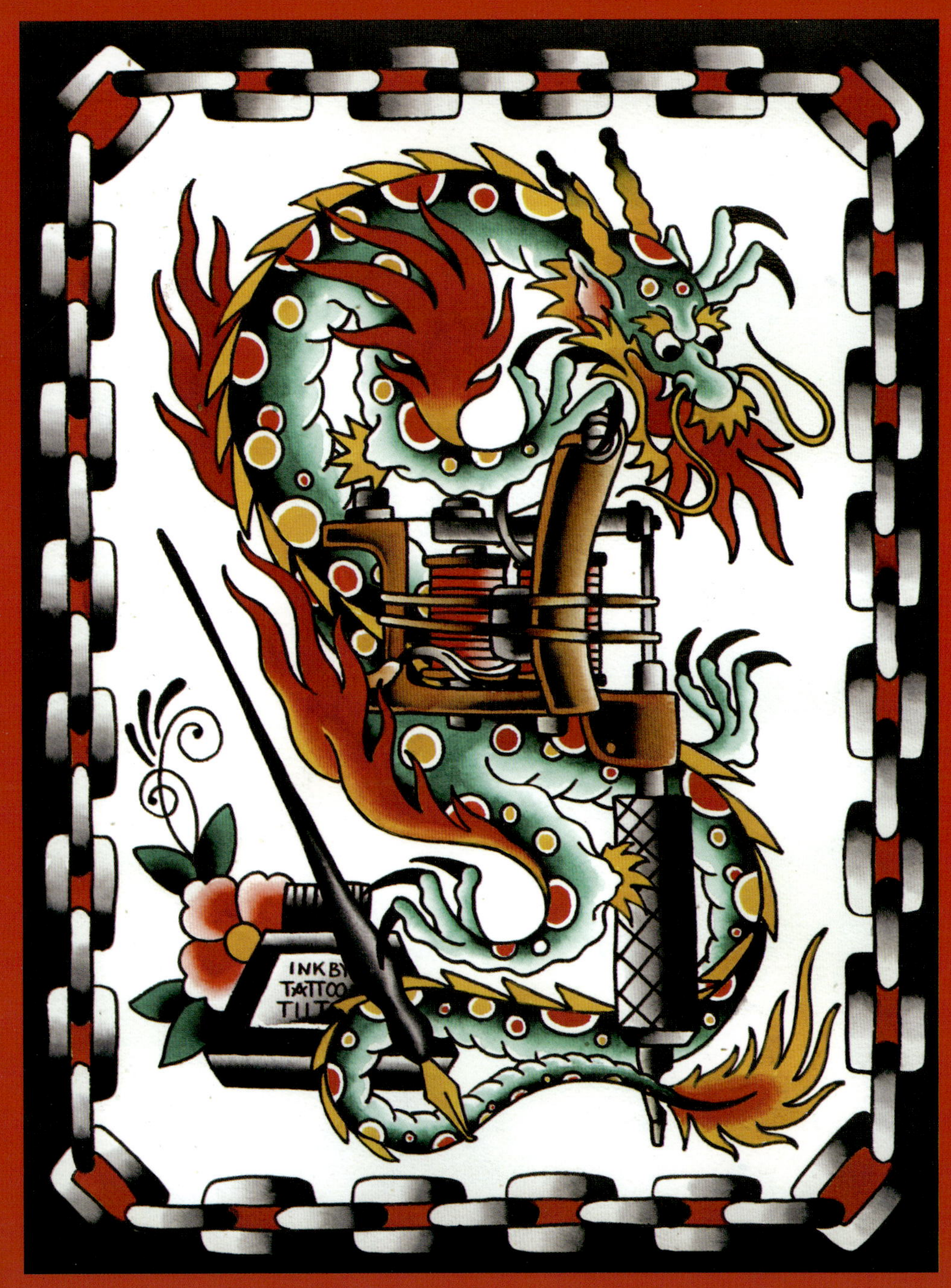
INKBY
TATTOO